The Life and Death of Olof Palme

BY PELLE NEROTH

TWO RAVEN BOOKS

For you, Catharina

This edition first published 2018
Two Raven Books
53232 Skara, Sweden
www.tworavenbooks.wordpress.com

British Library Cataloguing in Publication Data

ISBN 9781520483177 (paperback)

Typesetting and origination by Two Raven Books Publishing

Printed in the UK

"There were forces working across national borders who aimed their hatred at Scandinavian Social Democracy." – Gro Harlem Brundtland, Prime Minister, Norway, 1986

PROLOGUE: 11.21pm, 28 February 1986

Stockholm in late November, some 30 years after the murder in 1986. It gets dark not much beyond lunchtime, this far north, this time of year. It was now three pm and the sky was pitch black. I strolled alone in the snow, huddled figures around me, down the main road of the Old Town, full of souvenir shops: I bought a Viking plastic helmet with artificial Helga pigtails attached to the rim for my colleague at the newspaper back in London.

I crossed a bridge into Kungsträdgården, a park-like large square that used to be the King's Garden, hence the name, with Christmas stands, cradles of lightness and family in the inky late November darkness, selling fluffy toys, glazed peanuts; amber jewellery, tombola tickets, soft toy Santas and Swedish straw goats.

I walked up Sveavägen and stopped. Pedestrians flowed past, ignoring the plaque on the ground which shone dully in the bright lights of a nearby shop.

Here, at the junction of Sveavägen street and Tunnelgatan street, the assassination of Olof Palme, Swedish prime minister, took place at 11.21 pm on 28 February 1986.

A short timeline: At around 11.10 pm, leaving the Grand cinema, where they had seen a Swedish art-house film called the Brothers Mozart, the Palme couple turned right down Sveavägen, one of the main streets of Stockholm. His wife Lisbet was with him. No bodyguards: he didn't need them, this, after all, was Sweden, a couantry that had been at peace for two centuries and had for some decades been one of the world's most renowned democracies, the very epitome of harmonioaus utopia. One hundred and fifty metres from the Grand Cinema, the couple passed a grill kiosk whose owner recognised the couple and saw the couple followed by a thickset man in a dirty grey coat. The couple crossed the street because Lisbet wanted to look in at the window of a shop that sold Indian clothes.

They walked another 150 metres arm in arm until they reached the junction Tunnelgatan- Sveavägen. There, folded just inside the narrow side street Tunnelgatan, his silhouette visible in the glare of the window, stood the killer: He stepped out and killed Palme with one bullet and fired another at Lisbet, missing narrowly. He then turned on his heels and ran into the dark depths of Tunnelgatan, disappearing up some outdoor steps, gone forever

On 1 March 1986, the day after the murder of Olof Palme, footage showed a young policewoman in a blond ponytail gathering roses from mourners; by the end of the day, the pile was taking up much of the space of the sectioned off area outside the Dekorima store. Not just roses but notes, letters (often from children and immigrants), poems. Alas, because police had roped off such a small area, useful evidence, like fingerprints on the Dekorima window, was obliterated.

Over the next few days, there were torch-lit marches through Stockholm. People sang the socialist dirge "We Shall Overcome". Stockholm was gripped by an intensity of emotion that probably equalled and perhaps even exceeded that felt in London after the death of Princess Diana. From around the world, condolences were coming in. US President Ronald Reagan said: "I have learned with great shock of the tragic death. My sorrow in the face of this senseless act of violence is profound.

"Olof Palme was one of the world's most respected leaders, a man who made compassion the hallmark of Swedish policy. The world will remember him for his devotion to democratic values and his untiring efforts to promote peace."

It did not escape the notice of the Swedish ambassador to Washington, however, that while the Vice President and former head of the CIA, George Bush, was due to speak at his memorial service, held in Washington, Bush cancelled at the last moment.

TASS, the official Soviet news agency, said Palme's death was a punishment of peace activists by "militarists of all stripes". It did not blame the CIA directly, but claimed that Palme had been under surveillance by the CIA for several years because of his "fervent opposition to America's illegal wars". TASS also speculated whether the air crash death six months earlier of Samantha Smith, the 13-year-old Maine schoolgirl who visited the Soviet Union on a "peace mission" and became a little heroine in the Soviet media, was a matter of foul play by the Americans.

Few paid any attention to either allegation as anything but yet another example of Soviet propaganda.

A few days later, the Congress of People's Deputies in Moscow passed a resolution calling Palme a "man of peace" and held a silent two minutes in his memory. Palme had, after all, been vice president of the Socialist International, a body, though comprising mostly Western Social Democrats, the Soviet leadership respected.

The socialist governments of Tanzania and Nicaragua, primary recipients of Swedish aid largesse, sworn enemies of the United States, declared three days of national mourning. Other friends of Palme included the leadership of East Germany, a country whose media had given Palme plenty of favourable coverage over the years. The queues outside the Swedish embassy in East Berlin to sign the condolence books were a kilometre long. The funeral took place on 15 March 1986. Palme's white coffin lay on the white catafalque surrounded by red roses, the symbol of socialism, and wreaths of yellow and blue flowers, the Swedish national colours. There were the massed standards from the regional labour movements. Most of Europe's prime ministers were in attendance. One exception: Margaret Thatcher, who sent her deputy, Willie Whitelaw. Over a hundred governments had received invitations to send up to three representatives each. Only the right-wing governments of South Africa, Paraguay and Chile were not invited, even though PW Botha, the South African president, had sent his condolences. Instead, two opposition figures to the Apartheid regime came. Palme had been a staunch opponent of South Africa and Apartheid all his adult life.

Palme had spent his whole adult life making powerful enemies in international politics; in domestic policy too. (He also made many friends.) A biography of Palme, Sweden's leading twentieth-century politician, which this is, becomes not only the biography of a country's development, but a kind of detective story. As we go back and look at his life, his many activities again, we can ask ourselves this question. If he was killed by foreigners, which one of his many international engagements irked his opponents in that country the most – to the point that they actually assassinated him? Were representatives of that regime in attendance on the day of the funeral? Or had they stayed away?

One of Palme's friends, the left wing writer Pär Wästberg, described the scene at the funeral: ascetic, socialist, tasteful. There was mild jazz and one child from every local municipality sang in the choir. Palme had always liked children, and they often wrote letters to him – this, at least, was the myth promoted by his Social Democratic party. Palme aspired to recreate Sweden as a Barnens ö, the haven, the island, or refuge, of children.

There were not many national or religious symbols present at the funeral. The red flags of the workers' movement dominated over the Swedish blue and yellow national flag. The head of state, King Carl Gustav, was given secondary billing as speaker after the Social Democratic Party Secretary. Such a downgrading of the king's importance would have been unthinkable for most of Sweden's proud regal history, but Sweden had changed much in the 20th century, into becoming a secular and modern state, and Palme had done much to change it.

At the wake afterwards, Palme's wife Lisbet had gathered Palme's friends. The Swedish left wing writers and artists who had urged him on in his reforms. The ex-chancellors Willy Brandt of West Germany and Bruno Kreisky of Austria – his two closest allies in Western Europe, who had carried out liberal social reforms in their own countries, modelled on the pioneering work done by Palme in Sweden. Israel's Labour leader Shimon Peres. Socialist African leaders or future leaders. Oliver Tambo, Sam Nujoma – men who were enemies of the United States and UK, whose representatives were also in attendance, but friends of Palme's Sweden.

Robert Mugabe, the leader of Zimbabwe, was not at the intimate gathering of the wake, but he did attend the funeral itself. One of Palme's less wisely chosen friends, Mugabe was now out of favour with Palme's entourage for the enormous human rights problems of his country. Mugabe had once been the African guerrilla leader Swedish intellectuals liked best.

The day after Palme's funeral, anti-Apartheid politician Allan Boesak gave a fiery sermon at the Storkyrkan, the Old town church in Stockholm. The coloured South African priest and leader of the underground UDF movement had been given permission to leave a South Africa in turmoil – under emergency laws – to attend the funeral. He had had his passport withdrawn by the Apartheid regime but was given a one-off travel document for this occasion. He said: "From time to time, there appears in the world a figure with the stature of Martin Luther King, Mother Theresa or Olof Palme. He represented something we cannot afford to lose."

At a press conference afterwards, Boesak said that the name Olof Palme was legendary in the Third World. He declined to tell journalists his views on the pioneering Swedish sanctions on South Africa – that was one of the conditions for his permission to travel. He did say, though, that his meeting on the funeral sidelines with ANC leader Oliver Tambo, who lived in exile and who was one of Palme's closest friends, would not be seen positively by the South African government. He would have to deal with that when he got back. Swedish newspapers, even those that had attacked Olof Palme while he was alive, were impressed by the network of international contacts who had come to pay their final respects, and ruefully admitted there would be no one else in Swedish public life with the stature to step into Palme's shoes.

It was a funeral not just for a man, but for a particular idea of Sweden.

Palme's Sweden represented, to many, one of humanity's peaks of progress: high taxes, but generous social benefits, remarkably fair and prosperous, a country defined as a place where there was freedom from want. As one admiring Associated Press writer put it at around the time of the funeral: "A doctor's visit is $8, whether for a torn fingernail or for or brain surgery. School is free up to a PhD. There are no slums, and Stockholm's three bag ladies are local figures." There was also an activist foreign policy. Lots of third world activism, sanctioned as far up as Palme himself: for decades, Sweden had sent politicians, advisers, doctors, engineers to "clear up the mess" in the Third World of the newly decolonised states left behind by the colonial powers, countries like Britain. That was the Swedish self-narrative. And the large number of leaders from developing countries who attended Palme's funeral, the days of mourning, seemed to prove his popularity in the developing world. Amid the sorrow, Swedes felt proud.

In the years that were to follow, as Sweden changed rapidly in the 1990s in a neoliberal direction, commentators in Sweden came to talk about the death of Palme as the end of one era, and the beginning of another, not necessarily better, one. What was to follow was a political shift to the right, a greater openness to investment, foreign ideas, capitalism: a weakening of the total welfare state Palme had built up. Less glad-handing with leaders of the developing world, less moralising about the evils of western colonialism. And – a foreign policy away from Palme's moral neutrality towards a system increasingly aligned with the United States and NATO. For some, the death of Palme marked the beginning of the end of Sweden's geopolitical independence.

But was Palme's Sweden really that utopian? There is a whole school of thought that Sweden was and is – though less since Palme – a rather authoritarian welfare state. Certain conservative Danish journalists and historians are especially critical of Sweden. Denmark, they say, has a much freer, less conformist, intellectual climate. Recently, Denmark's biggest conservative newspaper called Sweden a "controlled democracy." Another critic was Roland Huntford, who spent some years in Stockholm as the London Observer's correspondent. He complained, in a famous book (The New Totalitarians 1971, new edition 1979) that was ignored or savaged by Swedish critics, about an intrusive bureaucracy and a politicised justice system aimed at achieving the political goals of the welfare state rather than protecting the rights of the individual.

Many of course didn't see the problem, or argued that this was a legacy of an older Sweden, which liberal social democracy and Olof Palme inherited, but did not impose. It's a tricky matter, a picture at odds with Sweden's reputation, in various international rankings, of being one of the world's best democracies. But consider this.

The Social Democrats had been in power for 44 years nonstop by the end of Palme's first period of rule. (Palme was the statsminister from 1969 to 1976; then once again from 1982 to his assassination in 1986.) One Social Democrat female minister exclaimed, when the Social Democrats finally lost power, the first time in four decades, in the elections of 1976 : "It feels like a coup d'état". The Social Democrats were unused to it; a change of government had not happened in Swedish politicians' adult lifetimes, not since 1932. The Social Democrats were back by 1982 and ruled with one brief interruption, until 2006. Bar

Japan, in no other country with regular elections has a single party ruled for so long.

SWEDISH HISTORY: 1611-1918

To understand the hatred Palme endured from his countrymen, especially in the last term in office, 1982-86, you have to understand how his friendly attitude towards the Soviets went against powerful traditions of Russophobia in Swedish history.

Sweden was once upon a time an imperial conqueror. Russia, and Poland and the Baltic territories, were once Sweden's playground. This fact had been written out of Swedish history by the Social Democrats. The past was not attractive. Only the future was. As a result, there was a lack of insight into the dark forces that not only bubbled under in Swedish society, but the motives and ways of thinking of other geopolitical players. This makes for a certain naivete in the Swedish mindset. Perhaps that is one reason why the murder has not been solved.

In Swedish school history lessons in the Social Democrat heyday of the early 1980s, I remember, Sweden's modern history was sketched very much in terms of coming out of the darkness of conservative inegalitarianism of the beginning of the twentieth century into the light of Social Democrat-ruled mid and late twentieth century Sweden. The Social Democrats' rule since 1932 more or less uninterruptedly was the central reference point. Pre-1918, old autocratic, monarchical Sweden, first a great imperial power, then poor and isolated, was regarded by the politicised educational establishment very much as an embarrassment. It was the same in the fifties, sixties and seventies. SO Swedish businessmen who travelled to Eastern Europe where the effects of Swedish invasions had been felt found they knew less about Swedish history than their hosts. They were told about Swedish invasions and massacres they had never heard of. For example, the destruction of up to a third of the Polish population between 1655-1657 – the years the Poles call "the Deluge".

Critics have said the school system was politicised to perpetuate the Social Democrats' hold on Swedish life, which was already growing by virtue of their unbroken hold on power. Sweden was a democracy, but the conservative and liberal opposition just couldn't get its act together to find a way to appeal to the working class majority. There was a price to pay. Political variation is good. By the seventies, the Social Democrats were increasingly seen as synonymous with the state. Clever people who were not so ideological gravitated to the Social Democrats, which was the only chance to sit in government, and many civil servants, supposed to be politically objective, thought it politic to adopt Social Democratic views, and make this be known. The Social Democrats also controlled an extremely powerful confederation of trade unions, LO, with much higher unionisation rates than the UK. There was social pressure in many workplaces to vote for the Social Democrats, not least because joining a union – practically compulsory if you wanted unemployment insurance - conferred automatic membership of the party.

This only began to change in the 1980s. The conservative bourgeois coalition found fresh confidence in the new right of Margaret Thatcher and Ronald Reagan. And they found a new cause. Russophobia and activism in favour of a new cold war..

Here the Swedish political right found allies in military Sweden. Sweden, at least in the fifties until the early seventies, was one of Europe's most militarised states, a European version of the Israel, with an unusually politicised and independent-minded military leadership. These values did not conflict with the Social Democracy of the time, which was far more pro Western and defence oriented than the 1980s, by which time, under Palme, it had become more anti-militaristic, pro blacks in Africa and much less anti Russian.

You could therefore talk about two Social Democratic parties, the militarist and later the pacifist, third world engagement one, which relied on multilateral UN solutions and believed in helping the global South. To the average English speaker, Sweden was, in the 1970s and 80s, and perhaps still is, to an extent, despite the neoliberal advances, the world's moral conscience and the embodiment of the United Nations idea of the generous welfare state. A paradise of decent values, a cosy island of progressive goodness. An influential minority of diplomats, journalists and conservative politicians in America and the UK felt that Swedish foreign policy was led by finger-wagging moralists; but many average people who didn't think about Sweden from one year to the next had a generally positive feeling about the place. And that is why the murder seemed to come so much out of the blue. The cognitive dissonance of a brutal assassination in utopia. But there are also, as we have already begun to explore, other realities. Other Swedens.

The Social Democrats had actually had a strong pacifist streak before Palme, from the 1880s to the 1930s. The Party only made peace with the military during and after the War. So you could argue that the tensions between Palme and the military was a resuscitation of the age old conflict. In WW1, the Social Democrats were regarded as unreliable and peace-loving by then government, in which the king was still a powerful influence. We also have to look at Palme's personal history. He was born in the 1920s into the Stockholm upper class. His family were aristocrats and soldiers. And the young Palme was an enthusiastic officer. After national service, he stayed on as a reserve officer for years, and briefly worked in military intelligence. And then he changed utterly after he embraced Social Democracy. One theory is that his pro African, pro Latin American "moral imperialism" in later life – helming an outward-looking Sweden that aggressively promoted peace and anticolonialism in the world – he attempted to channel the ancient Swedish desire to dominate the Baltic region, into an aspiration to impose Swedish socialist moral influence in a decolonising world, far from Sweden's own shores. Some people thought Palme was a Russian spy for doing this.

IF YOU DO just one tourist thing in Stockholm, avoid the Abba tours and the Stieg Larsson "Girl with a Dragon Tattoo" walks and head for the army museum, an elegant classical building in white stucco covering a whole block in Östermalm, the posh quarter, the Mayfair of Stockholm.

I visit the museum, one late summer's day a year or so after my initial interest in the Palme murder is piqued. Despite its size, the museum is off the beaten tourist track, perhaps because few foreign tourists associate Sweden with military prowess. But how wrong they are. A small plaque near the entrance informs the visitor that the army museum has a collection of four thousand standards from the 17th, 18th and 19th centuries belonging to other nations. Standards were critical and symbolic items of loot, since the standard was used to communicate messages in war as well as motivate the troops. Once they was taken, standards were counted as a symbolic victory over the opposing army. Standard bearers were defended tenaciously. And this is the astonishing thing: the Swedish army museum claims to have the world's largest collection of other nations' standards.

If you talked to an educated European of say 1910, this would not have come as a surprise. Sweden was, at the beginning of the twentieth century, not about Olof Palme's "peaceful progressive state" but was associated with winning wars and occupying other countries. In the beginning you had the Vikings of course. But in the 17th and 18th centuries, a couple of warrior kings, among them Gustavus Adolphus and Charles XII, mobilised the country's small population and turned Sweden into a very successful military-administrative warrior state. Perhaps Europe's first military state, a model for others, such as Peter the Great in Russia, later still Prussia. Russia was much larger but had been beaten by Sweden several times because Sweden was more organised, more disciplined, more autocratic. So Peter the Great's Russia modelled itself on Sweden in order to become a successful conqueroring nation itself.

The first famous Swedish warrior king was Gustavus Adolphus, who fought Poland and Russia, annexed the Baltic lands. Famously, he intervened in the German wars of religion, 1618 to 1648, also known as the Thirty Years War, and made a crucial difference with his revolutionary tactics of sword cavalry charges and manoeuvrable artillery. His organised military state, funded by high taxes on the peasantry and a church under state control that whipped up fervour for the war from the pulpit, was imitated by other countries, who wanted to keep up with the Swedes. It was easier to get Swedes to follow a single will than in the well-populated European states where the power of the king was undermined by a powerful rural nobility. Sweden had a weak nobility and few towns and so the country could tolerate a power system where the king alone dominated. Sweden also developed an ultra-competent administration. Thanks to this, and a church that organised, educated and monitored the population, the Swedish kingdom was able to mobilise the country's economic and human resources with an eafficiency that exceeded its neighbours. The army was characterised by immense discipline – there were 44 crimes to which the death penalty applied, including not turning up for morning prayers.

SINCE 1814, Sweden has been at peace. But even a hundred years later its old warrior reputation still stuck to it. Then Sweden was a neutral in world war 2, early Social Democrats had a reputation for progressive labour reforms, and then Sweden really began to shift leftwards with Palme. Of course, Palme lived through only part of this period, but more than anyone else he perhaps embodied the changes Sweden underwent. And he hurried them on. He came from one of the richest, most conservative, "old school" families in Stockholm – and one of the most militaristic ones. And while he did become an officer as a youth, and had traditional conservative views, he crossed the line and became a Social Democrat: not only that, but the most radical, most self-consciously "modern" leader the Social Democrats have ever had. And one who preached the humanitarian message all his life.

Who was he really?

On my way back through Stockholm, having visited the military museum, I try to conjure up some visuals.

Public man: Palme as the young politician: the suntanned, 30-something with rolled-up shirt sleeves, sweeping his blonde fringe back, on some political tour of Northern Sweden, talking from the back of a lorry about why he was a "democratic socialist", the face of Swedish progressivism. Family man: here he was, on the Swedish Baltic holiday island of Gotland, jumping down the dunes, in worn jeans, shorts and a faded old shirt, laser-eyed and flashy smiled, carrying his blonde 4-year-old son on his shoulders.

Media man: talking in excellent British English to David Frost; hesitant, slightly shyly about why he was against violence on television as it "affected young children quite badly". Later, there was also sneaky Palme: the ageing bureaucrat: telling sour lies, or cruelly putting down political opponents, ignoring friends and allies, blind to growing domestic right-wing critique of Sweden: its naiv foreign policies, its economic policies, its bloated welfare state. And finally there was dead Palme.

Palme's admiring biographer, Henrik Berggren, compares him to a James Bond-like existentialist: a brave radical, a man before his time, not socialist but almost a liberal rationalist, decisive. A thinking action hero – a creation of Berggren's that, in my opinion, creates a figure the whole of the new post-assassination Sweden 25 years is able to unite around, and heal its wounds. In Berggren's and others' analysis, he was a genuinely great man, influential with global politicians, a big friend of foreign "freedom movements" and on first name terms with every leader in the Bandung Conference of nonaligned states. A kind of political rock star. To other fans, he was a left wing, basically pro-American guy, who got it "right" on the main issues. Palme was in favour of equality, women's rights, combating third world poverty, world peace, nuclear disarmament – and, above all, he was against the Vietnam war, where he was western Europe's most publicly outspoken critic. Others thought Palme was a nationalist, of sorts: in his own, Swedish way, not in terms of military conquests, but in moral influence. The Danish writer Mogens Berendt called it Sweden's narcissistic megalomania . The Swedes liked to claim theirs was the most desirable social and political model, an example as a society for the rest of the world. A self-proclaimed moral superpower that exploited the static global situation between the two superpower blocs during the cold war to show Sweden's virtues off.

Colleagues could say Palme had a temper that was like a "planet exploding" yet who would cry when he saw suffering. He enjoyed being a decider and had high demands of his staff: he ranged across his ministers' expert areas and liked to intrude on their press conferences. In other subjects he was not so interested and ministers in these less favoured subject areas complained they had about thirty seconds to catch his attention before he tuned out. His family thought he was warm, generous and incredibly anti-authoritarian as a father (if frequently absent, despite his proclamations of feminism) who read Pippi Longstocking and Lord of the Rings to the children when young and discussed Russian poetry and Solzhenitsyn with them when older. Yet others thought he was a naïf, a fool. He was not very popular in Britain or America, inasmuch in that they were familiar with him. Nixon thought Olof Palme was loud-mouthed, self-righteous and ignorant.

The American conservative William Buckley writes him up – in Palme's obituary, March 1986, written for the wire services, published in hundreds of American newspapers - as a kind of Dostoyevskian idiot.

"There is something appealing about Olof Palme, even if he did his best during his long career to make Sweden uninhabitable. His dream of the beautiful socialist society totally interrupted any view of anything that stood in the way of his ideological dogma, If it is socialist it has got to be good. There were no anomalies recognised by him visible to the non-Swedish observer. His idealism was total."

And the self-exiled novelist Sven Fagerberg, one of the biggest critics of Palme, talks of an unbelievable simpleton with blue eyes (this had nothing to do with Palme's high formal IQ), good intentions and a steel toecap in his voice. Someone without integrity, full of fancies and whims, who went with the left wing flow of the times, interested only in power and jealous of genuine talent.

One thing everyone can agree on is this scion of the upper class changed his class loyalties. I suppose many revolutionaries did. Consider Danton, or Robespierre, or Bernardo O'Higgins, the liberator of Chile, or Cuba's Fidel Castro.

HAVING LEFT the army museum, still in the Östermalm quarter, I find myself in one of the most well-heeled main streets, Östermalmsgatan. I pause for a while. I look up at the cream-coloured four-story building in front of me, today the Romanian embassy, complete with menacing aerials on the roof. Back in 1927, it was the family home of Olof Palme's parents and grandparents, and here he was born on 30 January of that year.

As we have seen, Sweden, this country with a proud imperial history behind it, had just granted the universal franchise in 1918, late by European standards. This when Britain had already long had parliamentary rule and France universal male suffrage for 70 years.

The Palme family belonged to the old ruling class, martial in its outlook, commercial by its profession, conservative in disposition. Sweden was then an extremely pro German society. Swedish policemen wore pickelhube helmets and the elite easily read German newspapers like today they read American ones. Olof Palme's uncle, also called Olof Palme, went out to fight in the Finnish civil war of 1918 as a volunteer. Finland had been an inseparable part of Sweden for several hundred years until 1809, when the Russians seized it. (In the long history of wars between Russia and Sweden, Sweden was more often the sinner than the sinned against, though.) Although many Finns welcomed Russian rule, since it allowed Finnish culture and national feeling to develop amid virtual complete political autonomy, the Swedish elite thought Russian control of a country that had been an indivisible part of the Swedish state intolerable. As the 19th century progressed, the Swedish language lost its status in Finland as the utterly dominant medium of public life and education and Finnish took an ever larger role. Many right-wing Swedes were almost as unhappy about the growth of Finnish culture as they were about Russian rule of Finland. And people like Olof Palme Senior wanted a Finland reattached to Sweden. Many aristocrats and leading figures wanted to join Germany in the attack on Russia in 1914. They were denied this by a cautious government. But they bided their time. In 1918, after the Bolshevik revolution and the collapse of the Russian empire – which led to civil wars between "reds" and "whites" in Finland

– a Swedish volunteer movement saw its opportunity. Battalions were formed and sent over to Finland to fight on the white side.

The elder Olof Palme was killed by machine gun fire at the battle of Tammerfors on 3 April 1918. He was 33. He left behind a widow and four children. The other uncle, Nils, also fought in Finland, but survived. Olof Palme the younger's grandfather, Sven Palme, the chief executive for Scandinavia's largest insurance company, whose wife Hanna was a Finnish-Swedish aristocrat, was, like his sons, fanatic about getting Finland separated from Russia. He wanted a Finland under Swedish tutelage, a kind of restoration of Swedish empire, and Sven Palme was one of founders of Finland's Friends, the committee for Swedish aristocratic support for the Finnish Whites.

Upper-class men who wouldn't have minded "giving the workers a good hiding" in an increasingly fractious Sweden itself got the opportunity to do so in Finland instead. The letters of Adolf Hamilton, a young earl, a typical upper-class Swedish volunteer, have been published. His father was one of the most influential conservative politicians in Sweden: the speaker of the larger of the two Swedish parliamentary chambers, the Senate. Since the Finnish soldiers on the White side were mainly conscripts, the Swedish volunteer officers brought in plenty of expertise to the White Side. The handsome, chiselled, duelling-scarred Hamilton's skill was artillery, and he became head of the artillery school behind White lines. He was later dubbed the "father of the Finnish artillery". His letters to his prominent father are characterised by a kind of militant optimism. In one letter to his father, he says, "We [the right-wing Swedish volunteers] are going to march on St Petersburg...and after that we are going to seize Stockholm. If I was a member of the current Swedish government [of left-wing liberals and Social Democrats], I would wish I was elsewhere."

He added. "When we get to Helsinki, let's hope we catch Ivar Vennerström and Carl Lindhagen. It would be a great pleasure to hang both of them." Vennerström and Lindhagen were both left-wing Swedish Social Democrats, active agitators against the military. There were suspicions among the military class and bourgeoisie that the Swedish "reds", like their Finnish counterparts, were Trojan horses for a Russian takeover of Scandinavia. The Finnish reds were indeed supported by the new Bolshevik regime in Petrograd (St Petersburg) which was not, however, in much of a position to help out.

Hamilton described to his father how, on a whim, he and some friends, having had too much to drink, took a couple of Finnish "Reds" out of the jail cells into the yard to be executed. The corpses were then dragged to the entrance of the workers' union cafe where they lay the whole day to deter others. The letter from one of the men written to his children and wife moments before he was shot was quite pathetic.

It was part of an orgy of White death squad activity, 10,000 people over three months, many executions led by Swedish officers, against working class Finns who had nothing to do with the war. Bjarne Stenkvist, a Swedish historian, contrasts this orgy of killing unfavourably with the deeds of the right wing Pinochet regime in Chile, which shot a smaller number, 3,000 leftists, over a longer period, 18 years. Leeway to these "courts on the front" was given by the central White command to maintain deniability. Since the White actually won and formed a government, records were later destroyed. The victims were Social Democratic members of the local administration; members of the Finnish parliament, and members of Red tribunals and police. On snowy nights, trade union representatives were asked to walk down country roads and shot in the back. Patients were ripped out of hospital beds and manhandled into courtyards where they were machine-gunned down. One man was shot in the temple when told to look away because he stammered. On this occasion, a number of privates stood on the sidelines, quiet and upset. While records of the incidents were destroyed by White officials after the war, these slaughters were well known at the time and far outnumbered the Red killings of estate owners and priests at the beginning of the civil war.

When the Swedish volunteers returned to Sweden in late 1918, and marched to Stockholm's stadium to a patriotic celebration, Swedish Social Democrats along the marching route spat and called them butchers. There were scuffles and several were arrested, charged and convicted for disturbing the peace. It was traumatic for at least some of the returning volunteers who had fought on the white side. Colonel Harald Hjalmarson, the leader of the Swedish brigade, committed suicide. Ex-volunteers found themselves blacklisted and ostracised from workplaces by the Social Democrat labour unions. But other Swedish veterans prospered by entering and advancing in the regular Swedish army. The ex-volunteers later counted among three heads of the Swedish army, one chief of staff to the Swedish supreme commander, and the pro-Nazi head of the Swedish military intelligence service during the Second World War, Carlos Adlercreutz.

Tensions between the militarist royalist right, and the Social Democratic republican left were big, but Sweden avoided Finland's civil war, despite the hunger riots and class differences that were every bit as big as in Finland. One factor may have been a personal friendship between Hjalmar Branting, the Social Democrats' leader, who had an upper-class background, and Gustav V, the king. They had attended the same private school. The radical wing of the Social Democrats – who had wanted to abolish the monarchy or start a revolution – were shifted out of the party and formed their own radical leftist party, which went nowhere.

Instead, Sweden developed peacefully and became, over the next two decades, a kind of corporatist state of consensual, constantly negotiating interests, the emblem of which was the Saltsjöbaden agreement of 1938 that guaranteed labour peace between employers and employees. Left and right could somehow agree on the idea of the People's Home, (folkhemmet), a conformist but safe place. The folkhemmet is the most used and abused word in the Swedish 20th-century political vocabulary. It was a right wing idea initially, with overtones of soft fascism. But the Social Democrats appropriated it when they came into power. In Finland, meanwhile, since the Whites won, the history of Finland tended to be written from their perspective, and, as memories of those who lived through the events faded away, a delicate veil placed over the atrocities until a flood of books on the subject in the last few years. In the autumn of 1917, there were 92 Social Democrats in the Finnish Landtag, or parliament. Six months later, only one remained. The others had been murdered, imprisoned or escaped the country.

In 1918, the Swedish Social Democrats looked at what had happened to their comrades in Finland, at the hands of the mostly Swedish speaking upper class, combined with the efforts of volunteers from Sweden, and counted their blessings. The bitter, hateful war that took place in Finland had somehow been avoided in Sweden itself. But the grounds for tension were still there. Olof Palme (the young one, the subject of this book), scion of a military famly, got into conflict with the military at the end of his life, almost a throwback to the deeply divided Sweden of the early twentieth century. Indeed, some have speculated whether these tensions played a part in Olof Palme's assassination.

PALME'S CHILDHOOD AND YOUTH: 1927-1944

Only one of Sven Palme's three sons failed to fight in Finland: Gunnar Palme, the man who was to become the future prime minister's father. Gunnar Palme did, however, function as recruitment secretary for the volunteer brigade. Quieter and less impulsive than either his elder brother Olof, the historian and soldier, or the younger brother Nils, the entrepreneur and timber businessman, Gunnar was groomed to take over from his father Sven in the family insurance company, Thule. For much of that time, he stood in the older man's shadow. After the outbreak of the first world war, Gunnar married an aristocrat from the German-speaking minority in Latvia. Like his father, Sven, he had chosen to marry a woman from across the Baltic. But while Gunnar's wife, the future prime minister's mother, Elisabeth von Knieriem, was a "real" foreigner, from the cosmopolitan city of Riga, a Latvian-Jewish-German port city in the huge Russian empire, Sven's wife, Gunnar's mother, was from the well-established Finlandish Swedish elite in Finland with numerous links into Swedish society. While Riga had some historic links to Sweden, the elite's language was German, not Swedish. So Olof's mother found it much harder to adapt than his grandmother.

Hanna von Born, the grandmother, Sven's wife, was an extremely domineering woman, who in widowhood ran her country estate of Ånga, south of Stockholm, with an iron hand, Elizabeth was a quieter character and never quite found her feet in the Swedish environment. Born in 1890 in Riga, her father was a successful academic, trained at Heidelberg University in agronomics.

He later headed the technical university of Riga. He also ran the university agronomy department estate called Peterhof outside the city, which combined regular estate management and farming with various plant science studies. When war between the German and Russian empires broke out in August 1914, the university had to change its teaching language to Russian and Elizabeth's mother was sent into house arrest in Moscow, for alleged fifth column activity on behalf of the Germans. Elizabeth was at Freiburg University in Germany, studying medicine. Because she was a Russian citizen, her studies were interrupted by the outbreak of war and she had to return to Moscow, to meet up with her mother. As a Red Cross nurse tending German prisoners of war, she wrote letters home complaining about the terrible treatment German soldiers received. The letters came to the Russian authorities' attention.

The Russian secret police came to ask questions. It was dangerous to stay. The Swedish consul in Riga came to Elizabeth's rescue by arranging for her to leave for Sweden in early 1915. As it happened, in one of those amazing coincidences that influence the history of nations, the diplomat was good friends with Gunnar Palme, and asked his friend, then a 32 and a bachelor, to take care of the refugee. Elizabeth was quartered in the nanny's room of Sven Palme's flat and taught Gunnar's younger sister German. After intrigues to avoid the gimlet-eyed scepticism of the family matriarch that Palme's biographer Henrik Berggren compares to a bedroom farce, Elizabeth and Gunnar got together and were married on an idyllic Swedish June day in the summer of 1916. So that is the story of how Olof Palme's parents got together.

Gunnar's best man was Folke Bernadotte, the king's nephew and a young officer's cadet. Much later, Bernadotte would have been an inspiration to the young Olof Palme. Bernadotte had a future ahead of him as a hero and man of peace. Thirty years later, in 1945, when Palme was a teenager in his last year at boarding school in a sedate part of Sweden, Bernadotte saved 31,000 Norwegians and Danes, including many Jews, from the German concentration camps, by bringing them back to Scandinavia in the so-called White Buses campaign.

In a royal family where pro-German sympathies were rife, and there was at least passive acquiescence to the Nazis, Bernadotte stood out of a man who did the right thing in the name of humanitarianism. Deputy director of the Swedish Red Cross, Bernadotte travelled frequently between Stockholm and Berlin to try and convince Nazi leaders that Sweden should be allowed to take responsibility for Scandinavian prisoners in Germany's crumbling concentration camp system. This was in early 1945. He got to know the Nazi leadership quite well, so this he was granted. So with the Reich collapsing and every road crammed with vehicles, refugees and soldiers, 40 or so buses marked with the Red Cross and the Swedish flag edged their way from the Danish border to the camps deep inside the collapsing Reich.

Books by participants in the rescue actions describe tense moments when British and American dive bombers, which had complete air superiority, flew low and consider strafing the column, but on each occasion they were spared. Bernadotte wrote a book about his experiences and it became a best seller even in Britain and the USA when it came out in 1946, as it offered the first journalistic pen portrait of who the Nazi leaders were and how the Nazi court functioned. Bernadotte went on to become the United Nations' first peace broker in Palestine, in 1948. But within days of arriving was murdered by a gunman from the Israeli terrorist Stern gang who poked a machine gun through the rear windows of Bernadotte's official car, killing not only Bernadotte but also the French commanding general Andre Serot of the UN operation. Ironically, the general only came only on the ride because he wanted to thank Bernadotte for saving the general's wife from the Holocaust – she had been rescued from Dachau by Bernadotte's white buses. One of the planners of the Bernadotte assassination was Yitzhak Shamir, later Israeli prime minister. But Sweden never did make a big effort to bring the perpetrators in the Stern gang to justice.

SWEDEN HAS produced four statesmen of peace in the 20th century, and they were all assassinated or otherwise killed for it. One was Folke Bernadotte, killed by Israelis, another was Raoul Wallenberg, who saved tens of thousands of Jews in Budapest. He was arrested by the Soviets and died at the hands of the KGB in 1947. The third was Dag Hammarskjöld, the UN's most effective director general. More about Hammarskjöld later. His air crash in Congo, termed an "accident", was probably an assassination. Palme, younger by a generation than those men, grew up with his life defined by their achievements - perhaps tried to match them. And Palme was also assassinated. And in all four cases, the Swedish state has done little to seek to bring the nations associated with the killers to justice. Perhaps Sweden has too much to lose by offending powerful foreign states...

But Bernadotte's unfortunate end was decades away, and Palme was not to be born for another 12 years, as Bernadotte officiated at Palme's parents' wedding in 1916. After they married, Palme's parents lived relatively quiet and unassuming lives, both of them shy and retiring by nature. Elizabeth gave birth to three children, Claes, 1917, Catharina, 1920 and Olof Palme, 1927. She was frustrated in her career. Having broken off her studies in medicine at Freiburg at the start of the war, she tried to resume them at Stockholm's prestigious Karolinska medical institute for a while, but gave up her medical studies when pregnant with her eldest son. Instead, she took up voluntary work for the Red Cross, worked at a forerunner to today's childcare centres, and was voted into the executive committee for the feminist organisation Fredrika Bremer. Perhaps her frustration, communicated to her son, is what made him push through the widespread reforms to get every woman out into the workplace once he became prime minister. Meanwhile, Palme's father completed his law studies at Uppsala University, worked in the courts for a while and was employed by his father at the Thule Life Assurance company where he slowly started working his way to the top.

Sven Palme and his son Gunnar (and family, including Olof) lived in two separate mansion flats on the top floor of the house at Östermalmsgatan, separated by a landing. Servants, children and various pets crossed freely from one residence to the other. It likely resembled something from the Ingmar Bergman film Fanny and Alexander; richly textured wallpaper, mountains of presents at Christmas, glögg (mulled wine) and gingerbread houses. Little girls with bands in their hair and boys in sailor's uniforms. Christmas dancing from to room-to-room, candles everywhere and sleigh bells outside.

Summers were spent at Olof Palme's mother's parents' estate at Skangal outside Riga, a steamer ride across the Baltic away. At the end of her long life, Olof Palme's sister, Catharina Palme, wrote a very evocative memoir of her summers in Skangal with her mother Musi, her elder brother Claes and Palme, the baby of the family, seven years younger. She described the summers at Skangal as a "sequence of days without variation, one much like the other like pearls on a pearl necklace. The monotony gave a sense of security and harmony. Children need less variety than one thinks." Her book offers a splendid evocation of estate life in Eastern Europe in the 1930s. Long summers, little or no electricity, long northern summer evenings sitting on the veranda with gossiping womenfolk and a silent, ageing, tired patriarch, Olof's grandfather Woldemar. Feeding the pigs, helping with the hay, running barefoot in the dew covered morning grass. At breakfast, they drank coffee of corn and chicory, black bread baked twice a month with cheese and jam. They ate jellies for dessert, red on the top, white on the bottom, and gooseberry flavoured cream. At five, Olof was often ill, in chest infections or eczemas. His mother was prone to hysteria and letters went back and forth across the Baltic as soon as Olof's temperature reached

37.5 degrees Celsius (99.5 degrees F). To be fair, these were the days before antibiotics, and pneumonia could be fatal.

Opapa, Olof's mother's father, sat quietly at the head of the table in his later years, using his combined fork and spoon, a useful utensil that is seldom seen these days. The estate was mostly self-sufficient. There was a country shop a few kilometres away where you could buy essentials that could not be made at home: sugar, yeast and occasionally a bottle of schnapps which Opapa drank one glass of for supper. Illiterate home helps had long red hair and could not be persuaded to be serious about hygiene. The kids Olof, Claes and Catharina went barefoot from the first day to the last. The home helps' task was to wash the children's feet every night when they sat on benches outside the kitchen door and had their feet scrubbed. Baths were reserved for special occasions and for Opapa. The water was heated in large pots on the stove. Elder brother Claes was responsible for bathing Opapa. He helped him in and out of the bath and scrubbed his back with a brush.

The children were bilingual in Swedish and German but spoke no Latvian, so Olof's and Catharina's mother made sure to invite Baltic German children to play. The Baltic German community left for Germany after the Second World War started a few years later. His elder brother, Claes, helped out in the stables from morning till evening, while Catharina picked fallen apples to give to the pigs.

When the womenfolk sat shucking peas around the large table on the veranda, the gossip and the chat flowed. It was regarded as impolite to sit with one's hands in one's lap. Grandmother had a special chair made of velvet which no one else was allowed to occupy. When they weren't shucking peas they worked, read aloud or played games. On these occasions, Olof would sit playing in the sandpit visible from the veranda. A toy dog that did not move when Olof called it Tom Heraus {after the German komm heraus, come out) the dog had a new name Tom Heraus. Thirty-five years later Palme's own children played with the same dog, wrote Catharina. Olof was very intense in his play and would not be disturbed. When called for supper he once refused and said Ich bin angeklebt, I am stuck. Already then, said his sister, he was witty and had a quick repartee. Their grandfather had excellent contact with Claes, less with Catharina and Olof, who was too young. He talked less and less and sat in a chair attended by a nurse. He was always reading the same book by Schiller, the German poet.

On summer evenings they played cops and robbers. The "cops" waited in the tree-lined road that led to the estates. It was quite unpleasant because it was so dark she said. Otherwise, Olof was always playing by the little pond full of weeds. He built small rafts and managed to entertain himself quite royally. They also brought their bicycles and made trips. Catharina had few dolls. But she was very glad of Olof. "It matters a lot for a little girl to get a baby brother."

If Olof Palme was not paid so much attention to by his mother's father, the Baltic German academic, he got all the more attention from Grandpa Sven, his paternal grandfather, back in Stockholm, where the family lived the other nine months of the year. They lived in the same building, after all. Olof learned to read from a very young age. Aged five, he had used to read the headlines of the newspaper to the old insurance man when shaving. The family was international and curious about the outside world. Palme learned German from his mother and maternal grandparents, as we have seen. His nanny taught him French. And he was very precocious in Swedish, being frequently called from the children's nursery and asked to recite the poetry of the Viking Sagas to dinner guests. Despite the surroundings of privilege, his biographers say, there was a glimmer of the socialist-to-be. Unlike his noisy, self-centred grandparents, even as a privileged child he noticed the Little People. Sweden at the time was very much a class society, still, even though the Social Democrats had made their breakthrough – and his relatives were at the apex of the pyramid of this class society. Much later, after Olof Palme had died, the family's old maid put flowers at the assassination scene and a note saying. "Olof you were different, I remember you, as an eight-year-old, always helping us maids carry out the dishes and talking to us as equals."

When Olof Palme was six years old, in 1933, tragedy struck. Olof Palme's father Gunnar, died of an asthma attack, aged 48, just weeks after his own father, Palme's grandfather, the insurance magnate Sven, passed away of old age. Rather than seeing Palme raised in an all-female environment – the elder son, Claes, being away at Uppsala university - his mother Elisabeth sent him to Sweden's top boarding school, Sigtuna.

Sigtuna boarding school, Sweden's Eton, trained the Swedish elite in the idyllic surroundings of an ancient cathedral town overlooking an inlet of lake Mälaren. Two years into his school career there, the Second World War broke out. When the boys sang in revues and played tennis in gently wooded surroundings by the lake, the war raging around Sweden's borders must have felt far away indeed.

Yet boarding schools were their own self-contained world, and Palme was fighting his own battles. What motivated Olof Palme when he became Sweden's most radical prime minister? Maybe it was to purge Sweden of all its remaining autocratic, aristocratic tendencies. He was bullied at school, and maybe he blamed the upper class for all his negative experiences. Some journalists wondered, when, as prime minister, he made some particularly savage attack on the right of centre political bloc – the common name was the "bourgeois" bloc -- what had been the wellspring of his hate. His face would contort and his spittle-flecked curse "the Bourgeoisie" came twisted out of his mouth, in four syllables. "Bour-ge-ois–ie." Maybe this was it. School days.

One of Palme's biographers, Henrik Berggren, paints a forgiving, indulgent portrait of this young man. At 174cm (five foot eight) fully grown, Palme was physically smaller than many of the other boys, accelerated academically and thus younger, accentuating the size differences at this most sensitive age. He was subjected to bullying, despite his best attempts to be one of the guys by enthusiastically participating in sports. Indoor hockey was one favourite, where he was the goalkeeper. He was regarded as incredibly clever. This did not endear him to his classmates. Despite his exceptional intelligence, his grades were good, not brilliant. Personal hygiene was a problem. His nickname was "Skit Olle". Skit is the Swedish word for shit.

He was understimulated, when not being bullied, and escaped into his favourite interest: literature, especially modernist literature, where he had a highly mature, even avant garde, taste. When he was 17, he read the Swedish modernist Harry Martinson and James Joyce's Ulysses. "He was self-important, combative and always had to be right," said one individual who confessed he had once been one of his bullies.

THE POLITICAL breakthrough of the working class Social Democrats in 1918 had introduced some of the culture of the Swedish peasant community into Swedish daily life, and even coloured its foreign relations. The old Sweden that had dominated until the first world war - the aristocratic and royal Sweden, with its great power nostalgia, its military past, obsession with Russia, sense of destiny, and frustration – was gone. Instead, the thirties saw the rise of a self-contained, self-sufficient national egoism of a rural Sweden where the psychology of the peasant community came more to the forefront. Bernadotte's policy of neutrality created a hundred years earlier suited the peasant mind much better than it did the aristocratic mind. For all the autocracy at the level of the strong central state, the country had been too thinly populated, too inhospitable to allow the creation of major feudal estates. In the interwar period, Sweden as a state took on some of the flavour of a large peasant village, indifferent to the outside world, asking only to be left alone.

Instead of being engaged in international affairs, the Social Democrats consolidated and depolarised Sweden, which had been rent by strikes through the twenties, the Social Democratic breakthrough notwithstanding.

The Social Democrats also fell in love with functionalism. A critic of Swedish social democracy might say they combined the ideology of social engineering with the culture of the old peasant community to create a new era of peaceful social control, prosperity and welfare. Despite the formal democracy, the traditions of the powerful central state lived on, some might say, in Social Democratic paternalism. A number of new bureaucratic institutions concerned with watching over people's welfare were set up. Workers' homes were regularly inspected by a new cadre of social workers who might apply to the unclean and dissolute any number of penalties, including confiscation of the rationing card that allowed upstanding citizens three litres of alcohol a month from the state liquor store. Denunciation of neighbours who "behaved inappropriately" was encouraged until the 1940s as a "citizen's responsibility". Tens of thousands of women with unsuitable lifestyles or health problems were sterilised for the common good of the Swedish community. Personal integrity carried little value in relation to the wishes of the collective, or against the state's well-intentioned desire to help the workers lead better lives. As prof Yvonne Hirdman, who has specialised in the history of the Swedish control state, argues, "The politicians wished to create a new kind of healthy citizen and a stronger nation."

Because Sweden had been a society of a small autocratic monarchy and a vast peasantry, with no large urban middle class or bourgeoisie, the intermediate institutions of civil society had always been weaker than in the classically liberal states of western Europe.

The economic depression of the thirties affected Sweden less than other countries. Everywhere buildings in the new unadorned functionalist style were springing up, so photos of Sweden in this period show a level of visual modernity not achieved in other countries until the decades after the war. As recently as the turn of the 20th century, Stockholm had some of the worst slums in Europe, writes the historian Jenny Lundberg.

In 1936, Marquis Childs a young American journalist, published Sweden, the Middle Way, the country that had tamed the excesses of capitalism and where unions worked hand-in-hand with employers to improve productivity and avoid labour strife. It became one of the best sellers of the New Deal America of the late thirties, and Childs later won a Pulitzer Prize for commentary. The Middle Way referred to the fact that Sweden had avoided the extremes capitalism that, on the one hand, saw a massive concentration of wealth in the hands of the USA; on the other, saw the hardships of life in Russia. Roosevelt was impressed. He sent a commission to Sweden to look at how the country handled labour relations. Swedes, according to Childs, "cultivated their garden, their rocky, remote, lonely garden, with patience, with courage, and with an extraordinary degree of intelligence." The book was a paean of praise to Sweden, written partly out of ignorance, because of course Childs spoke no Swedish. But Sweden was fortunate to have Childs: he established this not entirely correct image of Sweden as the perfect, ancient democracy, when in fact Sweden was a very new democracy, and helped eclipse the reputation of the other, more liberal, Scandinavian countries. One reviewer in the 1980s called it "the fountainhead of mythopoesis about the Swedish welfare state that for more than four decades served as a textbook for numerous American would-be Fabians." Sweden became a place of pilgrimage for socialists in search of solutions to the crisis of reformism in Europe: Democratic Sweden, published in 1938 by the Fabian Society in London, is the first extensive compendium of the transformation implemented by a functional socialism". Sweden had been ruled by the Social Democrats for twenty years. They were not interested in glory on the Baltic, but in building up Sweden. They were rewarded with positive foreign coverage. Sweden was becoming a new kind of society, more like the society we know today.

SWEDEN IN WORLD WAR 2:1939-1945

The Social Democrats, building the welfare state and cultivating their rocky garden with "extraordinary intelligence", may not have been very interested in foreign affairs in the 1920s and 30s. But foreign affairs eventually intruded, whether they wanted to or not, with the Nazi rise to power. To the outside world, Sweden seemed to be a country increasingly in domestic political harmony. But the war exposed the ancient divisions in the country. The group that dominated was the one that wished to preserve Sweden's neutrality, and it has salience down into our day.

This is relevant to our story about Palme. Later, in the Palme's time, leftist governments everywhere in Europe came under suspicion about appeasing the Soviet Union. Did the British and American governments and military establishments trust Sweden and Olof Palme to stand up to Soviet pressure in the 1980s?

The roots of Sweden's modern reputation as a sail-trimmer par excellence were arguably established in the Second World War. The future British prime minister Harold Macmillan had served with distinction as a captain in the Grenadier Guards in WWI. In the Somme, he was wounded. He spent a whole day in the trenches with a bullet in his pelvis, reading Aeschylus in the original Greek while waiting to be rescued. Of the 28 freshmen who had started Balliol with Macmillan, only he and one other survived. In the 1930s he made a career on the backbenches as an arch-critic of appeasement and later served in a series of important posts in the wartime government. So he knew of what he spoke when he referred to Dag Hammarskjöld, the Swedish UN secretary general. "Hammarskjöld was a Swede, and although we admired the Swedish people we could not forget their long history of skilful abstention from the great causes which had torn the world apart." He sums up a prevailing view in the British military and political class: that Sweden had no fighting spirit, the result of a century of peace brought about by Bernadotte and the near total dominance, since the 1920s, of pacifist Social Democracy.

The war began when Olof Palme was in his third year at Sigtuna, this boarding school that was one of the many islands of the old social order, aristocratic, pro German, Russophobe. Many of his fellow pupils had pin-up photos of German soldiers with their "streamlined helmets, handsome uniforms and steel blue eyes." The 14-year-old Palme preferred American jazz, Jack Teagarden and Louis Armstrong. To an extent, the Second World War was a rerun of the first for Sweden's part. The same instincts, sometimes even the same people, urged allegiance to Germany, whose Nazi excesses were not then well known. A difference was that the Social Democrats were in government – more precisely, they formed a wartime coalition government which they absolutely dominated. While in 1914 they had been a semi-revolutionary party trying to get accepted by the establishment. The Swedish Social Democrat-led coalition government resisted early calls to join the German side. There were many military officers who still had "great power dreams" for Sweden – sharing in the German mastery of Europe, especially Eastern Europe. But the government resisted and generally played a very pro appeasement strategy. Norway and Denmark had been occupied in April 1940, Sweden avoided such a fate, as long as it kept on providing much-needed iron ore for the Nazi war machine. Which it did.

WHILE BRITAIN stood alone, and eastern Europe was suffering the almost unimaginable depredations of German occupation, Swedes lived in a bizarre little haven of near normality, neon light and food sufficiency under the Nazi umbrella. It is an underexplored perspective. Anglo-Saxon historians have emphasized a condition of permanent war between 1939 and 1945, and it is true for the British, and the Russians even more so, but the Swedish experience, more than any other country's, traces out a sketch of a post-war Nazi hegemony in Europe that might have occurred had not the Germans attacked Russia and America joined the war. Britain may well have survived in this alternative future scenario, impotent, on the sidelines: whether at peace or at war, its opposition a tiresome sideshow. Book fairs, business travel, sports events, between Stockholm and Berlin, took place. For Swedes, the German Neuropa was a reality. While maintaining its prosperous, calm, way of life, and selling goods to the Reich, Sweden was paid up front for its exports, chiefly iron ore, with gold looted from the occupied territories.

The first shocking news of this did not come out until January 1997 – it took about fifty years generally before Sweden's World War 2 secrets seeped out. A retired diplomat and a radio journalist reported in the newspaper Dagens Nyheter that, after examining the Riksbank central bank archives, it was clear that the central bank had evidence that Sweden was receiving looted Nazi gold in payment for war materials, but chose to continue the practice.

Another report, from US intelligence officials, details how the German legation in Stockholm sold diamonds, from 4 to 13 carats in size and looted from the Netherlands, to "dependable" Swedish purchasers. The vast majority of the diamond merchants in Antwerp and Amsterdam were Jews whose possessions were stolen as they were sent to camps.

What surprised the researchers Göran Elgemyr, a radio producer, and Sven Hedin, a retired diplomat, was the fact that it was they, non-historians, who broke the story. Before they looked into the Riksbank records in 1997, no Swedish scholar had looked at the tainted gold issue at all.

Sweden was at its most adaptable to Germany in the early years of the war, when Germany was militarily all-conquering in Europe. The high point of Germany's success – and consequently the high point of pro-war agitation among the Swedish military - was in early 1941, just before the invasion of Russia, about which the Swedes had early warning.

There was still hope from the Swedish military that they might join on the German side. The same aspiration as they had had in world war I. The Swedish army secretly printed up Russian-Swedish phrasebooks for their troops, in preparation for an invasion where they hoped to take part, the Swedish air force even rehearsed bombing runs in northern Sweden for the planned attack on Leningrad.

The Swedish government, dominated by pacifist Social Democrats, said no, again, to a petition by the supreme commander, but allowed some concessions to head off German diplomatic pressure, and the wishes of their own military. The Swedish government allowed German troop transports – armed men, not just soldiers on leave as previously – to and from Norway, from Norway to the Russian front. The Swedes set up food depots for the German army in the northern town of Luleå, escorted German ships through Swedish territorial waters en route to Finland to avoid attack by Russian submarines. Not all the activity was aimed against the Russians. The Swedes tapped British and American embassy cables and passed highly secret information on to Germany.

Against the Swedes the British tried some covert action, Special Operations Executive (SOE) operations, headed by Peter Tennant, whose official job was press attaché at the British embassy. SOE operatives blew up trains carrying iron ore to Germany. Part of Tennant's job description was spreading malicious rumours about the enemies of Britain, and he liked to circulate jokes at diplomatic gatherings about the Swedish king Gustav V's homosexuality – true, but covered up in Sweden – and relished spreading the rumour he was able to put his feet behind his head, which may or may not be true, to make the king seem ridiculous and thus discredit his pro-German proclivities.

PALME AS A YOUNG MAN: 1944-1953

At the end of the war, the teenager Palme was not yet a Socialist. Palme's left-wing radicalism in middle age might have come as a surprise to those who knew him as a young man. For example, on graduating from Sigtuna in 1944, he went into the army, serving in a top cavalry regiment, according to a list of wishes his father had once scrawled down on a piece of paper before he died. His elder brother, Claes, ten years the elder, had done the same. The cavalry still employed horses – the horse was thought effective in the forested, vast, area that was Lapland. By all accounts, Olof felt proud about serving in the army. He qualified as a reserve officer.

At a psychology test carried out in 1947, when Palme was 20, by an army psychologist, and which did become public knowledge until 15 years after Palme's death, his political views came out as conventionally conservative. He was not that knowledgeable or wise about politics, but he was creative and artistic, the psychologist said. "Palme has vast intellectual horizons in arts," he wrote.

But also this, given that he later instituted a most draconian tax regime ever seen in any western European country, was an especially interesting finding. Aged 20, Palme wanted lower taxes, "not quite halved", and he wanted no nationalisations of business, tougher prison sentences, and no democratisation of the officer corps. He was extremely anti-communist. When a journalist, Jonas Gummeson, published a book in 2001 with the findings of this test in it, along with other allegations that Palme had right-wing roots, some less substantiated admittedly than that black-on-white test, Palme's sons were furious – it destroyed he hagiographic myth of Palme as a lifeling leftist. According to the tabloid Expressen, Mårten Palme refused to meet the journalist Gummesson for a debate in a TV studio. Instead, he called him a "shithead" and said the book was completely twisted. The article did not explain if Palme junior thought Gummesson had got his facts wrong.

Palme's more recent biographers, like Henrik Berggren and Kjell Östberg, seem to agree that his journey leftwards was a gradual process. A scholarship to the United States sowed the seeds of personal and political change away from inherited conservative values. While registering to study law at Stockholm University in 1946, studies he did part-time over the next couple of years, he got a scholarship from a worthy cultural body called the American Scandinavian Foundation to study at Kenyon College. Kenyon was a liberal arts college in the Mid-West, now full of tough young ex-GIs who had served in the war and now enjoyed free tuition through the GI bill. There was no tradition of embracing America in Palme's strongly Germanophile, traditional family. So it was a kind of conscious break with the past.

Palme remembered the year he spent at the Midwestern college with its mock-Gothic environment as one of the happiest times of his life. With his crew cut, lopsided smile and college sweatshirt he became just one of the guys, a regular guy, Berggren says in his affectionate biography of Palme. He loved the informality of America compared to what he was used to, the upper-class life of Östermalm and Sigtuna. He acquired an encyclopaedic knowledge of American presidents. He had something of a passion for making sports lists. There was a shortage of girls, true, but he acquired two good friends, both war veterans, one of whom had escaped Germany as an anti-Nazi refugee in the thirties, both of whom later became academics. And spent the weekends travelling around Ohio on local buses, visiting local factories. His neighbour next door in T barracks, a temporary structure for overflow students, was Paul Newman – the actor, who was to share, in the sixties, Palme's passionate engagement against the war in Vietnam.

Berggren writes how America had won the war through its democratic, open and equal society, how it was evident that America, as the world's leading democracy, was going to play an active and positive role in the post-war world. The inheritance from the much-loved Roosevelt, who had died in office in April 1945, still very much framed the terms of reference and debate of American politics. The American trade union movement was stronger than it had ever been before. And for many, writes Berggren, who takes an optimistic and left-liberal stance on the world, victory in the second world war created an imperative in America to rectify all the injustices at home.

Palme described the atmosphere of America when he came back, as being full of "life-affirming materialism and naïve idealism." Politically, compared to the wave of sixties radicalism Palme was successfully to ride as a politician, the atmosphere at college was innocent and hedonistic. The Kenyon Review, the college magazine, did print some articles about foreign affairs. One was about the atom bomb: the article strongly objected to the idea of using an atom bomb against the Soviet Union, already, in 1947, transformed into cold war opponent. America had, for a few short years, a monopoly on the bomb, so had no fear of retribution. Still, the magazine reasoned, "We would probably discover we have turned a greater part of the world into an ash heap and driven its inhabitants to barbarianism and hopelessness."

Palme graduated from Kenyon with straight A's. His majors were economics and social sciences. He studied American history and the American constitution. His economics teacher, one Paul Titus, came from a background of Midwestern populism that was suspicious of the gold standard and big corporations and banks. The son of a train driver, Titus taught Palme to examine both Marx and Adam Smith on an equal level, something that got Titus into a minor trouble with the authorities during the McCarthy era which began a few years after Palme had left. Berggren thinks this broadened Palme's horizons, though there was no evidence as yet that Palme was in any way a socialist. Palme later claimed to have been a member of a socialist society while at Kenyon, but this claim has not been able to be verified.

It is probable, though, that Palme took part in a seminar organised by prof Titus where a member of the small American socialist party was invited. Palme wrote an essay on Hayek's The Road to Serfdom, one of the most cited texts in modern economics, a clarion call for libertarianism and a furious attack on the big state and central planning. Sadly the essay has not been preserved. Judging by his underlinings in his copy of the printed book, which has been preserved in the Palme archives, he took issue with Hayek's rhetoric where Social Democrat welfare policies were equated to Nazism and communism. "Kenyon awoke Palme's interest in economic doctrines," writes Berggren. The other thing Palme took away from Titus's lectures was an interest in industrial relations and labour market policies, and his final degree paper was on the American autoworkers' union, United Auto Workers, UAW. Palme spent several weekends at a ball bearing factory near Kenyon, almost certainly part of the research he was required to do as part of his degree for prof Titus.

During his summer trip across the United States, he visited and interviewed the legendary head of the UAW Walter Reuther at General Motors' headquarters in Detroit. Reuther had started out working at the conveyor belts and in his youth worked as a factory hand in the Soviet Union. In the hard strikes of the thirties, he had been roughed up by anti-trade union thugs from Ford. He had given up his socialism and called himself an American Social Democrat. As an enthusiastic New Dealer, he was looking to create a modern welfare state out of America with the help of the powerful trade unions.

Reuther was successful in negotiating extensive packages of rights for American car workers, including medical insurance, employer-funded pensions and extra unemployment benefits. His tactic was to target one of the big three automakers in turn. If they did not deal, he would go on strike at that plant and that one of the big three targeted would lose market share to its two rivals.

Later, Reuther became a champion of the Civil Rights movement and was so powerful he managed to frighten conservatives. In 1958, future presidential candidate Barry Goldwater declared Reuther a "dangerous menace" and "more dangerous than anything the Sputnik or the Soviet Union might do to America".

Reuther died at the age of 62 in 1970 with his wife when the Learjet they were travelling in crashed 260 miles from Detroit. The death has always excited speculation, since he had survived a near-fatal crash 18 months before approaching Dulles airport in another Learjet. His brother

Victor always maintained Reuther was the victim of a plot, mechanical sabotage. He was assassinated.

Anyhow, Berggren speculates that a significant shift in Palme's attitudes about his identity came when he realised in how high esteem Sweden was regarded in New Deal, US labour circles, like the much-admired Reuther. Thanks to the Social democrats' progressive efforts before the war, and books like Marquis Childs's, Sweden was held to be a prosperous model country with a well-organised trade union movement and where collaboration between the Unions and the Social Democrat ruling party was always close.

FOR THE YOUNG Palme, it must all have prompted a rethink. In his russophobic family, he was raised on myths of wars, like those fought by ancient kings Gustavus Adolphus and Charles XII. The latter frequently defeated Russian czar Peter the Great and penetrated deep into. But that was long ago. And his uncles had not exactly covered themselves with glory in Finland. A focus for his pride, the military education he had had in Sweden, despite being impressive by Swedish standards, counted for little when he was in the company of veterans who had fought on the beaches of Normandy or the islands of the Pacific Palme was a young man with strong national feelings, and whose family background had certain strong military traditions, but here he realised that what Sweden was actually well known and well regarded for in these post-war days was not its military achievements, for it had none, not for 200 years anyway – but for its left-wing reforms.

"Sweden's WW2 neutrality was usually a burden for those Swedes travelling around in the world at this time," writes Berggren. Sweden's welfare model, based on harmonious industrial relations, reforms that the Social Democrats had carried out in the thirties, was something Swedes genuinely could be proud of. Perhaps Palme drew the appropriate conclusion. He should appropriate this genuine Swedish achievement and make it part of his identity, and forget about all the military stuff.

After his year at Kenyon, Palme spent the summer of 1948 hitchhiking and greyhounding it across the States, staying at YMCAs, eating cheeseburgers in drugstores and sleeping on night buses. He had lived a sheltered life in a series of elite Swedish institutions, from boarding schools to the Guards cavalry. But in America he was free to escape the straitjacket of his background for the first time, and he clearly had some defining experiences. He once sat at the back, with the blacks, on a bus in the South, rather than near the front, with the other whites. When he was asked by a couple of young white males to move, he refused - and escaped being beaten, he said in a letter home, only because they "took me for a crazy foreigner". In the eyes of his biographers, this was a pivotal event in his life.

Later, he would exaggerate the suddenness of his conversion to the left, focusing on a couple of easily explained incidents such as the one above, when he encountered racism in a very stark way. But his faith in socialism was a gradual process, which he worked through after digesting his experiences, thinking about his essays, going over old conversations, both with college friends and people he met on his travels. A few months after his return he wrote an article in a Stockholm evening paper on a book recently published by the British left-wing intellectual Harold Laski, about the Communist Manifesto, which showed a deep appreciation of Marxist ideas that would have been unthinkable before his trip to the United States.

William Shirer, the great American journalist, author of the Rise and Fall of the Third Reich, visited Stockholm in the late forties and found it a society of profound class barriers, despite twenty years of Social Democrat rule and 50 years of labour movement activism. Social relations were still formal. Stockholm had lost some of its lustre of the war years, having then been a nest for spies, journalists and diplomats from all sides. Doubtless Palme found the city less than dynamic after his American experiences, particularly as he had returned to his old room in his mother's home, a short walk away from the University of Stockholm. He had started reading law, about which he was less than enthusiastic, but which was the wish of his family.

THINGS CHANGED when he was contacted by two young co-chairs of the Swedish union of students, who had seen a very well written and intelligent article Palme had written about American youth in a long feature article for Svenska Dagbladet, the conservative paper of Stockholm. The Swedish National Union of Students, SFS, lacked an international secretary. Unbeknownst to Palme, his thoughtful article became a kind of job application, and the student chair met Palme for tea at Palme's mother's home. The meeting passed off in a mutually satisfactory way, and Palme accepted the unpaid post of international secretary a few days later.

The late forties was a time when student groups from Europe spent a lot of time planning for and thinking about a better post-war world. Students would meet and spend the summers helping to build, say, a railway through the mountains of Bosnia. Sunburnt and thoroughly exercised, they would talk and drink the nights away. The various student groupings were also very politicised, a battleground for the hearts and minds of the future elites of Europeans. The communist bloc had infiltrated and taken over the International Union of Students, based in Prague, already in 1946.

The communists had a lot of credibility because of the Soviet Union's overwhelming, role in defeating Nazi Germany. They also had some good arguments: the colonial question. The Soviet Union had a lot of prestige as it posed as an anti-colonial great power. Palme was appalled by the Stalinist demagoguery, though, and was appalled by the Communist takeover in Prague in 1948, whose aftermath he witnessed at first hand. He worked hard to set up an alternative student's union comprising the student unions of the West. He struggled, but eventually succeeded, in forming the breakaway grouping called the International Student Congress and gained the backing of the British NUS as well as all the Commonwealth and Scandinavian student organisations to do so. In 1967 it was revealed that Palme's organisation, that is, the ISC, had been funded by a front group of the CIA. His group was not the only body thus funded. Post-1945, the Americans were very keen to win the hearts and minds of Europe's intellectuals and workers. The CIA supported literary and current affairs magazines like Encounter in the UK and Der Monat in West Germany. It also paid for the workers' equivalent of Palme's student organisation, the Free Trade Union international. Palme always denied knowing where the money came from when the scandal broke in the media in 1967, by which time he was a junior minister for the Social Democrats. Having started up the organisation, with headquarters in Holland, he refused repeated American requests for him to be the foundation's chairman. In retrospect, it is easy to see why the CIA would have wanted a charismatic young man from a neutral country as the perfect front man for an organisation they funded.

But Palme had other fish to fry: a Swedish future, which he continued to nurture. In 1951, he graduated in law from Stockholm University. That autumn he did his military repetition service in military intelligence. He joined the Social Democrats' student movement. In 1952, he became chairman of the Swedish union of students, SFS. It was a full-time, but unpaid, job, where he acted as a lobbyist on education questions, helped provide service activities for students and advised on matters concerning course literature. Palme was never very good with financial issues, it has been said: and indeed, the organisation suffered economic losses from some bad business decisions. The climax of his year in office was the student parliament in Lund in the summer of 1953. Palme held the keynote speech, where he contrasted the anti-Semitic, conservative student movement of the thirties – which voted for a resolution to exclude a number of Jewish doctors seeking asylum from Hitler in Sweden – to the progressive, idealistic, liberal student movement it had become under his aegis. It was one of his most important ever speeches, says his biographer, since in it Palme sketched an alternative to the painful self-examination over Sweden's passivity and profitable neutrality in World War Two. Berggren writes that the "subtext of his speech was that Sweden would atone its guilt through action". Palme set the framework for his own actions later to make Sweden's role in the sixties and seventies world conscience and support of the poor, particularly in Africa. This route was to put him and Sweden on a collision course with Britain, the United States as well as the Apartheid regime in South Africa. The course may, as we will see, have played a critical negative role in his destiny.

IT HAD LONG seemed that Palme would be heading into the diplomatic service, or possibly the intelligence services. There were many routes open to him, even journalism. But his important career choice came in the late summer of 1953. Palme was doing one last job for the ISC, the CIA-funded (it later emerged) pro-western international student organisation. It was a three-month trip to Asia. He visited India, Burma, Malaysia, Singapore, Indonesia. His task was to interview local student leaders and assess the opportunities for collaboration with anti-Communist student groups in these countries. It was difficult: the West, or at least the old colonial powers, had little credibility. Palme, unconsciously or not, appealed to the anti-Colonialism of the ISC's true paymaster's, the Americans. Perhaps his conclusions also reflected his own growing convictions. In his 100 page report to the ISC's secretariat in the Netherlands, he was appalled at the intellectual hold British culture still had over Indians, with their command of Shakespeare and Shaw and their love/hate relationship with Britain. He was rather more admiring of the tough doers of the Indonesian nationalist movement; who had totally rejected Dutch culture in 1945. In preference to the over-intellectual and alienated Indian student groups, the Indonesian student groups were actively engaged in a project of national reconstruction. The Indonesians were confident, not oppressed by the weight of western culture. He was also impressed that the students had formed their own military unit during the war of liberation from the Dutch in 1945. That had contributed to their self-confidence, he argued.

Palme was recovering from malaria and was visiting the University of Rangoon in Burma as part of a study trip to Asia as his last task for the ISC when he was reached by the news that his application to join the intelligence section of the defence staff in Stockholm had been accepted. He did not stay long in his new job, though. The Social Democrat prime minister, Tage Erlander, shortly after that hired Palme to be his assistant and translator. Palme, son of a wealthy, conservative family, was to make a meteoric career in the workers' party. Fifteen years later, he himself was to become prime minister.

THE PRIME MINISTER'S ASSISTANT: 1953-1961

Palme was the conservative turned renegade leftist. Why the conversion? There were his youthful experiences, with Paul Titus, at Kenyon, his meeting with Walther Reuther and his encounters with racism in the American South. In his political journey to the left, I would also add that his then fiancée, soon-to-be wife Lisbet was genuinely a big influence on her husband, constant dialogue and conversation radicalising him. Moving in the circles she did, the radical left wing, proto-feminist, child psychologists of Stockholm, she had her ear to the ground as to what modern urban women were thinking. Later, powerful independent women provided substantial support for him. Palme's focus on the rights of children, and the mainstreaming of children's needs into all walks of Swedish life in the 1970s, undoubtedly owed something to Lisbet's child psychologist influence. From television, to housing design, schooling, smacking bans and other safety measures – Sweden invented the seat belt and the child seat – Sweden was a pioneer in child-friendly strategies. Under Palme, Sweden acquired a bit of a reputation as a nanny state. Strangely, no biography has even been written in Swedish about Palme's strong-willed wife.

Lisbet and Olof met while Palme was on a skiing holiday in Lapland, organised by the Swedish students' union. As Berggren puts it, a Swedish skiing holiday was exotic and challenging even for Swedes, in the 1950s. Sweden is a big country. The distance between Southern Sweden and Lapland is the same as the distance between Stockholm and Rome. The train journey was long and indirect, living quarters were primitive. The trips, writes Berggren, were characterised by the "smell of wet wool drying on the Aga". The evenings were filled with wholesome folksongs ´and fireside lectures on the history of the Lapps. There were no ski lifts. The skiers had to walk up the slopes with the skis on their backs. In one of the cottages was a group of young women, including Lisbet Beck Friis, a psychology student at Stockholm University. She had spent her holidays teaching a school for challenging and violent youths and sympathised with the Social Democrats, despite an upper middle-class background. Legend has it they started talking after Palme spilled some coffee in her lap. He was charming, eloquent, but shy with women. He had dated women; he had had no serious romantic relationships – but he had in fact been married.

During a trip to an international student conference in Prague, just after the communist coup there, as a student leader, Palme had met a Czech girl his age who was desperate to get out of the country and be with her boyfriend, who had fled to Sweden. The new communist regulations forbade travel, unless you married a foreigner. So Palme obliged, two days before the rules changed banning even Czechs who married foreigners from leaving the country. Palme divorced the girl when she arrived in Sweden, and she continued her life with her boyfriend, studying and eventually becoming a doctor in Uppsala. Palme almost certainly did not receive money for it. Rather you could look for the reason in his family history. His mother too had been an east European medical student. As we have seen, desperate to flee chaos and oppression of tsarist Latvia, she had headed for Sweden in 1915 and was lodged with Palme's father as a favour to a mutual friend, and eventually they married.

William Buckley, the legendary conservative American journalist, mentioned the event in the surprisingly well informed obituary he wrote of Palme that was syndicated in the US on 10 March 1986, a week after the murder, and used the example to highlight Palme's underlying idealism – not yet, in 1950, quite poured into the mould of Social Democrat pacifism. "One had the feeling about Olof Palme that, had the law permitted it, he would have married all the women in the world who wanted to move elsewhere. As scholar James Burnham once remarked about Eleanor Roosevelt, she turned all the world into her personal slum project."

Palme's keen Swedish biographer Berggren takes a less satirical view and appreciates this gesture as an example of his emerging selflessness. This event, too, has become, among the Social Democrat party faithful, an example of Olof Palme's concern for the weak, for the vulnerable, his lifelong interest in refugees.....

Palme and Lisbet hit it off, though none of the two dozen or so books that have been published about Palme have really any in-depth psychological account of their relationship. Berggren's book's greatest book is that he doesn't analyse her at all. If the 1950s were still a conservative era, Lisbet was radical and knew what she wanted. She had originally wanted to be a nurse but when he father, an engineer to whom she was close, died she resaddled and started getting interested in psychology. That interest took her to the foster home Skå Hedeby, where a kind of radical, pacifist antitraditonalism was practised, on the model of England's Summerhill. Many of her generation of child psychologists spent time working there. Newspapers gave the institution acres of favourable coverage. It influenced Palme and it arguably had an influence on Swedish culture as a whole.

If Lisbet Palme was to become one lodestar of Olof Palme's life, Tage Erlander, prime minister from 1946 and mentor, the man who recruited Palme into the Social Democrat party, also played a huge role in influencing Palme. He was Palme's political father figure, and one possible motive for Palme's doing what he did was surely do go one better than Erlander and Per Albin Hansson, to complete the Social Democratic project, export it abroad. Erlander and Hansson had exported it to the furthest reaches of Sweden.

Erlander had been looking for a competent assistant for years. As head of the student's union, a trained cavalry officer, and recently qualified lawyer, Palme's name had cropped up on various occasions as a promising young possibility, but he was far from the only candidate. Assar Lindbeck, later the economist who chaired the Nobel Economics Prize committee, was another brilliant young man, who later became a fierce critic of Palme's economic policies. Palme and Erlander had met on a train from Uppsala to Stockholm in 1951, introduced by a trade union official they both knew, and Palme had given a favourable impression. Erlander wanted to have another look at Palme in the summer of 1953, but Palme was on his Asia trip and the meeting had to wait until the autumn. On 20 September 1953, Palme, recovering from a bout of Asian malaria, duly took the train to the prime minister's country residence, Harpsund, south of Stockholm, sometimes dubbed the "Swedish Chequers". They went on a fishing trip on the estate's lake, caught a pike and wined and dined through the evening. Erlander noted in his diary after he had complained about the hangover that resulted. "Palme is very intelligent. But does he have the moral strength to be a politician?" He also wondered whether Palme really was the Social Democrat he claimed to be. Nevertheless, he decided to give it a punt and employed Palme on a part-time basis along with another young man. From 1954, the other man went onto other things and Palme became sole assistant and went full-time, having resigned from his job in military intelligence service.

Berggren's biography of Palme focuses on Palme's youth and is really a book about two men. Palme himself and Erlander. Of the brilliant sorcerer's apprentice, indulged by the good father who had extremely high hopes that Palme would carry Social Democracy further than ever before. Tage Erlander, a jovial, academic, collegial type, who ruled Sweden for 23 years, 1946-69, arouses very little hostility in the Swedish historical profession and a lot of affection. In polls of experts, he usually comes near the top as the best prime minister Sweden has ever had. Of course, it helped that his long rule coincided with Sweden's economic golden age, the thirty year period between the war in 1945 and the early 1970s.

A COMPROMISE CANDIDATE between the party left and party right in 1946, Erlander was initially seen as a bridging solution until a strongman in the traditional Social Democratic mould came along. Erlander, the Christian village teacher's son, grew up in a traditional small Swedish community in the western forest county of Värmland, bordering Norway: the county of the prettiest girls, best storytellers and the best folk songs, it is said. He grew up in the bell-ringer's home, a typical three-story red painted wooden house, the 16th-century church visible through a line of silver birches. A representative of the new meritocracy, Erlander completed his studies at Lund University, then went on to be elected MP in 1932 for the Social Democrats. In 1941 he became state secretary, a senior civil service position (there no Chinese walls between politics and administration in Sweden) and helped form some of the important social policy decisions in wartime Sweden. He was appointed education minister and, in 1946, prime minister. He was said to have an enormous capacity for work and an eye for creative solutions. One reason why he emerged so quickly as a compromise candidate was his lack of egotism, dosed with an academic's sense of self-irony.

So he became Sweden's longest-serving prime minister – and Swedish historians, both right and left, ascribe his longevity in part to the unstinting support he got from his loyal, bright and hardworking assistant, Olof Palme. It was a fluke for Palme, too, that Erlander had so quickly identified his talents as a political fixer and player. As we have seen, Palme, the reserve officer from an upper middle class background, had no traditional links with the labour movement, and while he had spent years of his adult life engaged in student politics, student politics was traditionally made up of those with bourgeois views. But Palme became totally committed to his new job. Having got engaged to Lisbet in 1952, he put off marriage so that he could travel light, as he told her. They waited four years before tying the knot in Copenhagen.

Within weeks of being hired by Erlander in 1953, Palme was thrown in at the deep end when he was asked to interpret at Erlander's meeting with the German SPD leader Erich Ollenhauer. Palme's language skills were put to full use in his subsequent travels with Erlander. Civil servants who feared that Erlander would put his foot in his mouth talking to foreign leaders sometimes consoled themselves that no foreigner could possibly understand Erlander's English, or "Swenglish". But Palme was a language genius. He had learned French from his childhood au pair, he was bilingual in German, since his mother spoke to him in that language, and he had had plenty of experience at practising his excellent English during his student engagement years. Erlander was also far less experienced at foreign travel than Palme, despite being more than twice his age.

Palme not only spoke foreign languages, he understood all the nuances of discussion like a true interpreter. Erlander's diaries, published after his death, are full of praise for his young new assistant, even if Palme did have youthfully strong and often negative opinions of the elder statesmen he met, including Ollenhauer. But Erlander put up with Palme's youthful arrogance, especially came with constructively critical observations about Erlander's own manoeuvres on the diplomatic stage. Palme's advice became more and more appreciated, and soon the young man was writing Erlander's speeches.

With his ability to absorb new situations, Palme soon became a man with whom Erlander could discuss the whole arena of politics in all its complexity. Within months, everybody started noting how if Erlander was around, Palme could be counted on as being not far away. They had offices next to each other in the rather unassuming cabinet offices in Mynttorget square in Stockholm's old town, facing the far grander Royal Castle on one side and the turn of the century Riksdag (parliament) building on the other side of a narrow canal. Most of the time, in the beginning, when he was still formally working in military intelligence,

Palme worked nights and weekends mostly, constantly smoking Kent cigarettes as he wrote speeches, took notes, prepared election manifestos, scribbled assessments of Erlander's speeches and functioned as a general sounding board for the prime minister. Sometimes he slept on a narrow couch under a woollen blanket provided by a kindly janitor. Sometimes Erlander would arrive in the morning to see a draft to a speech Palme had left in the early hours on Erlander's desk.

Senior members of the Palme clan were deeply disappointed with his career choice. His grandmother Hanna von Born, whose eldest son we will recall had died in the battle against the "Finnish barbarians" in the Finnish civil war, was very fond of her "most talented grandson" but now she was sad. "I regret the fact that Olof has placed his great gifts in the service of a party that is busy destroying our country," she said once, rather hyperbolically. Other family members, according to the right-wing journalist Gustav von Platen, who often mixed with the Palme clan, talked about Palme's career choice with an apologetic tone of voice, "as if he was a relative who'd started playing guitar in a rock band."

The media were quick to notice that Erlander had a new adviser at his side. One witty Swedish newspaper columnist said Palme was like the scheming secretary Rastignac straight out of a Balzac novel. Referring to his nose and sharp fringe, the columnist described Palme as "half hawk, half weasel".

That Erlander had quickly developed an almost dependent relationship with Palme was a common theme, One right-of-centre newspaper wrote that the "prime minister, like the potentate of some totalitarian country, surrounds himself with a shadow, OP, an intellectually superior upper-class youth, a promising cavalry officer, with brilliant tactical skills, who for some completely unknown reason prefers the modern corridors of the cabinet office to the high ceilings of the defence staff." If Palme had left the bosom of military Sweden joined the "other side", the Social Democrat leftist side, was one theme, so was the idea that Erlander was a bit of marionette. One report of parliamentary proceedings said, "Mr Erlander became very angry with his opponent, presumably on Mr Palme's advice."

Usually, Erlander tolerated Palme's missteps, if Erlander's published diaries are any guide, though it is possible that his responses in them are toned down compared to his real feelings. His treatment of Palme was a reflection of his accepting personality. Another biographer, Bertil Östergren, more sceptical of Palme than either Berggren or Kjell Östberg, yet another biographer, argues it was probably a good thing the tolerant Erlander was boss and the energetic Palme the subordinate. Judging by the way Palme handled some of his subordinates later in life, the relationship would have been loess far less harmonious if the more abrasive Palme had been in charge and the more sensitive and forgiving Erlander the subordinate.

Despite their contrasts, the two men grew into having had a "love affair of the intellect", finishing each other's sentences. Underneath his kindly and unassuming manner, Erlander was a melancholy man, almost consumed, his diaries show, by political anxieties. It was difficult for him to talk openly about his political problems with his working-class cabinet colleagues. They had, says Berggren, the self-confidence of men who had risen from simple workers' homes to become the King's Ministers. They were deeply engaged in their departmental duties and often had little interest or time to delve into Erlander's self-doubting and sometimes depressive interior thought processes. Erlander, as a Christian scholarship student from the rural middle class, kept his distance from his tough, self-possessed, urban working class cabinet colleagues. What Erlander needed was a companion, someone with a big intellectual capacity, who respected the prime minister, could challenge him yet who outwardly was totally loyal. Which Palme was. Palme seemed to give the older man stimulation and energy, and Erlander appreciated him a lot. Thanks to Palme's support, Erlander achieved numerous political victories, and it is arguably thanks to the younger man's unswerving support that Erlander was able to last the political course as long as he did, for 23 years. One cartoon of the time had the duo standing in a Roman chariot, Palme whispering in his master's ear, "Remember, you are immortal".

MILITARY RELATIONS: 1953-1968

One of the challenges Erlander and Palme had to deal with in the first decade of their partnership was the relationship to the military, a world Palme had abandoned when he left military intelligence in 1953. Erlander had chosen not to join NATO in 1948; instead he had proposed a Scandinavian Defence Union with Norway and Denmark. Not trusting Sweden to be a reliable partner in security, Norway opted for the Atlantic alliance and Denmark followed suit. It took some time before Sweden's reputation was restored with the UK and especially the United States after the pro-Nazism of parts of the military and the appeasement of the political class during the Second World war, but by the fifties Erlander had built up rapport both with his military – with whom the party of pacifism had traditionally had bad relations – as well as the UK and US. This period lasted until the late 1960s, when Palme, taking ever more control of government affairs as Erlander approached retirement, alienated both the Americans and the Swedish military with his very vocal hostility to the war in Vietnam.

Between German unification in 1871 and the end of the Second World War in 1945, Sweden had been a cultural and political satellite of Germany. After the war, overnight, loyalties changed. Symbolically, Swedish schools ditched German as the first foreign language in 1946, introducing English instead. The diary of the new supreme commander, Helge Jung, who replaced the compromised pro-Nazi Olof Thörnell in 1944, is filled with entries for his new intensive course in English, at 2 pm every day for two hours. Clearly an adaptable fellow.

The context of the military-political rapprochement with the Western powers is a Swedish cultural reorientation that was genuine enough in time. Erlander did much to improve relations with the UK, historically not a very important destination for Swedish politicians, writers or cultural figures. British culture came flooding in and is still dominant. Today's sixty plus Swedes grew up with The Forsyte Saga, the Onedin Line, Upstairs, Downstairs, Monty Python; today's fortysomething generation grew up with The Tube, Not the Nine O'Clock News, Mr Bean, Spitting Image and Inspector Morse. Very few Swedes speak German today, read German literature or follow German television. As a result of which Swedes are slightly alienated from their own history, culture and thought processes from before 1945.

Sweden had a couple of talented young diplomats who had dealt extensively with Britain during the war. Among them one Gunnar Hägglöf, who became the ambassador to London. He stayed so long, until 1967, he eventually became the doyen of the London diplomatic corps, and also formed a close friendship with Anthony Eden. Their wives were friends. Hägglöf was astonished when he arrived that there were no links between the political parties in either country and set about to change that. The closer ties were encouraged by the new king, Gustav VI Adolf, who was actually rather old when he acceded. The old king, Gustav V, secretly homosexual, who reigned between 1907 and 1950, was inveterately pro-German on account of his German wife. In contrast, his son, Gustav VI Adolf, married English women, and the constitutional monarchical attitudes did much to wash away the whiff of old autocratic, Russia-obsessed Sweden with which his father was associated. His second wife, also English, was Louisa Mountbatten, sister of Lord Mountbatten, who did much to try and counteract German sympathies in Stockholm during the war. Gustav VI Adolf made a point, after the war, of visiting London every year. He was a respected archaeologist, a member of the British Academy. He always paid a call to the British Museum and the academics associated with it. The extent to which this popular old king brought Britain and Sweden closer together, in a pre-Palme era when the monarch still had some socio-cultural influence in the country, mustn't be underestimated.

While both Sweden and Britain were to stay out of the European Economic Community, formed in 1957, at other transnational for a in which both were numbers, like the OEEC, the organisation founded to help administer the Marshall plan, the default position of Sweden, in the absence of instructions from Stockholm, was "always to vote with the British".

British politicians were actually a bit puzzled by the workings of Swedish democracy, which experienced none of the changes of government experienced in other advanced western democracies. Only Japan and Mexico, with their advanced systems of clientelism, had such extended periods of one-party rule. They were generally extremely ignorant of Swedish history; but there was no reservoir of historical resentment to keep Sweden at the forefront of British politicians' minds. Just a peevishness in some quarters that Sweden had been a freerider in the war, its industry and country unaffected while other nations fought the Nazis.

ERLANDER KNEW Herbert Morrison well. Morrison, the senior Labour politician, former foreign and home secretary, always asked Erlander how his party always managed to win every election. Erlander replied, "You have to ask the opposition". Swedish politics was different, much more settled. Behind the façade, Sweden was still a conformist place, its democracy relatively fresh and not very supple. Erlander, in fact, said to Morrison once he thought the British style of buying the floating voter with promises – politics as a marketplace – was vaguely unethical.

British politicians, in particular on the left, enjoyed Erlander's company. If Swedish politics left them puzzled, they were more impressed with the economics. They tried to learn from the Swedish miracle, which was becoming increasingly apparent as the fifties wore on. The Swedes were lucky about the war. There was a legacy of social discipline in Swedish culture: many decisions were made outside the executive arena in high-level negotiations between government and special interest group representatives. The historian Roland Huntford calls the system corporatism.

The bureaucracy was efficient. Sweden had an excellent education system and Swedes were extremely talented organisers. Swedes, while no nation of intellectuals, were innovative in the practical sense. Several of Sweden's leading companies were based on great inventions dreamt up in workshops by solitary inventors. What Sweden also excelled in, since the Social Democrat came to power, was worker retraining, peaceful worker-employer relations and a culture of easy acceptance of new technology. The aristocratic but impoverished Sweden of the 19th century was but a memory. A new class was in the ascendant. The Social Democrats, sons of peasants and workers, had little cultural or historical baggage. Societies could be designed and engineered. Functionalism was the rage;

optimism about technology was boundless. It's revealing that many Swedes regarded 1960s Britain as an endearingly backward country of almost Mediterranean inefficiency. Sometimes Britain lived up this image, as the following citation in a book about Harold Wilson shows.

"On one occasion not long after he had become Prime Minister, Harold Wilson was travelling on a Sunday to Blackpool with the Swedish Prime Minister, Tage Erlander, as his guest. Wilson was explaining his plans for building the New Britain. The train clanked to a halt. For half an hour it stood stationary and then shunted slowly backwards down the line. British Rail never failed to provide us with metaphors as Wilson travelled the land preaching modernisation and progress."

Erlander's response is not recorded, but it is likely to have been quietly humorous.

RELATIONS HAD been good-natured on a defence level between the two countries, and doubtless Erlander's Anglophilia played a part. Having failed to inveigle the Danes and Norwegians into a Scandinavian defence union after the war, with little apparent self-awareness about how Sweden's wartime neutrality still rankled in Norway and Denmark, Sweden headed back into non-alignment. But what sort of neutrality was it? This is endlessly disputed.

After the war, the Swedish military bought British equipment – including Spitfires and Vampire jets - and the intelligence services started collaborating with MI6 on secret missions in the Baltic, against the Soviet Union. For a while, relations with the Americans were trickier. Despite the good rapport that an insinuating pro-Nazi Swedish military commander struck with general Patton in 1946, to the chagrin of a British diplomat reporting, the Americans were more sceptical in general towards the Swedes. Throughout this period the American ambassador to Stockholm, the intensely anti-communist and also anti-Swedish Freeman Matthews, thought the Swedes were a nation of unreliable, self-interested flip-floppers who had switched overnight from being pro-Nazi to pro-American and wanted the enemies of Communism to stand up and be counted. Sweden's decision to remain neutral in the face of the Soviet threat – while Denmark and Norway joined NATO – turned Matthews purple with rage. He wanted Sweden ostracised: "isolationism repaid with isolation".

Britain's softer approach was partly due to a lower level of idealism about international relations, an understanding in some quarters that Sweden had done as well as she could in the Second World War. Some Brits appreciated Sweden's neutrality as providing a centre for British diplomatic, intelligence gathering and espionage activity, which would have been impossible had Sweden joined the war or been occupied. Sweden's reputation got a boost when it became more widely known that nearly all of Denmark's 7,000 Jews were shifted across the Öresund straits in small boats and given safe harbour in Sweden when a crackdown by the Nazis threatened in 1943. Thanks to Sweden, Denmark was the only country in occupied Europe where no Jews died in the Holocaust. Perhaps a softer British approach could also perhaps be explained by economics. Sweden consented to join the Sterling area after the war . Britain, impoverished, exported less to Sweden than she imported, and had a constant balance of payments crisis which Sweden tolerated. In fact, after the war and until the mid-50s, Sweden was the UK's largest trading partner in Europe and third largest in the world.

By 1952 or so the western allies had reached a modus operandi with the Swedes when even the Americans had reconciled themselves to Sweden's formal decision to remain neutral, and stay out of the emerging Atlantic community.

The Swedes could retain their cherished non-alignment, but there might still be useful collaboration, if the Swedes rearmed and defended NATO's Northern flank, the Swedes would get access to top western technology to fill the gaps in the jet planes and tanks they were churning out of their own factories. Other small countries, with the possible exception of Switzerland, couldn't match Sweden's arms output. A generation of plane spotters everywhere admired the SAAB Tunnan jetfighter, nicknamed the Barrel, or the SAAB Draken fighter, the Dragon. There was also a lively exchange with NATO of intelligence information and many informal discussions about the perceived common threat from the Soviet Union. Just how much collaboration was there, and how much of it was serious? During Erlander's long rule, Sweden's stated aim was to stay out of a third world war but, if attacked, and only if attacked, get help as early as possible from the western powers. Was there an active secret alliance with the West to facilitate this help, or was there just a passive reinsurance policy that would only be activated after an invasion broke out? This is still a subject surrounded by an enormous amount of confusion, ignorance, disinformation, uncertainty, confidentiality and competing agendas. There must have been huge issues about Sweden's reliability, which both NATO and Swedish actors would have an interest in quietening down in retrospect. Sweden had been calculatingly neutral in the Second World war. Just whose side were those Swedes planning to be on – next time? Despite or because of the new anglophile orientation, memories of Sweden's incredibly ambiguous positions in two world wars did not fade so easily. Perhaps the Swedes would have tolerated living inside a totalitarian Soviet hegemony, possibly as privileged members, rather than choosing war, just as they had done regarding the Nazis in WW2? It has been made more sensitive by the growing awareness that, the event that the Soviet Union might not oblige by invading Sweden, which was possible . In that eventuality, NATO might well not have wanted Sweden to stay out of an East-West war, and tried anything to make Sweden's participation happen – possibly against Swedish interests, by "friendly occupation" in the run up to a war – which in turn would force a Soviet attack on Sweden.

But it is a mistake to talk of one Sweden; in geopolitical and foreign affairs, there were two Sweden, with the old class divide manifesting itself. Just as there were pro-Nazi sympathies in favour of engagement in WW2 from the upper classes and the Swedish armed forces, the Swedish armed forces, while paying lip service to their working-class government's neutrality, consistently favoured NATO in the Cold War.

Robert Dalsjö, a lecturer at the Swedish School of Defence Studies, and formerly of King's College London, recently wrote of the difficulties surrounding of his research into the links between Sweden and NATO from 1945 to 1989 in his dissertation "Lifeline Lost". He explained that the scope of the task was immense and challenges were numerous. "Very little of all this was set down on paper of what was put down on paper was often destroyed. The documents still in existence are still classified. Though it is possible to go the long way around and find things stored in foreign archives. I had to give up my ambition to give a detailed account and instead focused on turning points in Sweden's relations with the West."

Dalsjö also had to deal with the fact many participants were dead and that many of those still alive had faded memories. He also came across many actors who did not feel Sweden's and NATO's biggest security secrets were anything to talk about to researchers.

Whatever Sweden and the West's armed forces may have secretly and unofficially agreed to, officially Sweden did take its neutrality policy requirement seriously, which was to have a strong defence. At least during the fifties, sixties and seventies. Surprisingly so, given the pacifist reputation Sweden often has. The idea was not to defeat the attacker (ie the USSR) outright, but make an attack too costly to be worthwhile given his other likely. Not kill the bear, but at least tear off a leg. A strong defence would assuage fears of one side that the other side would take advantage of Sweden's weakness, and invade it – and so force the first side to invade in order to pre-empt a situation where the other side got a military advantage by occupying Sweden.

From the early 1950s onwards, Sweden built up an air force of 800 fighter jets, which were domestically designed and produced SAABs (for a long time the cars were a sideline business: SAAB is an acronym in Swedish for the Swedish Aeroplane Limited Company). Sweden produced its own tanks and artillery. Bofors was an artillery manufacturer that was famous worldwide. With an extensive conscript system, Sweden could theoretically mobilise 750,000 men under arms, almost. A US military confidential briefing paper admiringly noted that Sweden had one of the strongest air forces in the world and that could "mobilise in minutes". Swedish jets were patrolling the Baltic Sea 24 hours a day, and the paper reserved special praise for the new distinctive double canard-shaped Viggen, or Thunderbolt, aircraft, that could take off and land on short runways. All this was Erlander's doing. The civil defences were extensive and well integrated with the military. All children were given dog tags in case of war. There were siren exercises on the first Monday of every month: the air raid wails filled the streets of every town and area for five minutes. Every block of flats mandated to have underground or basement bomb shelters, built to typical practical, thorough Swedish standards, with thick doors.

EVIDENCE OF readiness in the event of the Cold War turning nasty was everywhere, if you knew where to look. Even when I was a child, in the seventies. Sweden is comprised mostly of forest, and some country roads were a little wider than others for short stretches. Since the end of the Cold War, the purpose of these broadened roads has been made public. They had an alternative wartime function as fighter aircraft runways. In the event of war, Sweden's air force would leave its regular air bases and disperse to these, as well as to a number of underground installations, hangars carved into the granite that forms Sweden's subsoil, which were very difficult to target. Once war had broken out, the jets were to park under the trees adjacent to the forest road/runways and be serviced and refuelled there by their ground crew. Swedish aircraft were specially constructed for short takeoffs and landings.

In contrast to England, where the military has a low profile, often you could see in Sweden men in uniform on trains and sometimes buses: after the compulsory 9-month military service, people were called up every few years for a month, to rehearse what they had learned during their initial national service. The binding commitment to a unit ended only when a man had reached the age of 47.

The Swedes were confident they could pull it off since their system was very similar to the Israeli one, and that country had mobilised a similar proportion of its population for the six-day war in 1967. The military's traditional resentment against the Social Democrats that had existed ever since the party's founding in 1889 had calmed down by the Erlander years in the fifties and sixties due to the generous funding increases Erlander had given them to protect Sweden in the Cold War. Some senior military men were Social Democrat, partly out of convenience, perhaps, but partly also because the military had a much broader recruitment base compared to before the war. The extensive national service system could be said to have a political role, in that it induced, or anchored, young men of all social classes and backgrounds in the values of Erlander's corporatist state. As said, there was an extensive civil defence system. The country consisted of 96,000 lakes; everything else lay on a table of granite. Once it had been a curse: a third of the population had emigrated to the United States in the 19th century from this unfertile land. Now, the granite table finally came good, and helped provide Sweden with an extensive network of air raid shelters, subterranean command posts, air hangars, government headquarters and fuel depots. Southern Stockholm hosted the biggest air shelter, excavated out of the cliffs of the quarter of the Södermalm. It had a capacity of 35,000 people and cutaway diagrams of the multi-storey underground structured graced featured in international technology magazines of the time. Every home had by law to have a bombproof air shelter. It was more extensive than in most other countries, One high official of the civil defence association told a New York Times reporter that "When the Martians make it to earth after a nuclear war, we may have to greet them with the explanation. 'There is nobody left but us Swedes'."

Because the Swedes were "behaving", at least until the independent minded, assertive left wing Palme became prime minister, the Americans had allowed the Swedes to buy 20 radar stations and Falcon sidewinder missiles. To stop the equipment from ending up in the wrong hands, Swedish workers in sensitive industries were closely watched by Swedish intelligence. Swedish military intelligence exploited the Social Democrat Party's local labour union representatives in every Swedish workplace to keep tabs on local Swedish Communist Party sympathisers. (They had about 5% of the national vote.) They reported back to the military intelligence, and these people found it impossible to get jobs in areas which require security clearance, such as dealing with American materiel. It is not clear how much this was demanded by the Americans, and to what extent the Swedes just pre-empted American fears.

Sweden was a well-defended country, at least in the fifties and sixties. But many in the military, and even leading Social Democrats, traditionally (but not under Erlander) a pacifist party, wanted the atomic Bomb. Sweden had become, in a short time, very advanced technologically. It was within the country's grasp. Being the fourth country in the world to develop the bomb (after the UK, the USA and the USSR, but before China and France) would give the country of just eight million people an enormous reputational boost. In the end, Erlander and Palme decided not to, to the military's intense chagrin. Palme started to be an object of suspicion in military circles. Surely his influence on the otherwise pro military Erlander was decisive. Palme started to become suspect in other ways. His intense opposition to Vietnam came a few years later. And there came to be other stuff, too.

CRITICISM OF THE 'CONTROL STATE': 1958-1986

It ought not be surprising that the Swedish state's power has grown unopposed, creeping into all the cracks of daily life, regulating people's doings in a way without precedent in free societies - Hans Magnus Enzensberger, West German essayist

Another big challenge to Social Democracy after Palme took over – apart from criticisms of his foreign policy and growing alienation from the military, as we will explore in future chapters – was a reputation for illiberal controlling behaviour. We will go slightly ahead of ourselves and deal with the whole issue, up to the point of his assassination, in this chapter. Many leftist parties everywhere engaged in redistribution and social engineering have had to endure this kind of attack. It goes with the territory. During Erlander taxes were rather low so the government did not have much power or ability to socially engineer. Palme changed the tax system though, and hiked rates.

Of course it was during the Palme era that Sweden earned its reputation for being a utopia, where the weak were really taken care of, and everyone was granted by the strong state the opportunity to realise their life projects. At the same time, it made him unpopular – not only with the bourgeoisie and business community, who professed to feel overtaxed. But also a growing number of intellectuals, who, perhaps feeling an ancient Swedish inferiority complex towards Britain and France, argued that Palme had unfortunately tapped into an older Swedish autocratic culture. Good for discipline and getting things done. Bad for free speech or personal freedom, the freedom not to conform; of which the freedom to make money and not have it taxed away, as well as not being bossed about by the state, were a part..

The debate reached a crescendo in the 1980s when some people argued that Sweden was not culturally (let alone militarily) quite part of the Western camp. Just as East Germany's autocracy had Prussian roots, Sweden was a kind of DDR Light, or even a bit Soviet, and so a candidate for being dragged into the East bloc. (Just as another country on the same longitude, East and West facing Czechoslovakia, had had a Communist takeover in 1948.) Actually, if Sweden's control state was older than the Social Democracy, you couldn't blame Palme for it. But maybe Palme exacerbated it, with his strong dominant personality. And the tax-funded strong state – with power to put money in various places to improve people's lives – can build on prior cultural trends. Some would say to compare Sweden to East Germany is monstrous. The important thing is that people were having these arguments, and British journalists who visited Sweden often the same thing.

This criticism chipped away at Palme's popularity as he became a lightning conductor – if not an active enabler – on issues concerning the over-mighty welfare state. These sentiments were set aside after the assassination, and the funeral guests would not have guessed that behind the utopian facade, these sentiments were active among various Swedish groupings.

You might say that there are two axes along which tensions exist between various historical forces that define the Swedish character. On the one axis, an outward-looking "great power" Sweden, aggressive and militaristic, above all Russophobic, contrasts with the left-wing, provincial, inward-looking pacifist "little Sweden" more concerned with the national development of all domestic resources. Another axis concerns freedom versus control.

In the so-called warfare state period, during Sweden's 17th and early 18th century military empire, the Swedish everyday people's lives were carefully monitored and controlled by the church, which mobilised opinion behind Sweden's conquests. Internal passports were required for travel outside the parish until 1860; the local Lutheran priest signed the travel warrant based on a history of good behaviour. Sweden has the world's oldest population records, maintained by the church, which were essential for the warfare state's recruitment process. The local recruitment agency, the king's local officials, knew exactly the identities of boys coming of military age in every municipality. But even in periods of "little Sweden" the control state was at work, which had its positive sides. It contributed to the fact that the Swedish working classes had among the world's highest literacy rates. Knowledge of religious texts was compulsory. When Sweden became industrialised, it had an excellent supply of educated labour to man the new industries.

The church records contained all results of church interrogations of the individual's knowledge of the Bible; his weaknesses: adultery, laziness, literacy problems; church attendance was compulsory until the late 19th century. It wasn't possible to leave the Swedish church and become an atheist until 1951. The social control may have been restrictive; however, the social discipline and community cohesion it created has stood Sweden in good stead, economically and socially.

The same intellectual culture produced 19th-century regulations like the "conventicle law", which banned private gatherings of bible readings. The archives of the British library are full of reports from appalled Victorian British travellers visiting Sweden, finding people furtively gathering on forest clearings to discuss religion without the presence of a state-employed priest, enforcing standard thought processes and common values on the whole community. Someone has said that the dominant church has been replaced by a powerful media, who see it as their role not to report on the misdeeds of the powerful and hold politicians to account but to impose the correct social and political attitudes of the day on to the populace, whether it be patriotism and imperial conquest of Russia in the 17th and 18th centuries, socialist redistrubition in Palme's seventies or uncritical acceptance of mass demographic change in the 2010s.

In the 20th century, as the oligarchic aristocratic state was replaced by workers' democracy and Social Democrat rule, you had mandatory housing inspections to ensure the worker "lived cleanly" – but also, alas, compulsory sterilisation of women thought unfit to have babies. A ruthless technocratic decision, it led to the sterilisation – in their best interests, of course – of 60,000 women between 1933 and 1976. Palme put a stop to the practice.

Sterilisations were things that took place under the justification of medical and social necessity and was something casual visitors seldom saw. Everyday life in Sweden could seem remarkably free, and certainly prosperous, to some. Life was calm and peaceful. Sam Falla, a British ambassador to Stockholm in the 1970s, was so enthusiastic about Swedish life it provoked snide comments from Whitehall bureaucrats that Falla had gone native.

But there was international criticism too. Perhaps because Sweden aimed high, there were plenty of critics willing to take it down a peg or two. TIME magazine wrote in 1951 that Swedes lived in a "well-meaning despo-Socialism". They were not exactly unfree, but they lived in a controlled freedom, the magazine argued.

There were some other common themes in the sceptical take on Sweden. That life was boring and people were uninteresting and cold. The old aristocratic oligarchical state was being replaced by a rationalist, functionalist, Social Democratic one, and that both were a bit controlling. That the welfare state that smoothed the path of progress also removed the pleasures of achievement and all sense of personal responsibility. That, in the country's headlong rush to material welfare, the human angle of social relations was neglected. There was scepticism from visitors from more cynical societies about Sweden's confidence that technology and rationalism could solve everything, and they had doubts about the "rule of men in white coats". A few visitors, like the writer and Observer correspondent Roland Huntford, worried about Sweden's positivist justice system, which put expediency and the needs of the state over the rights of the individual, in the name of ideology and progress.

Perry Anderson, newly graduated from Oxford, later a well-known British academic, was deeply impressed by the modernity of daily life in 1961. In the recently started New Left Review, in an article called "Tony Crosland's dreamland", he was genuinely taken by the telephones, beige and shaped like drooping tulips, made of "featherlight plastic". The newspapers were 30 pages thick and there were private airfields solely for their distribution. In the suburbs, automatic stainless steel dispensers sold geometrically stacked foods from cucumbers to chickens. In the railway station cafes, there were coin-operated radios at every table.

ALTHOUGH ANDERSON was admiring on the whole, he did worry about the technocratic tendencies in Swedish Social Democracy. He interviewed the young Olof Palme, then still Erlanders's assistant and adviser, who explained that social welfare was not only there to prevent poverty but was also supposed to guarantee a good standard of living. Anderson was impressed by Palme, an unusual politician. Not ingratiating, but direct, and very intelligent. But he thought Palme's ideology was a bit crass. In the eyes of the British left, socialism was about something more than rational planning and rising economic growth. Drawing inspiration from the younger Marx's texts, he argued that British socialism was more aware than Swedish one about the alienation and powerlessness that the industrial society created.

David Jenkins, an American journalist, wrote in Sweden and the Price of Progress, something "fairly unoriginal", complained Palme's biographer, that the Swedes were a materialistic and boring people. Jenkins said the Swedish genius expressed itself in the mechanical arts, and the most prestigious occupation was that of an engineer. Swedes had a "sure talent for organisation". "With his interest in the mechanical, the Swede is thing oriented rather than people oriented," wrote Jenkins. He said a lot of absurdity had been written about Sweden, and that the country brought out the worst in writers, taking as an example the claim that it was a "Nordic love nest compared to which romantic tropics are a puritan's paradise."

"Sweden's excruciating dullness" Jenkins maintained, lay in its food and its lack of nightlife and added: "A great many people dislike Sweden, and there is no reason that everybody should like Sweden any more than that everybody should like toasted marshmallows."

The Palme era, from say, the mid-sixties, when his cultural influence began to be felt, offered up more of the same in terms of foreign criticism. The era represented a paradox. The sixties brought liberalism in personal morality, free sex. Palme personally at least always claimed to be a supporter of free speech, and spoke often of freedom. If justice was sometimes arbitrary, sentences became increasingly lenient.

And yet, like the message in a broken stick of Brighton rock, criticism, both domestic and international, of the conforming Swedish state, and the culture which was enmeshed with it, took on new forms. For a while, everyone in journalism seemed to sing from the same hymn sheet in the necessity of helping third world liberation movements, however despotic they may be. Social Democracy – which was about enforcing equality and universal standard on the whole country – inevitably took on authoritative impositions in smoothing out local differences, and thus eliminating regional variety in this large country. It could also be claimed that judges seemed to behave more like social activists who wanted to create a better society than professionals concerned with protecting the individual from abuse by the strong state.

Writers like Vilhelm Moberg, who wrote the bestselling epic about the Emigrants, the Swedish settlers who went to Minnesota, was an intellectual opponent of the new developments.

Moberg's family came from a peasant background and he grew up on a farm in Småland, the unfertile, stony, forested county of the southern Swedish highlands that provided the largest number of emigrants to America in the 1800s. He worked as a volunteer for many local newspapers in Småland and eventually wrote some of Sweden's best-loved epics, a trilogy about a smallholding farmer and his wife who emigrated to America to escape the bossy local priest and the intrusive local tax collector. Björn and Benny from ABBA later turned the story into their most famous musical, Kristina från Duvemåla, and in 1971 it was made into an Oscar-nominated film, the Emigrants, starring Max von Sydow and Liv Ullman, both actors making a big international career in the seventies.

Moberg was also known as polemicist with a sharp pen, and spent the 1950s in America, which he compared favourably to Sweden for its independent-minded citizenry and outspoken media which held politicians to account. Moberg was not an opponent to the welfare state per se. He had been a member of the Social Democrat party when younger, But he felt that the workers' movement, having taken control of the levers of state, exhibited the same arrogance in power as the old bureaucratic monarchical state. He warned that the Social Democrats were opening the door to the authoritarian state where the individual is subsumed into the collective and turned into an object for the furtherment of the state's interests.

Highlighting a couple of scandals in fifties Sweden, including an incident where an awkward individual exposing police corruption was put in a mental hospital, Moberg wished to put some moral courage into the Swedish citizenry.

To stand up for their rights, and not to stand cap in hand, head bowed, in front of the new Social Democrat masters. He wanted them to dare to break the atmosphere of consensus which meant that the will of the collective was more important than the freedom of the individual.

"We lack the public opinion in this country of people who are deeply disturbed by judicial persecutions carried out against individuals."

Moberg was particularly negatively inclined towards the legal positivism that ruled the roost particularly in the law studies faculty of the University of Stockholm, Palme's alma mater. In the dystopian satire The Old Kingdom from 1953 he lets a professor at the University of Flamonia, capital of the country of Idyllia, explain that man has no God-given natural rights. "In the democratic state under the rule of law, the citizen's best interests were identical to the collective's best interests."

There were other problems, and the old authoritarianism found new manifestations. The American sociologist David Popenoe, who spent a year in Sweden, was sceptical of the growing power of social welfare bureaucrats.

They were interested in controlling basically psychologically healthy families because it gave them an excuse to exercise power. The Swedish spanking ban – first in the world – and the general feminisation of public life weakened the authority of the father in the home, he argued, to a harmful extent.

THE STATE CAME in and took over the father role. Human Rights Groups like the Nordic Committee for Human Rights, led by a Jamaican-Swedish lawyer, Ruby Claesson, found that increasing numbers of children were being taken away from their families to give them a "proper upbringing" in foster homes. She and her maverick organisation were generally ignored by the Swedish media. By the late 1970s, she showed the rates of forced child removal were much higher in Sweden than in Denmark or Norway despite the fact that, on objective grounds, wealth levels were similar – and child poverty was extremely low in all three Nordic countries. The "mass" confiscation of children was picked up by Der Spiegel which turned it into a large, critical article on Sweden's "children gulags" ."Kinder Gulag in Sozialstaat Schweden." The phrase children's gulags was an exaggeration. The foster homes were hardly prison camps. It wasn't picked up domestically until it became a worldwide news story. Bo Edvardsson, a lecturer at the School of Örebro University, who had spent thirty years covering the issue, said that Swedish welfare bureaucrats use dozens of different "persecutory strategies" in child protection investigations, like exaggeration or falsifications of negative evidence.

Doubtless, there were many cases where the social workers' involvement in family lives were justified, where parent and child were better off separated. But the zeal with which so many children were put into custody often seemed to be, family rights lawyer Siw Westerberg said, in a speech to the Family Education Trust in London because the social workers just wanted to demonstrate their power. She argued that the foster homes the children were sent to were often worse than the original families, much worse. Foster care remuneration was generous and tax-free, and it appealed to people from poor or even criminal backgrounds. A big government commission, announced in 2010, into the foster care abuses of the 1960s, 70s and 80s seemed to vindicate her. Thousands of cases of compensation for children who had been abused were quietly announced.

The enforced child custody cases reflected in some way, a change in family life, a family as comprised of individuals each of whom had a relationship with the state rather than a unit. The state took on a paternalistic relationship towards the individual, taking the lead in inducting modern norms. Alternatives poles of power, father figures, were weakened.

And yet Palme's Sweden had many defenders. The philosophy of Palme's Strong State was this: it meant freeing the individual from the contingent burdens of his surroundings. Freeing the middle-aged from the burden of looking after old parents, or being prevented by the existence of young children from being free to go out and work. For young children, Palme's philosophy meant if parents were "bad parents", the child had the right to start again with "better opportunities" - an argument that could be seen as justifying foster care. For the elderly, freedom meant the right to be free from humiliating dependence on their children. So decent care for the elderly. In theory, it sounded good. But there was always a problem when delegating and concentrating powers to a single focus, that is, the state. The state must be powerful and intrusive to prevent abuse by individuals or institutions against individuals. But here is the challenge: how do you prevent the state itself from abusing individual rights? Even the Swedish state was not infallible. Quis custodiet ipsos custodes? Who guards us against the guardians asked thoughtful critics of Social Democrat Sweden.

The weakening of the family and above all its formal head, the father figure, was one thing. Secularisation and a certain kind of progressivism being others, which acted like red rags to a bull to certain American conservatives who painted Erlander's (and, later, even more so Palme's) Sweden as a godless, faithless dystopia where family disintegration led to huge social problems. At a time when Sweden led the world in working mothers, having two working parents was believed to lead to child delinquency and divorce, mental illness and suicide. In 1960 Republican President Eisenhower fed a myth that still persists with some right-wing Americans that Swedes have found hard to live down when he talked of "complete paternalism in a friendly European country. This country has a tremendous record for socialistic operation, following a socialistic philosophy, and the record shows that their rate of suicide has gone up almost unbelievably and I think they were almost the lowest nation in the world for that. Now, they have more than twice our rate. Drunkenness has gone up. Lack of ambition is discernible on all sides." Much opposition to the Social Democrats' long rule from 1932 to 1976 came from a group of judges and professors of jurisprudence. People like Gustaf Petren, the government counsel, Lennart Hane, and Jacob Sundberg, the latter the professor of law at Stockholm University.

Their accusations went like this: Palme and his senior justice officials, Carl Lidbom and Lennart Geijer, were passing a huge number of laws in 1979 to 76, one every eight hours; Palme said. "Give Calle Lidbom a couple of hours and he will have a new ready for you." They were badly constructed – perhaps deliberately. They were called general clauses, said Sundberg, who called them rubber laws because of their flexibility as instruments of the state. Judges never looked to the constitution but interpreted these statutes with one eye at what the government's general political goals were. It wasn't helped by the abject dependence of the judiciary on the government for promotion and the revolving doors between the judiciary and jobs in the government chancellery. Sundberg, for one, welcomed the fact that Sweden started losing cases in the European Court of Human Tights with greater frequency than other countries – a fact the Swedish media were not keen on publicising.

Sundberg was particularly busy at publishing papers in international publications, and even appeared in a German ZDF TV programme looking into Palme's Sweden. The West Germans were in general much more alert to Sweden's political characteristics than the French and British, largely ignorant of Scandinavian affairs. Its title was "1984 – not far off" and it was only shown on Swedish television after the ZDF producer taunted a Swedish journalist at an international TV seminar with the words, "Of course, it will never be shown in your country". It was – but after it Swedish press corps referred to Sundberg – Sweden's most prominent jurist, as a "weirdo. Of course we must accept their right to say what they have to say but that is no reason to take them seriously."

And Sundberg was disappointed that his courses at Stockholm university were never once attended by government officials; nor did he ever receive one invite to lecture on human rights, despite being Sweden's premier expert on the ECHR. Sundberg knew that Palme hated the idea of an extension of judge–based rule – Palme called Strasbourg "Petren's little kindergarten" – but he believed some of Sweden's "human rights problems" could have been avoided had it been implemented earlier.

Hans Bergström, the former executive editor of Dagens Nyheter, therefore formerly Sweden's most influential journalist, now a freelancer, called Palme's Sweden "a one-party state". He qualified this by adding that the country is a democracy of course – though if people are brainwashed into voting for one party that means nothing more than to say it was a formal democracy – and that Sweden was a market economy embedded in Europe. But he criticised the lack of checks and balances, the weakness and lack of independence of the courts, the centralisation of the government. The long rule of the Social Democrats, he said, had "hollowed out civil society, diminished civic courage, created ever narrower demarcations of what constitutes an acceptable opinion in Swedish society."

"Don't forget, these are very subtle mechanisms. We mustn't forget that Sweden has for centuries been an authoritarian consensus society where the social exclusion mechanisms are very strong. Everyone knows everyone, and there are networks. You don't need the police to stop someone. There are much more subtle methods: who gets appointed, who is under consideration for appointment, who is allowed to participate and seen as legitimate in the debate."

He also added:

"You have to remember that Sweden is as if made for a one-party state: there is no division between the legislature and the executive; no dispersal of power between different levels; no constitutional court and a labour movement hand in glove with the government."

"Few people anywhere have personal experience how the world hangs together and so rely on the media to give them a picture of reality. The problem is that radio, TV and newspapers in Sweden are thoroughly socialist." Bergström continued: "Everywhere in society there is the assumption that, in one year, in five years, in ten years, the same party will be in power, and trim their behaviour thereafter."

Bergström emigrated to America; from where he writes occasional columns critical of Sweden.

WHAT TO conclude from all these fragmentary snapshots? It is obvious that most normal Swedes do not feel they lived, or live, in an unfree society. In fact feel exceptionally privileged. Prosperity and the easy, good, life calms things down anyway. Physical freedom is undoubtedly great. It is a large, empty country with good communications links. Efficient administration and a welfare state that tides people over, takes some of the burden of childcare away, also adds to the sense of freedom. Freedom means many things.

What about intellectual freedom in a country nearly all foreigners complain is conformist, and a bit disciplined, a bit politically correct? "The strangest thing about Sweden, to the English eye, was always its tremendous conformity. It did not matter what the orthodoxy might be. The point is everyone knew what was acceptable and proper to believe," writes longtime Sweden resident Andrew Brown, author of the award-winning Swedish memoir Fishing in Utopia. Brown lived and worked a journalist through the Palme era. The London Times Guide to the Peoples of Europe noted that "the Swedish character values security and tends to place the interests of the group over the individual. This tendency is characterised by the concept of lagom which translates as just the right amount. Hence it is not done to stray too far from the average...the social pressures to conform can be considerable." Swedish patriots might say that all countries have their faults, and this had fewer than most. That critics like Bergström were disturbed mavericks with an axe to grind. Various international organisations always put Sweden near the top of the list of the world's democracies.

On the other hand, a small minorlity of Swedes, and some unimpressed foreign writers, including the very well respected German leftist intellectual Hans Magnus Enzensberger, felt intensely that Sweden was a soft "totalitarian society" that somehow got away with it. After a visit to Sweden in 1982, Enzensberger wrote a series of articles for Dagens Nyheter (which later became a book, available in English) in which he complained that Swedes had given up their sense of freedom and personal autonomy in exchange for faith in a benevolent state. "Whether it is a question of using a 'hotline', of bringing up children or having their wages taxed, Swedish citizens are always prepared to come to the authorities innocently and full of trust, as if their benevolence were beyond question," he wrote. "It ought not be surprising," he added, "that the state's power has grown unopposed, creeping into the cracks of daily life, regulating people's activities in a way without precedent in free societies."

Mogens Berendt, a Danish journalist, built up a case for a society where everything was prohibited in his 1983 book, Faeldet Sverige. (The Swedish case). He picked on a theme I mentioned earlier: Palme's modern Social Democrat Sweden was a continuation of the right-wing bureaucratic Sweden of old warrior kings, who harnessed the church to mobilise opinion through very effective application of early propaganda in favour of the state's endless wars in the sixteenth and seventeenth centuries. The Swedish Social Democrats and the labour movement had gained political power and, according to Berendt, used it to repress deviations from their socialist egalitarian welfare project without mercy.

Berendt's book established a certain sceptical Danish view of Sweden, symbolised concretely by the inability of visiting Danes to buy alcohol from shops on weekends. But Denmark is a small, uninfluential country, and had always had a predictable rivalry with their larger neighbour. What Danes thought seldom influenced anyone. So that assessment of Sweden remained largely their own. Until the 1980s, Sweden mostly avoided flak from America's mighty cold war warriors (apart from some social conservatives concerned with social policy issues, such as David Popenoe.

But, come the 1980s, as tensions rose around Sweden's borders, the old questions about Sweden's political and cultural system became more contested. Was Sweden not a bit "eastern" and "autocratic" too? With such a dominant personality, Palme became a natural focus. He became a lightning conductor for domestic doubts in some circles about what kind of country Sweden really was, and if it, with its strong and sometimes controlling state, was a "soft totalitarian" society, a DDR Light. Sweden had a Germanic culture, after all, and Stockholm, geographically, was situated East of Prague and Berlin. There were groupings in Stockholm, at least, who convinced themselves that they were dissidents in a totalitarian society, that Palme, as a traitor to his bourgeois class, might conceivably have become a traitor to his country also. Palme was marching the country - then and always slightly autocratic - into the Soviet bloc. Some military figures were also of this opinion.

Importantly, they found friends and allies in the powerful Swedish business and industrial sector chafing at taxes and regulations which they claimed harmed the Swedish economy, more of which in a later chapter. These groups sometimes made common cause with American

Republicans as well as American defence and political thinkers, who, resentful that East coast liberals had always used Sweden as a stick to beat the Republicans and the American model of low taxes and free enterprise with, looked eagerly for any cracks in this idealised society's façade. Palme gave as good as he got, in international newspaper interviews where he argued that Sweden was one of the freest, most equal, most civilised and most peaceful countries on the planet – and certainly there were many Europeans and educated Americans who agreed with him on that. He could have pointed out that, despite Eisenhower's remark, Swedish suicide rates were not exceptional – that is a canard. Or, had he felt really nasty, he could have pointed out Time magazine's close links with the CIA. Which explained why it was sometimes used to attack rivals of the United States. Remember the despo-socialism articles? But he refrained from that. He was, in the end, rather pro-American, the quintessential Kennedy liberal. And we will recall that Kennedy also had powerful enemies, in the deep state and the political right. On that note, we return to the timeline of Palme's life.

THE SIXTIES: 1961 to 1969: cabinet minister

"Sweden, why is it always Sweden?" Keith Joseph, leading thinker of the British conservative party

In 1958, when Erlander was still only halfway through his long premiership, Palme took the step into parliament, becoming MP for the town of Jönköping, to some irritation of the local women's association, which had hoped to put one of their own in the seat. The Swedish parliament only started to achieve high figures for female representation in the 1980s. Let us take a snapshot of the era.

We have seen how Marquis Childs's books, Sweden, the Middle Way, from 1936, had painted Sweden as a technocratic, hypermodern redistributionist utopia. It had influenced the American union leader Walther Reuther and made the young exchange student Olof Palme really realise what Americans admired Sweden for But in some ways Childs's book described a happening trend in some fields rather than an accomplished reality in every part of Swedish life. Consider this: In 1960,. Social democracy had been in charge for 27 years nonstop. Although in many respects there were continuities throughout the period, Sweden was still a country in transition. It was still a one breadwinner per family country. Sweden, these days, has a reputation for being one of the most feminist countries in the world. Back then, during Erlander's last decade in power, there was a smaller proportion of women in the workplace than, for example, the UK. Sweden was a more male-dominated, military, traditional country than it is now. There is a photo of Erlander and his cabinet in 1960, half of them working class Social Democrats, at the opening of the Riksdag, all of them in top hats, in a picture that could easily have been taken 50 years earlier. Only one minister was a woman. People worked or went to school on Saturdays and schools began with morning prayer. The king, Gustav VI, open and attended every cabinet meeting, which took place weekly in the Royal Castle. The Friday radio news always began "the king opened the council today". Swedish embassies abroad were still royal embassies (as Danish and Norwegians still are) and the king's signature was printed on the leaflet sent out to every Swedish household saying Swedes had to do their patriotic duty and resist any attacker in the event of a war. By Palme's time, 10 years later, by 1973, a more pacifist winds dominated, the king's signature had disappeared as had the exhortation to fight any invader.

Sweden had overtaken France in per capita income already in 1937, and in 1957 Sweden overtook the British in terms of wealth per capita. By the mid-1960s Sweden had the second highest gross national product per capita in Europe. The Swedish growth miracle did not go unnoticed, even in a Europe where the economic success of a long post-war boom was enjoyed everywhere. Pompidou, the French presidential candidate, when asked what his plans for France were, said, to turn the country into "a Sweden with sunshine". British academics and journalists with an interest in Scandinavia were forever being asked to talk about the themes of Sweden: a model for Europe. And, as The Times put it, when Wilson's Labour government came to office it seemed to regard the government's historic role as being to recreate Britain as an image of Sweden. The White Heat of Technology and all that. "Sweden, why is it always Sweden?" said an exasperated Keith Joseph – the politician-intellectual credited as being Margaret Thatcher's "guru" – at around this time, after the latest handwringing in the British media why a strike-prone Britain couldn't measure up to the modernity of Sweden.

The Labour party were right to see Erlander's Sweden as a model: but, while it was socially radicalising, like the rest of the western world, it was still a corporatist welfare state, even though it revelled in the term "the middle way", with a highly efficient manufacturing sector, and rather low tax burden. Healthcare was not free at point of use. Nor was it, despite the explosion of massage parlours, permissive in every way. Abortion was banned for longer than it was in the UK – Swedish women went to Communist Poland for their abortions. For all the talk of a middle way of capitalism mentioned by Marquis Childs, not only was industry overwhelmingly privately controlled – more so than in the UK – but concentrated on 17 families, none of them flamboyant, the most famous of whom were the Wallenbergs. Through the Stockholm Enskilda

Bank the clan had an extraordinary influence over Swedish life. The head of the family, Dr Marcus Wallenberg, sat on the board of no less than 63 companies.

So Sweden was wealthy, profiting from its lucky break in the war, two wars, and despite Social Democratic rule since 1932 was a bit conservative– though not nearly as conservative as it was before the first world war, and not very radical, or "pacifist". Call 1960 something of a turning point. After that, politically, Sweden accelerated leftwards, due to many causes, not least some kind of indefinable spirit of the times, but also helped by Palme's growing influence over his mentor.

Immigrants started coming, guest workers from Finland, Italy and Yugoslavia. The beautiful women were an advert for Sweden, even if, or perhaps because, some of them appeared in insalubrious movies, which started come on-stream in the mid-1960s as a more permissive society blossomed and Stockholm's nightlife shrugged off its 1950s conservatism and expanded to include at one point several hundred massage parlours. For decades after that, the phrase "Swedish girls" was a guaranteed titillator in brothel windows or on telephone booth sex advert cards in other countries. Schwedenfilm remains the German word for pornography.

Palme changed too. His own radicalism blossomed. He both exemplified the changes that were to come, and, when he rose to the top positions, hurried them on. As a first indication of the kind of person he was, when he married his fiancee Lisbet in 1956, he did not stay in the area of Östermalm, where he grew up, and which is the Chelsea/Kensington of Sweden, but moved to a modern house, radhus, or "rowhouse", in the modest suburb of Vällingby. The houses were yellow bricked two-story houses built admittedly to a high standard, with shared gardens with their invariable upended tricycles and climbing frames.

As Sweden's first New Town, Vällingby, with its integration of social housing, lakes and wooded landscapes, became a poster child for a new Sweden, and town planners from around the world came to visit. Not everyone liked it: One writer who grew up there described the empty bottles being kicked and echoing between the concrete facades of the nearby blocks by lone teenagers or troublemakers as being the only sound on a Saturday night. Sophisticated nightlife was not then Sweden's thing, hadn't caught up with the advances in high standards of housing.

It was a good place to raise children, though, and the Palme family lived in the leafier, low-rise part. Lisbet at least must have liked it. She left their posh duplex flat in the Old Town and moved back to Vällingby after her husband's assassination in 1986.

In these years as a young family man with a feminist wife he seemed to truly slough off his identity as a reserve cavalry officer, and the martial instincts of his parents and grandparents who had been right wing, anti-Russian and sent a son to die in the Finnish civil war.

SWEDEN VS WASHINGTON, the beginnings

Palme made his first foray into foreign affairs in 1965. For over a decade, he had been a forceful influence on the domestic intellectual political scene, despite his youth, thanks to his job as Erlander adviser and right-hand man. A power in the shadows. He was the drafter of the speech that kept Sweden out of the EEC in 1961. He was also the leading light behind the manual that became the "bible" of the foreign aid bureaucracy.

Now, in 1965, in the town of Gävle, he made a speech excoriating the US intervention in Vietnam. It was true that he articulated what many European leaders thought, but did not utter, but he did go very far. Palme had been convinced by accounts of Sweden's radical young ambassador in Hanoi, the capital of North Vietnam, that were very critical of what the Americans were doing. Some leader-writers friendly to Palme had also urged him to speak up about Vietnam. Palme chose the Broderskap (Brotherhood) conference in Gävle north of Stockholm. Brotherhood was the Christian branch of the Social Democrat party; always, thanks to the history of Protestant missionary work in the developing world, the most outward-looking, even interventionist, part of Palme's Social Democrat party. Palme ran through his speech with prime minister Erlander and foreign minister Torsten Nilsson before delivering it. It contained phrases like "It is an illusion to believe you can counter demands for social justice with military power". And: "The fundamental values of democratic socialism place a duty upon us to stand on the side of the oppressed against the oppressors, on the side of the poor and impoverished against their masters and exploiters". On a hot summer's day in Stockholm restaurant, Erlander waved it through, despite the word "Socialism". Erlander's party was Social Democratic. This was one step further. Perhaps Erlander was growing old and tired.

Crucially, Palme made his speech a bit more explicit on delivery. Rather than talking about national liberation in general, he added, on making the statement, that "of course, it is really Vietnam that I am talking about". Any listener to the speech who had been reading the news could complete the equation. America was an exploiter and oppressor. Erlander defended Palme's speech in parliament some days later, even though it appears Palme hadn't cleared the reference to the United States with his pro-American boss. An ideological change of course had been made. The stage for an eventual breach with the United States was set.

The US embassy called on Erlander to issue a protest, and apparently began to keep a close eye on Palme at this point. In a long character analysis, forwarded to the CIA in Langley, the speech was seen as the creation of a power base that could lead Palme into the post of prime minister. He was a brilliant, hardworking assistant of Erlander which made him the "leader of the left in Swedish social democracy". The analysis also referred to Erlander's emotional dependence on Palme. Not everyone liked Palme, the US analysis noted: "Some of the older members of government regard him as a ruthless arriviste and particularly foreign minister Nilsson is presumed to be suspicious of him".

The disturbance in Swedish-US relations was brief, though – this time. Erlander visited the US in November 1965 to great fanfare. Vice president Humphrey welcomed the Swedish prime ministerial couple to a luxury weekend at one of America's finest hotels, Greenbrier in Virginia. They talked about Vietnam. In Washington, Erlander met Kennedy's widow Jacqueline and handed over Swedish gifts to the Kennedy Center in Washington. Peace was restored. Back in Stockholm, Swedish ministers continued to attend the Tuesday club at the American Embassy, rubbing shoulders and networking with American officials, spies, and diplomats.

Two years later hosting of the Russell Tribunal in May 1967 ratcheted up tensions again. The Russell Tribunal, which also dubbed itself, without official backing, the International War Crimes Tribunal, was co-organised by the British pacifist and philosopher Bertrand Russell, in his nineties, and the French superstar ditto Jean-Paul Sartre.

It was said that the Swedish government was lukewarm about the conference being held in Stockholm, but did nothing to stop it, despite Erlander being given a serious talking to by the head of the American National Security Council at the funeral in Bonn of Konrad Adenauer, the former West German Chancellor. At the conference, which neither US nor Swedish government officials attended, the attacks on the American military were unrelenting: one British newspaper reported that the tribunal intended to "provide the most passionate, thorough and well-documented challenge to American war policy ever delivered in the West."

A French doctor called Abraham Behar gave testimony on the first day, describing, with the help of photographs, alleged American bombing raids on churches, convents and hospitals. "Towns, villages and cooperatives seem to have been bombed contrary to all logic and against all determinations of a military character."

Roger Pic, a French photographer and filmmaker, showed a film he had taken of the results of American bombings. It showed shattered churches, sobbing old men and dead and mutilated children. Stanley

Faulkner, an observer from the National Lawyers' Guild in the United States, said he "felt ashamed" of his country that day.

The next day, the tribunal – which consisted of a panel of doctors, lawyers and historians, from many countries, including the third world – heard witness testimony from a South Vietnamese peasant, who stripped to the waist to show the severe burn marks had received from American napalm bombing. Thai Binh Dan, 18 years old, had grotesque burns to his face and body, and said that at the time of the attack there were no Viet Cong troops in his village that could have justified the American bombing attack. Describing the raid, he said that as American aircraft flew overhead he ran for shelter but before he reached it a napalm bomb exploded.

When the conference concluded, the predominantly (Swedish) student audience clapped continuously for twenty minutes. The final communiqué unanimously found the United States guilty of "aggression against international law" and illegal bombings against innocent civilians. The language of condemnation against the United States appears to have been intentionally similar to what the allies used against the Nazis at Nuremberg after WW2. The tribunal's secretary said his organisation had to do for oppressed peoples what "no tribunal did while Nazi crimes were being committed and plotted."

The Swedish historian Staffan Thorsell has shown that, while lukewarmly protesting the conference in public, in private Swedish diplomats did everything they could do to expedite the processing of North Vietnamese visas to Stockholm. If Sweden had really wanted to stop the conference, it could have created artificial bureaucratic hassles. When some Swedish newspaper commentators questioned the wisdom of baiting the United States by allowing the conference to take place, Palme went out with an article in Aftonbladet newspaper that anyone who worried that the Swedish government was worried about the American reaction was "ignorant".

A certain nonchalance about American feelings seems to have prevailed. Torsten Nilsson, Swedish foreign minister, proposed to visit Washington in the autumn of 1967 to propose a peace plan for the war. The Americans said no, and their new ambassador to Stockholm was astonished that "on the one hand they help our enemies by insulting us and on the other moment they want to show our friends in America and the world that they are okay people." How were the Swedes expecting the Americans to react?

The crisis that caused the Americans to withdraw their ambassador happened less than a year after the Russell Tribunal. January 1968 saw the North Vietnamese Tet offensive strike a blow at the American presence in South Vietnam. For a whole month, the North Vietnamese army occupied the old imperial capital Hue and a suicide squad attacked the US embassy in Saigon. The attackers were driven off, but the whole

Tet operation is regarded as a political disaster for the USA, since it crushed the myth of the almighty USA and breathed fire into the American peace movement that wanted to pull out of Vietnam. The Swedish Vietnam movement was growing and received sustenance from the Tet offensive. Support for the Vietcong was often uncritical in the media, and among activists. A torchlit demonstration for peace was set for the 21st February 1968. As it happened, on the day before the march, US ambassador William Heath, had just had lunch with Erlander, where he had lectured on Swedish one-sidedness. "You always criticise us but never say a word about the other side's murders and destruction. Do your relations with the United States mean nothing to you? Are you afraid of losing votes to the left?" The Swedish archives lack a record of this conversation, which was found in the US archives. Writing of archive gaps elsewhere, historian Thorsell notes that the Swedish authorities are often less frank and open than Anglo-Saxon ones, and, sometimes in sensitive areas, it seems some documents have simply vanished from the record.

Scheduled for the day after the meeting with Heath, the Swedish government had invited the North Vietnamese ambassador to talks on the latter's visit to Sweden, part of a "diplomatic equivalent of the Tet offensive". The Swedes hoped ambassador Chan would be carrying offers of a peace deal in his pocket, thus giving the Swedes a chance to pose as important dealmakers between America and Vietnam – again, the delusion that they had legitimacy as go-betweens in American eyes. Alas, Chan apparently did not oblige the Swedes, as he came with "tired propaganda messages and no openings for peace or anything else."

On the evening of 21 February 1968, in a snowy, wintry Stockholm, Ambassador Chan found himself marching side by side with Olof Palme at the head of a demo of hundreds of people, Palme carrying a burning torch, wearing a Russian-style bearskin hat and a demonic smile accentuated by the shadows caused by the torchlight.

Palme, who had a previous arrangement to attend the march organised by the Swedish Vietnam committee, always claimed it was a total coincidence that he came face-to-face with the ambassador, but a later historian had talked to Palme's assistant and found that Palme was well informed about the ambassador's attendance before it took place; it was all over the newspapers anyway; the historian Thorsell quotes close colleagues who speculate that Palme knew the ambassador was coming and saw it as an opportunity to advance his career. "It was a chance for Palme to get a big breakthrough for what he had to say." This despite the fact that Erlander was worried enough by the potentially explosive nature of Palme's march for Sweden's relations with the States to suggest to the organisers that Palme be replaced as keynote speaker. But Palme was no longer doing the ageing Erlander's bidding; he was staking out his own path.

At Sergel's square, where the demo had gathered up, Palme held his toughest speech so far on the Vietnam war to an audience of activists and normal members of the Swedish public, fired up by the media campaign against the USA. There were placards saying "Arm the FNL" (ie the Vietcong). One speaker protested against America's "genocide". Ambassador Chan, speaking through an interpreter, made seem clearly hyperbolic claims: 1,500 enemy, ie American, planes had been shot down, and millions of tonnes of enemy weapons captured and destroyed during Tet. Chan's speech was followed by Palme's where he described the war not only as a threat to the democratic ideals in Vietnam, but to the whole world. Carried along by the atmosphere of protest, Palme argued that American policy was either a misjudgement or, he added in Marxian subtones, a manifestation of Capitalist imperialism. He added: "If you are talking about democracy in Vietnam it is obvious it is represented to a higher degree by the FNL than by the United States and its allied juntas." This speech must surely mark the final purging of the conservative officer type Palme had been in his twenties.

The news photo of Palme on the demo, transmitted on the wires, appeared in hundreds of international newspapers, and put Palme on the map of American public opinion. In a negative way. Willy Brandt, onetime Berlin mayor, a friend of Palme and foreign minister, of Germany, in the late sixties (later Chancellor), wrote in his memoirs that he was unable to share Palme's stance on Vietnam. "I didn't know enough and perhaps I did not want to know enough because it would have brought me into conflict with American politics on which I was dependent on as mayor of West Berlin then and later. I couldn't take it upon my responsibility to be openly critical towards our protective power." Palme had it easier, he said.

WILLIAM Heath , the US ambassador, went to see Erlander: according to the archives, he had many complaints, but the torchlit march topped the list. Heath was angry. Erlander replied emolliently that, for all the differences over the Vietnam war, Sweden and America got on well. The main reason for the Social Democrats' approach was to capture public opinion and prevent the far left from having a monopoly on criticism on the war. Heath was not satisfied. The Swedish diplomat taking notes on the meeting later predicted a "further deterioration in Swedish-American relations" ahead. Heath, said he regarded Palme's speeches as a "Swedish kick in the teeth" against America.

Ambassador Heath wrote a personal letter to the American secretary of state Dean Rusk saying the Swedes argued the only way for America to improve relations with the country was to make peace on Hanoi's conditions. Later, reflecting back on the incident, Heath said that he felt sorry for Erlander: Erlander was ashamed over the whole affair, being basically pro American. With Palme it was different.

"I think he was unhappy here in the USA. I got the feeling he heartily disliked this country...that he wanted to be even worse than he was but realised it was not politically wise to do so."

Though only a junior minister, Palme's skill with words, and the fact he was known to be Erlander's protégé, and that he was side by side with America's official enemy, prompted the US to withdraw Heath for consultations in March 1968. It was a punishment accorded, since the war, according to historian Staffan Thorsell, citing US archive documents, only to countries the US considered rogue states, like Cuba and the Dominican Republic. A category to which Sweden, normally anyway, never could have imagined belonging to.

Palme told an interviewer on Swedish television that he did not regret a thing.

Again, these signs can be seen with hindsight as obvious warnings about the radicalism and the future poor relationship with the States A Swedish writer and diplomat, Leif Leifland, wrote a book about the next tricky six years of US-Swedish relations from 1968 to 1974 and called it "The Years of Frost". But Palme, blithely unaware, continued with his day job, the practical matters of his new portfolio. Erlander had continued to march his protégé through the ranks. No longer his humble advisor of the fifties, he had been elected MP in 1960, then become minister without portfolio, and now communications minister. One of his tasks was to preside over the switching of Sweden from driving on the left to driving on the right, a reform carried out – by necessity, of course – at once, at 5 am on a Sunday in September 1967, after years of preparation.

In 1968, he became culture and education minister, and the radical Palme had another big stage. Palme had always read widely, and the left wing writers and journalists who filled the TV's discussion programmes and newspaper debating forums were happy to have, as one said, "one of their own" in a high post in government.

They egged him on, and he encouraged them, and together they totally helped change Sweden in a leftwards direction. It is impossible to underestimate the importance of the Vietnam war, and people's disappointment with the United States, in this radicalisation process. "The whole of Sweden basically turned into an anti-war movement," said one left-wing American observer of Swedish affairs. "And it was thanks to the agitation by one man, Olof Palme."

Sweden became the only destination that accepted US deserters and draft dodgers in the Vietnam war. Some nine hundred came , leaving via Canada or West Germany, welcomed at first because it confirmed Sweden's emerging view of itself as a moral superpower. For young Swedes, the deserters brought in a whiff of the big world, marijuana and the fashions and music of US counterculture. Black deserters were particularly exotic. Many deserters started careers and families. Hundreds went home when president Carter announced an amnesty in

1977. But a certain number were for various reasons refused the right to return, even thirty years later. One Michael Bransome, whose career as a successful doctor in Sweden made no difference to his opportunity to return home, told a reporter that when he deserted he figured the harshest penalty would be a few years in jail, not permanent separation from his family. In all those years, his mother he had only been to see him once.

Some deserters were unapologetic about what they had done: Vietnam deserters was a favoured topic for American reporters when they swung by Sweden. One writer summed up his many interviewees thus. "They see the United States as an aggressive militaristic land, driven by greed and infested with crime, controlled by big corporations and unconcerned about the millions trapped in desperate poverty." They passed on those beliefs to the Swedes they met.

In 1972, an astonishing 40% of adult Swedes signed an anti-Vietnam war declaration – meaning the protests had a penetration far, far beyond radical circles - and the degree of self-righteousness was considerable. The young student journalist Britt Marie Mattsson, who was to become the foreign editor of Göteborgs-Posten, Sweden's second largest broadsheet newspaper, said she found it hard when she went to the United States, to argue against American young friends and critics of the Vietnam war that the Swedish government "dared" have a hostile opinion against the Vietnam war, which cost Sweden nothing. (Apart from the irritation of the Nixon administration.) But it had not displayed the same degree of courage in Europe in world war 2.

America had saved Europe while Sweden had crouched and not even after the war dared come to terms with its past, by declassifying material for historians. Americans protesting against the Vietnam war risked their careers while Swedes that criticised Vietnam, well, it was comme il faut in Swedish circles. It amounted to a kind of typical Swedish groupthink. Nilsson's American friends argued that the difficult thing was to stand up when a price had to be paid on a personal level, if they stayed in the country. Americans living in the US and criticising Vietnam were vulnerable. Swedes were protected because they held identical views to that of their prime minister, and they were immune to any consequences. The implied statement was that Swedish left-wingers and war protesters were not having their courage actually tested.

One of Palme's most enthusiastic supporters was the editor of Dagens Nyheter, the largest and most influential newspaper, Olof Lagercrantz. Like Palme, Lagercrantz was a bit of an upper-class renegade who turned sharply to the left. Lagercrantz's uncle was Adolf Hamilton – the artillery officer who dragged Finnish workers out and had them executed after he had had too much to drink. Lagercrantz, like so many of the upper class, had been engaged in Finland's affairs, and fought as a volunteer in the Finnish Soviet winter war of 1939, on the Finnish side. He was born in 1911. But by the seventies his critics averred that Lagercrantz had become a "useful idiot" for left-wing dictatorships. He travelled around Mao's China and wrote things like: "The difference between us and China is that, in China people mean much more than with us." Lagercrantz's comment came after the fact that, a few years earlier, Mao had killed 60 million people in the Great Famine. He also called Mao a "great writer and decisive man of action.....what an asset it is for China to have a man like Mao Tse Tung as the father of the nation. He is practical, experienced and filled with empathy for his people." This uncritical fan of Mao was the most influential opinion former in Sweden. But there were other leftists who became prominent in media, politics and academia.

In the mid-sixties, Palme had a succession of posts that testified to the esteem with which Erlander held him. He was clearly being groomed as Erlander's successor. Palme was highly influential in his job as education minister, and as his school and kindergarten reforms have lasted to this day they are worth paying attention to. He replaced student grants for a minority with a student loans system for a larger number of people. He expanded further education facilities for adults. There was the integration of preschool into the whole school system, and a massive expansion of day-care centres. The (nearly) free kindergartens are a key to understanding the Palme era, and Sweden since.

Along with the leftist TV output that replaced the conservative old television service, with its quiz shows featuring brylcreemed teenage boys in pressed suits, they put a generation of Swedes who grew up under Palme's influence – my generation – into a cultural conflict with the more conservative, Social Democrat generation that was the Erlander era. In the kindergartens, the values promoted tended to be pacifist and collectivist. Palme left the education ministry when he became prime minister in 1969.

By then he had abolished the student's exam, that extremely academic baccalaureate (studentexamen) taken at 18 by a small minority of students, fewer than one in ten 18-year-olds. It turned people who could sing patriotic songs, quote Latin and list the names and dates of old kings. It put a lucky tiny minority of students on a level of education similar to their best educated European counterparts.

But Palme argued it also created two classes of people. It was not egalitarian. It was a remnant of the old aristocratic and conservative Sweden. It discriminated against the working class.

With the abolition of the old school system, winds of radicalism swept through the common rooms. So teachers started to become radicalised during his tenure. The old style school teacher was male, politically conservative, specialist and a graduate of one of the old elite universities. The new teachers tended to be female, left wing, young, generalist and a graduate of a new university. Schools became less academic, more egalitarian, and a number of subjects fell out of the curriculum. History was downgraded in importance as subjects like Childcare studies became compulsory. History was regarded as a bit of a bourgeois and reactionary subject, while mandatory childcare studies, which every 15-year-old had to pass before being allowed to graduate from basic school, had undoubted practical benefits. Sex and procreation were explained in a straightforward and comprehensive way. Sweden had far fewer teenage pregnancies than, for instance, the UK. However, the argument that Swedes needed history to orientate themselves in their part of the world fell a bit on deaf ears with Palme and fellow ministers of his generation. The German writer Hans Magnus Enzensberger complained that Swedish youngsters knew more about the plight of the starving African poor than their own country's past. From being a country that, through the entire 19th century and the first few decades of the twentieth, seemed to live for its past as a 17th-century great power, Sweden, at least its younger element, now knew almost nothing about its (frequently conservative) past. Forgetting the past, Enzensberger wrote, made "the breathing of their explanations short and flat".

Another area where Palme's policies had an impact on the Swedish people was television, another of his responsibilities as communications minister. Since its launch in 1955, the television service had kept a conservative profile, helped no doubt by the watchful eye kept by the deputy head of television, whom, it has been revealed, was a prominent agent for the intelligence service. (He was later to become its boss). His job was to vet Swedish journalists to ensure they did not show left-wing or communist subversive influences. His presence in such a senior executive position was an indication of the right wing, anti-communist bias of Tage Erlander's Social Democrat Sweden and the close understanding between military and government .

Palme gave the impetus to a new state TV channel, TV2, which had a pronouncedly radical profile. A genuine and not untypical programme listing for one evening in 1975 comprised a Danish film about a boy in a psychiatric clinic, a programme about a railway in Tanzania built by Mao's China, a debate about paperback thrillers and the dangers of violence in literature affecting readers (the awfulness of violence on TV being one of Olof and Lisbet Palme's favourite topics), followed by a programme about socialist fighting songs against the Spanish dictator Franco. This typical worthy evening fare ended with a debating programme on the proletarian theme of "from the factory floor". Sven Ramel, a diplomat who later became a senior official at the Swedish royal court, summed up the attitude of many on the right towards the new reformists when he talked about the "collective autism" of the new reformist media intellectuals, not interested in the more down to earth, bourgeois concerns of the average Swede, who wanted to have fun and not be politically lectured to all the time.

British ambassador Guy Millard wrote to his superiors in Whitehall that Swedish television "has been penetrated by political fringe elements, and in the absence of competing programmes, the distortion of both news and comment tends to be uncritically accepted". One British bugbear was the uncritical attitude taking by this newly radicalised Swedish television towards the IRA.

American television cartoons were much criticised by Swedish child psychologists for their "violence" and were virtually absent from the schedules. Instead, complementing plenty of domestic stuff, like the Swedish production about the socialist superhero Captain Zoom who was going to "save the world from child poverty", the East German cartoon figure Sandmanchen's narcotically peaceful and inconsequential adventures were imported by Swedish television from the DDR and held up as exemplars of children's programming. While Donald Duck comics were not similarly censored in the way Disney TV cartoons were, children's comic books also took a left-wing slant. One, for older children, was a socially and politically aware graphic novel featuring a heroic feminist Swedish doctor taking on the Ian Smith regime of Rhodesia. Another comic book taught children as young as six how they could go on strike against their parents.

All these trends were part of Sweden's becoming a more egalitarian, less elitist and more left wing place. But critics were also to claim this had a price. In Erlander's traditional Sweden, Sweden won 11 Nobel prizes in the sciences between 1948 and 1981. Erlander's government poured a lot of money into physics in a period when Swedes believed they should be acquiring the Bomb. The old school conservative Social Democrats, with their workers' backgrounds, had always been "framstegsoptimister" (optimists about the future) and materialist technocrats, at the expense of being humanists – symbolised by a decline in scholarship in "dead languages", which they thought was vaguely bourgeois.

But now the new education system, along with declining defence research funding for physics, especially nuclear physics, its critics said led to a decline even in the areas of expertise that had been boosted by the Social Democrats. Other factors, such America's enormous growth in science domination, have played a part, but do not alone explain why Sweden has won one science Nobel prize in the thirty years since 1981. And elite scholarship in many areas of the traditional humanities is a thing of the past. It is interesting to note that Berggren, the historian and biographer who is otherwise incredibly positive about Palme, thought the dumbing down of the education system were Palme's greatest failure. Lena Hjelm Wallen, the school minister between 1974 and 1976, recently told Finnish radio that "We in the workers' movement stood for proper order and organisations, but some pedagogues were very radical, did go very far."

BY 1968, with several ministerial posts under his belt, including education and communications, the increasingly radical crown prince was almost ready for the top job. Erlander won his greatest ever victory in terms of the national vote in the elections that year, but he was tired, and was ready to leave though fresh from his victory. The elderly men, usually from working-class backgrounds, who had ruled with Erlander, some practically since the war, declined to stand, saying it was time for a generational change. At the party congress in 1969 Palme was voted in unanimously. He had been active in the party since the age of 27. He had had several hugely influential posts and already made his mark on society. He was now 42.

He was Erlander's protégé, but he was more than that. He had become a youngish man who seemed to embody the dynamic spirit of the age, popular with the young, with students, intellectuals and women. Partly it was his leadership over the Vietnam war issue. In the short term, his aggressive stance gave him a strong domestic profile. Sweden was standing up to one of the superpowers and telling it off - the very thought of it thrilled many especially young radical Swedes and helped fix their moral compass. Official Washington was boiling. Swedes didn't care. When the US sent an ambassador called Jerome Holland who was a black American as a replacement to the old ambassador who had stormed out because of Palme's Vietnam stance, he was jeered by a crowd of Swedish students and American war deserters who had sought refuge in Sweden as "Lyndon's House Nigger". Palme criticised the thuggish behaviour, unconvincingly to some.

But the Party sat up and took note. His activism raised his profile with the influential youth organisation, the powerful women's organisation and the unions. It showed he was not just Erlander's errand boy, his fixer and adviser, but someone ready to stake out his own, radical political territory. Erlander had taken a much more cautious approach to third world questions, which a category that included both Vietnam and decolonisation.

In retrospect, Western diplomatic dispatches already then betray a concern and anxiety over Palme's accession.

The British embassy records a conversation with Olof Palme during Harold Wilson's visit in the summer of 1969 to Tage Erlander in which Palme talks of increasing the Social Democratic youth vote - already at 60 percent - by introducing a "greater element of socialism into their performance". Palme said, to his British embassy interlocutor, at a meeting of Swedish and British party workers, that Swedish youth were increasing their demands on government and industrial policy, no longer just satisfied with material progress but demanding new standards to apply to what was produced. There were increased concerns about the environment and the young also wanted "increased worker participation in the decisions of industry," said Palme. One diplomat or intelligence officer, Denys Brown, gave an analysis for a friend and colleague on the Western Europe desk in Whitehall, in handwriting, on the notepaper of his gentlemen's club, based on his experiences of being stationed in Sweden. It shows a kind of ambivalence towards Palme.

"I hedged in answering your question whether he was personally unpleasant. My guess is no. But there are lots of people who would say so....What is odd about Palme is the degree of dislike and fear or hatred or contempt which he arouses in the Swedish right-wing establishment."

There was also some scepticism about an upper-class boy in the Social Democrats from the old guard Social Democrat establishment, but that had been overcome. But the conservatives felt a "degree of dislike and distrust towards him over and above what they would feel on political grounds". He had, after all, betrayed his class by becoming a Social Democrat, and quite a radical one at that. Brown compared it to the loathing felt by right-wing Americans towards Roosevelt in the thirties, or of British conservatives for Churchill when he joined the Liberals. Whether Palme would ever achieve the same stature was another matter, added Brown.

Brown went on to say Palme was academically brilliant, but, from talking to old school friends, he heard that Palme was sickly, studious and bullied at school. One of Palme's contemporaries told Brown that young Palme "didn't wash and smelt appalling". "I gather that because of his oddity and cleverness he was rather a butt at school. Unlike his elder brother, who has turned into a blameless right-wing lawyer."

Palme's own ideas seemed "orthodox progressive" but some of the most credible charges of his right-wing opponents was the "extremist appointments in the information media". "Was it simply a rising politician's determination to be well with press and TV. Or should he be regarded as giving political backing to some of the wilder young men?"

Palme was also something of a romantic. At the Soviet invasion of Czechoslovakia in 1968, he said all the right things about the invasion but ended his speech with "You cannot stop ideas with tanks". Brown was doubtful of that, adding, "Well...Judging from his collection of speeches" - which he praised as extremely literate, remarkable for the number of quotations from classic literature –" reason and persuasion may be given too large and force and violence too small a role in his picture of how things actually work." He ended up saying Palme was a "man to watch".

In early 1970, six months into the prime minister's job, Palme paid a visit to London, part of a whirlwind tour of Europe's capitals to establish himself, in the words of one confidential Whitehall briefing, as someone to be taken seriously. "Palme was not altogether a popular choice and has not been altogether popular in his attempts to win the respect and confidence of Swedish business...his aim is to improve his image with the electorate as a whole and to establish himself both at home and abroad as a sound politician."

The Whitehall brief added that "With prosperity at home and few commitments abroad the Swedes have for years enjoyed the luxury of irresponsibility in some of their attitudes on foreign affairs. Under the guise of non-alignment they have indulged in criticism of the foreign and 'colonial' policies of some western powers." It talked about Palme the "enfant terrible" personally responsible to a large extent for the appalling deterioration in relations with the United States."

In advance of his state visit to Britain, The Times wrote in similar tones, a warning. Palme represented, in contrast to the Erlander era, "a new neutralism with a whiff of student radicalism and lecturing righteousness", especially given Sweden's dodgy wartime past. Palme was always critical towards America on Vietnam.

"There is an argument that in a world of military deadlocks between the power blocs only the nonaligned can be power brokers and moral arbiters...His is a voice of protest as an act of government. He is better qualified than any other political leader to fulfil the instinctive urge of Scandinavia in general and Sweden in particular to be the conscience of Europe and possibly the whole world community."

He had the "capacity and self-righteousness. It can be a useful role in international affairs, though, perhaps not quite as valuable as those who play it imagine," The Times wrote, superciliously. "Not everyone is attracted by the spectacle of any nation waxing indignant forever at those who bearing the responsibilities of power."

"Mr Palme seems to be around on the European stage for years to come, and seems certain to win much publicity. He could be the Nehru of the 1970s. But if he is to achieve his full potential he will have to display a sureness of judgment and timing that have not been apparent at every step of a highly successful political career."

PALME'S FIRST TERM: 1969 to 1976

From having been a conservative and a cavalry officer when embarking on adulthood, Palme was now truly a man marching in tune with his times. The late sixties and early seventies was a thrilling, radical period in which to be young in the West. And Palme was a youthful 42 at a time when most European leaders were a generation older. They had experience of war, were instinctively members of the officer class, took responsibility. Despite his cavalry training, Palme remained something of the schoolboy know-all, accentuated by Sweden's position somewhat outside the European mainstream. Palme had already radicalised Swedish television and education.

Radicalism suited him, and change, sometimes violent change, was in the air. 1968 was about street theatre and self-mocking slogans, "Je suis Marxiste, tendance Groucho". Thousands of young people demonstrated outside the Pentagon, trying to levitate it with the power of their thoughts, while Saigon's police chief shot a man, a South Vietnamese army deserter, in front of a photographer who caught the moment. It quickly became it one of the most famous news photographs in history. Having agitated for equal rights for blacks, Martin Luther King was assassinated in Memphis. Robert Kennedy, who offered a progressive American programme, was gunned down in 1968, while campaigning to be the Democrat Party's candidate for the presidency. Swedish writers have sometimes compared Palme to one or other of the Kennedy brothers: progressive, charismatic, promising hope, very much men of the sixties.

Later, Palme obsessed about the Kennedy murder. Dieter Strand, his campaign chronicler and close journalist friend, was not initially much impressed by Robert Kennedy, JFK's younger brother and the attorney general during the JFK presidency: too keen on the Vietnam war, linked to the mafia and the CIA. But then, accompanying his campaign, he saw RFK's last election, the one in California June 1968, how the poorest black and Mexican workers celebrated him when he came in his motorcade, tearing at the cufflinks and grabbed him so that their dirty fingernails scratched his skin and every night he had to be bandaged up. Strand and Palme spent a lot of time together on Swedish election campaigns, sharing whisky out of a toothbrush glass in some remote northern Swedish town. Palme never could get enough of these details. Perhaps he, too, fancied himself as a European Kennedy. In a fascination that foreshadowed the intense speculation that was to surround his own death, Palme was obsessed with who killed the Kennedys. Who killed Kennedy? Why? Why?

Indeed, who killed Palme?

In another development in 1968, Alexander Dubcek carried out liberal reforms in Czechoslovakia in what has become known as the Prague Spring. There was a new mood in the air, and Sweden was starting to think of itself as a country on the leading edge of progressivism. Palme had surrounded himself with young advisers, all postgraduate and cocky, and they were going to change the country after 25 years of Erlander's caution. In West Germany, Palme's friend Willy Brandt had just been appointed chancellor, and he was going to open up his country too, make West Germany more "modern".

As we have seen, after its period of robust post-war, pro-western caution under Erlander's conservative variant of Social Democracy, Sweden was undergoing a period of rapid social change, in education, media and social areas. Palme's Sweden quickly became alert to the environmental issue. Palme moved quickly. Sweden became the first country in the world to ban DDT, to show it "led the way" in environmental credentials. It also became the first country in the world to recognise North Vietnam. And Palme set about changing the Social climate in Sweden by boosting women's rights and creating an extremely egalitarian society: Childcare was expanded and women were encouraged to go out and work. The married tax allowance – which meant the single wage earner paid less taxes if his partner stayed at home - was abolished at the time as the maximum marginal tax rate was increased, effectively making it impossible for Swedish salarymen, however highly paid, to support their families on their income alone. A second income was necessary. Housewives basically disappeared. Nearly all women went, with varying degrees of enthusiasm, into the workplace. The media did their bit by stigmatising the "husfru", the housewife, as someone oppressed and if she reckoned she wasn't oppressed, she was doubtless suffering from "false consciousness". The results were drastic. In the 1940s Sweden was described as having the most gender-defined roles in Scandinavia; in 1966, two-thirds of women stayed at home. By 1974, a complete transformation, 80 percent of women were active in the workplace. Sweden, having been one of the most class-ridden countries in the world in Palme's childhood, soon had the smallest income differences of any developed country, and the highest female labour participation rate. From a country that shared a family structure with West Germany to one that shared it with East Germany. (Women in the workplace, a large service industry of carers and nurseries being one of the big things that set apart bourgeois federal republic West Germany and socialist DDR.) Current Swedish socialist writer and commentator Göran Greider calls the high female participation rate a launch pad for what he called "embryonic socialism".

"In Swedish society the expanding official provision of services became a veritable cultural and mental landslide. A huge female collective became visible in the workplace, where until recently it had been atomised in families or spread out in a still existing home help class." This large new collective could be used as an agent for further social engineering, writes Greider, who was not unsympathetic to what Palme did. "At the same time, the politicians had in their hands a new powerful instrument to push society in their desired direction."

THIS WAS accompanied by many social and cultural changes: Sweden became less patriarchal, less family oriented, less traditional, more feminist, more secular – judging by church attendance figures, the most secular country in the world outside the communist societies of Eastern Europe. (Some self-styled Swedish dissidents, and some in the military, of course, as we have seen, thought of Sweden as developing worrying East bloc tendencies – secular, socialist, non spiritual, anti family.) Cohabitation, divorce and single parenthood rates were very high compared to the rest of Europe. (although teenage parenthood rates were very low.) In time, the rest of northern Europe, including the UK, was to catch up on some of the secularisation and cohabitation bit (but not the low teenage pregnancies) but Sweden was an outlier in the early seventies. A lot of conservatives in the Anglo Saxon world peered at Sweden and saw the future. And they professed that they were distinctly ambivalent about what they had seen.

However, even if one is a fan of Palme, and accepts that he did a lot of good, one ought to be able to agree that the social victories had an economic price. Sweden under Erlander never was a socialist success story and poster child that some foreign progressives claimed: the reason that Sweden was at the pinnacle of global economic success, in 1970, after running a mostly capitalist economy, albeit with welfare elements. It was a corporatist system, with powerful capitalist players in creative tension with powerful unions. It was an enormously technocratic society that was competent at science and engineering and respected its uses. Material prosperity was the grail. The self-discipline, high literacy, conformism, peasant work ethic and memories of centuries-long poverty of an enfranchised and self-confident working class played a huge part in the Swedish miracle up to the end of Erlander's rule. However, even though the social classes remained at peace with one another, Sweden continued to be a society divided by class and gender differences. One of Palme's big goals was to set about changing that. Socialist idealism replaced Erlander's hard-headed technocratic Social Democracy.

Palme launched a most extensive welfare state with dozens of new lawss on social reform, as well as an unprecedented tax and spend programme. And it happened very quickly. A British embassy brief analysed the situation, talking of the "juggernaut of equality".

"Under the Erlander regime, progress would have been gradual and cautious, and there would have been sufficient discussion to show that the interest of the country as a whole was being served; whereas now it is as if government was forcing the pace and ramming the ideas of the Social Democratic party conference down the people's throats with scant respect for the Riksdag and with a minimum of discussion with those who traditionally helped in the taking of decisions. And of course all this is associated with the name of Palme."

He had already turned television and the school system into bastions of change. Now he was going solve income inequality, social inequality, female emancipation, and workers' rights. He was not concerned to introduce Socialism in the sense of nationalising the means of production, which was socialism under the classic definition, and was what the British Labour party had done in 1945. Ninety percent of business remained in private hands. As one wag said later, the state in Sweden had no need to own the cow – as long as it got its hands on the milk. But taxes on wealth, income, gifts and inheritance were raised drastically from the Erlander era and this spent on a large public sector. Political scientists have sometimes called Palme's highly taxed capitalism and the strong, mighty, redistributive state "functional socialism". It had the effect of socialism through capitalist means. Palme himself started calling himself "a democratic socialist". The party still called itself the Social Democrats, but it was different from Erlander's more right-wing system. One of his biographers, Kjell Östberg, writes that "the depth of the wave of reforms that washed through Sweden in the early 1970s made Sweden in many ways unique. International observers often asked if Palme's Sweden was on its way to becoming another country."

There were important constitutional changes at this time, too. The monarchy had still surprisingly influential presence in Swedish life under Erlander. However, in the 1960s the leftist Social Democrats expressed their very clear desire to abolish the remnants of the old conservative Sweden whose most powerful symbol was the still extant monarchy. Suspicions were mutual. The Finnish diplomat Max Jacobson describes visiting a Swedish royal gathering in white tails in the early 70s and one youngish man standing alone in a black suit, looking unhappy and desperate for someone to talk to. It was the prime minister, Olof Palme. Jacobson, who was Finnish ambassador to Sweden at the time, wrote. "I said hello and he looked happy someone had bothered to come over and talk to him." The Royal Family and their guests were clearly showing their feelings for Palme.

To show the monarchy was adaptable in these leftist times, the old king sent his grandson and heir, crown prince Carl Gustaf, on study visits to the centres of the new power dispensation, like the leftist LO trade union headquarters.

To little avail. In 1973, after the popular 91-year-old Gustav VI Adolf died, and was replaced by his callow playboy grandson, Carl XVI Gustav, 27, Olof Palme immediately signed a deal deprived the monarchy of all its functional powers. The new king's personal qualities probably played no part in the decisions in principle to change the machinery of state, but the death of the popular old king probably was a factor in the timing of Palme's reforms. Under the new legislation, the king no longer called on the prime minister to form a government, and no longer opened parliament with all the regalia. He no longer attended cabinet meetings. The king's chairing of cabinet meetings, a holdover from the monarchical period, even if just a formality, had given the Swedish monarch arguably more day-to-day informal influence on Swedish politics than, say, the British monarch, right into the 1970s and Palme's reforms.

Under a new constitution of 1973 which replaced the one of 1809, the opening of parliament was now performed by the speaker, in a regular suit. Sweden, under Palme, became a republic in all but in name, the most republican of all the Scandinavian monarchies. And maybe Palme expected to go further, to administer the coup de grace after winning the next election.

"THE MONARCHY can now be abolished by the stroke of a pen," Palme famously said. It never was – quite. But Sweden had changed very much indeed since the days when Sweden was one of the most royalist of all European countries as recently as 1914, when all men wore rows of medals on their chest and the Court was the centre of all Stockholm life. The powerless new monarchy remained popular with the "working people", as the rows of gossip magazines on supermarket shelves could testify to, but historians argued that parliamentary democracy had been deprived of one of its most powerful symbols without being replaced by anything else. Sweden also acquired a new constitution under Palme, but the German poet and intellectual Hans Magnus Enzensberger, who wrote the essay "Swedish Autumn", one of the most perceptive pieces of writing ever made about Sweden, which was an interesting German leftist take on Sweden in 1982, complained that none of Stockholm's bookshops seemed to stock it. And none of the Swedes he met even seemed aware that Sweden had a constitution that provided a reference point for individual rights.

The leftist Swedish professor Arne Ruth wrote a few years later, that the "marvellous story" of Social Democracy, of how the working class took power in Europe's most conservative country and created a society based on principles of equality and solidarity, was in danger of not inspiring the sense of loyalty it once did, since the workers now led bourgeois lives. Yet no other narratives, pace Palme's strong state, came close to replacing it. For Ruth, "there is no binding moral tradition in Swedish society" in a country where religion no longer played a part and "the constitution was too recent".

Some of the maverick Swedes, who gratefully found an audience with foreign writers and academics looking for a Swedish dystopia, complained that the human rights problems that seemed to occur in Sweden sometimes where individuals were trodden on came because Swedes were not legal-minded, or cared about their freedoms. And the new constitution did not protect individual rights. There was a discussion whether the new constitution of 1974 should contain individual rights enshrined in basic law. The Swedish Moderates (conservatives) and liberals favoured such a solution, in theory, but did not exactly push it. The Social Democrats demanded that the constitution contain the classic left-wing positive rights such as the right to work, home and security in return for the classic liberal negative rights – the citizen's protection against oppression from the state – becoming enshrined in the constitution. The upshot was that no compromise was found and neither positive nor negative rights were protected in the constitution. As we have seen, law professors such as Jacob Sundberg and Gustaf Petren thought that Palme's and the Social Democrats' compact hostility to any kind of control mechanisms against political power very short-sighted. It was true that the politicians' legitimacy was guaranteed by the mandate they got in regular democratic elections. But in a system where one party had been in power for 40 years nonstop when Palme came to power, you could question whether the public vote provided adequate checks and balances against political arrogance. By the end of the Tories' 18 years in power in Britain in 1997, there was much talk of elective dictatorship. Well, in comparison, the Swedish Social Democrats ruled 2.5 times as long without interruption. The Social Democrats even refused to create a legal council that would preexamine law proposals to see if they were consistent with the constitution. It was not even meant as a constitutional court on the model of West Germany, the USA or Denmark. The government would still have the last word. But Palme said he did wish to go back to the old Sweden of conservative judges against which the workers' movement had so successfully risen in 1918.

Would Sweden be the first country where a Social Democrat regime, under a democratic mandate, introduced full-on economic socialism?" That was one question posed by a biographer of Palme, Kjell Östberg, who went on to say Palme certainly did not lack for ambition. In a series of letters to his counterparts Willy Brandt in Germany and Bruno Kreisky in Austria, he debated the problems of capitalism and democracy, industrialisation and the environment. Their correspondence was later published as a book. Palme enjoyed speaking to star-struck individual intellectuals from places like France. He told his MPs that Sweden had gone further than any other country in fighting the big dilemmas of modern industrialised societies: the problems of growing inequality and income differences. America's Nation magazine said Sweden was the first country that tried to deal with the hangover of industrial society.

Östberg concludes, however, that Palme's genius lay in changing the message depending on the audience and that "the mixed economy" was a phrase you could sometimes fill with more, sometimes with less, capitalism. Many senior journalists remembered him from young Social Democrat days and said his moderate views hadn't changed since then. Östberg concludes that despite his rhetoric Palme was, in practical behaviour, a warm supporter of the market economy. Others, such as the former socialist Assar Lindbeck, now a famous economist, chairman of the Nobel memorial prize in economics committee, disagreed.

But again, there are other stories, other ways to look at it. Palme's Sweden broke several records. No other western country, not even Mitterand's France in the early 80s, before or since Sweden in the 1970 and 80s, has had so many public employees, as a percentage of the total workforce; in no other western country, before or since, was the state to make up such a large proportion of the country's economic output. Or ensure such small wage gaps between citizens, between the janitor and the executive. And yet, as Östberg says, Sweden did have, unlike East

Germany, with which critics occasionally compared it as a "DDR Light", highly competitive capitalist firms, like Volvo or Ericsson, that could compete on the world markets with the best of them.

A VERY CRITICAL diagnosis came, in the1990s, a few years after Palme's death, in an economics paper by Assar Lindbeck. Prof Lindbeck, who had started out as an ally of Palme, is one of Sweden's most distinguished economists, the man who for 14 years was the chairman of the committee that awarded the Nobel Memorial Prize in Economics. Hugely influential in that his committee had the capability to elevate certain economists to enormous global intellectual fame, Assar Lindbeck was one of Palme's intellectually most distinguished contemporaries, once tipped to be a leader of Social Democracy himself. In fact, Erlander once asked Lindbeck to be his assistant too. Lindbeck had declined, had in fact recommended Palme.

Lindbeck and Palme, both the same age, knew each other well, and, as neighbours in Vällingby had been in harness together in the late fifties as they wrote a few joint economics papers with ideas for how Social Democracy should look in the seventies and eighties. However, their views diverged and Lindbeck found Palme more and more radical, too radical for his taste. In the early nineties, after Palme's death, Sweden went through a big recession which prompted a lot of soul-searching among Sweden's policymakers and public intellectuals as to its origins. In 1997, Lindbeck wrote an influential economics paper criticising the high tax, strong state which had been allowed to develop under Palme. The paper, whose subject was Palme's period in office, was called "the Swedish Experiment".

Lindbeck explained how Palme had created a massive central government apparatus that sucked in taxes and spent them on a huge and expanding variety of welfare programmes. There were, of course, programmes to tackle inequality, kindergarten programmes, more generous sick leave and holidays; expanded elderly care projects - all planned from Stockholm by a growing and centralised bureaucracy and run locally by a massively expanded public sector. Eventually, however, the taxpaying sector of society was unable to bear the costs imposed by the tax demanding sector. Economic gravity would eventually take its toll, whether Palme and his ideological supporters liked it or not.

Palme's giveaway budgets were popular - the expanded number of public sector workers dependent on the state for their salaries became the bedrock of Palme's electoral support – but, as the saying goes, Lindbeck said, socialists always run out of other people's money. Top tax rates were over 90%, and they kicked in at much lower levels of income than in Britain, which under Labour also ran very high marginal taxes. The average worker was on a tax rate of 60%. Apart from the high taxes, this expansion was funded by cutting down on some other expenses, including the expensive military state built up during and after WW2, which, bit by bit, shrank in extent. While army numbers stayed steady, the number of aircraft dropped by 10% and the number of large navy attack ships decreased by 55% between 1965 and 1975.

Figures can illustrate how much more socialist Palme's Sweden was than Erlander's Sweden.

Under Erlander, Sweden's public sector was no bigger than any other western country's. Within a few years, Swedish public sector expenditures were something of the order of 70% of GDP, astonishing compared to the 45% that was the OECD average.

There were, for sure, good things about these policies, and Lindbeck lists them. The generous welfare arrangements made for "high-income security, a lot of income equality, little poverty." Excellent antenatal care funded by taxes gave the lowest childhood mortality rates in the world. The investment in human capital, particularly the poor, promoted economic growth - up to a point. Compressed incomes and generous benefits were good for social peace and social stability. Palme sometimes said to critics that "Sweden is the most civilised society in the world" and there was a lot be said for the Swedish utopia he was trying to create.

However, wealth distribution requires wealth creation. That was something, Lindbeck said, the left often forgot. You cannot hand out money unless you have made it. The trouble was, as the demands on the private sector's productive capacities grew, these productive capacities themselves shrank, precisely because inbuilt disincentives built into Palme's model.

The high tax wedges discouraged hard work. If you worked overtime, you would likely end up in higher tax bracket and up with very little extra take-home pay. On the other hand, sick leave benefits kicked in after the first day off and were generous and tax-free. So it became difficult to get the Swedes to work hard, wrote Lindbeck. The net salary increase from extraordinary effort was so small it wasn't worth it.

Instead, people often took impromptu days off if they felt they had to catch up on household work – just as in the absurdist economies of Eastern Europe. Companies like Volvo had to overstaff their shifts by 25 or 30 percent to precompensate for the number of people they knew would call in sick – even though they were, of course, perfectly healthy. "I always say there are more 'sick' people in a Swedish factory than a Swedish hospital," said Electrolux's Hans Werthen sarcastically. He was one of the many business leaders increasingly critical of Palme.

The motor of Sweden's prosperity in the Erlander had been shipbuilding, textiles, cars and engineering. The first two categories provided no household names, but in the areas of cars and engineering Volvo, SAAB, Ericsson, Electrolux and ASEA were famous worldwide. An upstart furniture retailer called IKEA was already expanding out of Scandinavia. Business leaders, who had always been sceptical of Palme, had their "I told you so" moment about his socialism. "Sweden left work sometime in the mid-Seventies," Werthen, chairman of Electrolux, said. Leading industrialists threatened to take their companies abroad to avoid the Swedish "low productivity disease" caused by demotivatingly high taxes and two – IKEA and Tetra Pak, the world's leading manufacturer of milk cartons – actually did.

People also did jobs on the side, bartering services or paying cash in hand to avoid the ferocious taxman. "I will do your teeth if you fix my drains," the dentist might say to the plumber. Alternatively: "I will pay you in cash so you won't have to declare it."

To crack down on this trend, laws were passed that granted extensive powers to the tax police to open people's mail or turn up and search homes without a warrant. Marianne Alopaeus, a Swedish-speaking Finnish writer, described high tax Sweden in a book aptly named Cursed by Sweden (Drabbad av Sverige) in which it "never pays to work a little harder, where the tax forms are so complicated that the signature under the 'on my honour and good conscience' gives you stomach ache and where workers who are paid cash-in-hand are hunted with a blowtorch."

Film director Ingmar Bergman, the author of Pippi Longstocking, Astrid Lindgren, and the pop group ABBA, literally Sweden's second biggest export after Volvo, all at various times got into very public trouble with the authorities over their taxes. Bergman was eventually cleared of tax cheating by the courts, but not before the sensitive film director had a breakdown over the tax authority's attention. The film director emigrated to Munich for several years and the case created an enormous international stir. Lindgren's case, in which she was taxed more than she earned, ie at 102% of her annual earnings, under a new law that put no upper limit on freelancers' own surcharge taxes, was a huge public opinion setback for the Social Democrats. The elderly writer of fairy tales was an untouchable icon for adults and children alike – she had always been a proud Social Democrat and never objected to paying taxes per se. Lindgren wrote a "naïve" fairy story in the Expressen newspaper about the country Mosimania and its mad tax collectors which was clearly about Sweden and Palme. Where law professors and radical right wing journalists had failed, the children's writer succeeded in striking a blow against Social Democrats' reputation.

The affairs were exploited by Palme's political opponents as weapons against both high taxes and the Strong State.

On a more general note, Lindbeck argued that the sky-high employer taxes were no way to revive the economy. Certain firms, like Volvo and Saab, continued to flourish, but Palme's Sweden also suffered from the fact that, in many of the large manufacturing sectors where Sweden had excelled, such as shipbuilding, Asian competition was beginning to make Sweden uncompetitive. That wasn't Palme's fault but happened under his watch. Sweden's energy dependency was greater than that of most other countries. But with the oil crisis of 1973, energy prices soared, putting further pressure on manufacturing. Sweden needed to generate new areas where it could be competitive. And yet, as said, the tax system discouraged new business start ups.

Lindbeck was not the only well-regarded mainstream economist who was critical of the way his own party was creating an economy with unproductivity biases. The respected Danish economist Gösta Esping Andersen looked at the policy of getting women into the workplace by (mostly) having them work in the public sector as one fraught with problems. While it was politically good in that it boosted for gender equality, and allowed women to harmonise childbirth and careers and helped absorb unskilled workers into well-paid employment, he argued it was an expensive luxury that didn't actually generate wealth for the country, and worked only as long as the economy was booming.

Let us be clear: Sweden remained prosperous. However, in terms of wealth per capita, statistics seem to show that Sweden actually went into a relative economic decline for 25 years from about 1972, under the years of Palme's giveaway largesse to women, public sector workers and the unemployed. While remaining a clean and organised place with a high level of income equality, Sweden fell from being the second richest country in the world per capita in 1970 to about the middle of the West European table. (Although the economy was to pick up again after 1983 as a new, more realistic economic policy was implemented.) Britain was the well-known sick man of Europe in the 1970s. But according to economists such as Lindbeck and others, Sweden was also an underperformer. As we have seen in an earlier chapter, fairly or not, one stick used to be at Palme was the alleged control state. This chapter has demonstrated how he opened himself up to charges of weakness on the economy. And then, depending on your perspectives, there was his foreign and security policy.

ATTACKING WASHINGTON: foreign policy 1969- 1976

US/Swedish relations had been cool since the torchlit Vietnam demo in February 1968 when Palme marched side by side with the North Vietnamese ambassador to Moscow, visiting Scandinavia to drum up support.

The US ambassador, having complained to Erlander, left for the US, then returned to Sweden, then left again. After an eight-month hiatus, he was replaced by Jerome Holland, in 1970. Holland was a friend of Nixon's, and black. Holland's reports about being on the receiving end of racism – from Swedish anti-American demonstrators, never from Palme – enraged Nixon. This soon came to a head. When Palme was invited to the United States to receive an honorary doctorate from his alma mater, Kenyon College in Ohio, in June 1970, he was keen to build bridges. He made it clear he was open to seeing the president. Would he be invited to drop in on the president which, in normal circumstances, would have been the polite thing to do?

Nixon was not keen. There was a battle in the White House about what to do about Palme. Nixon wrote in the margins on a memo about the event. "Let us totally ignore this visit". National security adviser Henry Kissinger said if the Swedes raised the question with them the White House should make it clear it was just a private visit. If they want to arrange meetings with Palme and American officials, we must indicate this is not possible, wrote Al Haig, a rising star on National Security Adviser Kissinger's staff. This was the diplomatic equivalent of a complete cold shoulder. The memo was circulated to Nixon and to the US embassy in Stockholm.

However, the State Department was less hostile, and some diplomats there said someone in the American government ought to meet the young Swedish premier, who might be around for a long time.

At the same time, Palme was being deliberately vague with his Washington ambassador, Hubert de Besche. De Besche was instructed to say that Palme was available for talks and meetings that the Americans might wish to suggest. But the actual formulations were left to de Besche's judgment. However, after much discussion, the State Department's bureaucrats successfully arranged for a meeting with Secretary of State William Rogers to go ahead. Rogers was a notorious dove in the Nixon White House and may have sympathised with some of the European criticism of the Vietnam war. He and Kissinger hated one another.

When Kissinger heard that Rogers was meeting Palme he fired off an outraged, top-secret memo. He warned Nixon and Rogers against meeting Palme for four reasons

- Sweden was the only western country helping Hanoi
- Palme was extremely anti-American
- His way of going outside the usual channels was bordering on personal insult
- Palme would turn the meeting to his political advantage when he returned home.

Kissinger argued that changed directives would damage Nixon's authority with the state department. Telegrams went back and forth, but it, at the end of it all, seemed that, at least, Palme would be seeing Rogers, for what Rogers emphasized would be just a "low-key event". As for Nixon, he told his subordinates to arrange for him to be completely busy when Palme came to Washington, preferably travelling.

The matter was still not entirely settled when Palme arrived in Washington on the evening of 3 June 1970. He moved into a suite on the eighth floor of the hotel Mayflower a few blocks away from the White House. Palme was nervous when he came to Washington. Although he was ostensibly only in America to collect an honorary degree at Kenyon, this was his baptism of fire across the Atlantic, in the same way he had visited the leaders of Europe in April to take soundings.

Palme was flying into an America that was boiling over on the issue of the Vietnam War. Nixon had just expanded the war by invading Cambodia to attack the North Vietnamese based there, The New York Times had revealed a number of bombing runs against Cambodia that were so secret not even the Secretary of Defense knew of them. In April, at Kent State University, not far from Kenyon, the National Guard had dispersed an anti-war demonstration with live bullets that ended up killing four people.

The Swedish foreign ministry had sent Palme a folder jam-packed with information about the United States and Us Swedish relations. A few handwritten notes are all that remain, but Palme had prepared the trip carefully. Canada's prime minister Pierre Trudeau, whose anti-American reputation and radical upper-class personality prompted some comparisons with Palme, had just held a speech at the National Press Club in Washington where Palme was also due to speak. Palme watched a taping of Trudeau's performance several times on the flight across the Atlantic. The American newspapers, surely briefed by Nixon's men, wrote that Palme was "an unwelcome guest" in Washington. It had not happened since Fidel Castro was in town that the United States had refused to see a foreign leader, The New York Times wrote.

The Los Angeles Times wrote that relations between Sweden and the US had not been so bad since the Second World War.

The meeting with William Rogers was more successful than Palme dared hope. The discussions dealt with the big problems of the time, in the Middle East, EEC, Vietnam and Cambodia. The Swedish ambassador wrote afterwards that "Rogers seemed genuinely interested in what Palme had to say".

Later, Palme's speechwriter Anders Ferm wrote that Rogers was sympathetic but that his advisers were more hawkish, which prompted an immediate angry reply from a senior Swedish official that Ferm, who was then only in his twenties, should be less indiscreet when talking on the phone, which was likely bugged by the CIA as a matter of routine.

Palme then went to Congress, where he had a positive meeting with William Fulbright, chairman of the Senate Foreign Relations committee and a staunch critic of the Vietnam war. Real friends dare say tell the truth, said Fulbright, gazing over his reading glasses. The Democratic senator had shown on many occasions views that agreed with Palme on the matter of American behaviour in the war. Press conferences and TV interviews followed. Many of them were sympathetic. However, when Palme spoke at Kenyon, a hundred dockers turned up with placards that accused Palme of being racist – because of ambassador Holland's troubles – and told Palme to "go home and take your Volvos with you."

Back in New York, Palme spoke to other public figures and was faced with more demonstrators, factory workers who accused him of being pro-Communist and anti-American. The Governor of New York State, Nelson Rockefeller, said he would meet Palme, on one condition: no photographers. In the summer of 1970, writes Thorsell, the historian of American-Swedish relations, Palme was politically radioactive. Still, considering he had "invited himself" to Washington (in extension of Kenyon) his trip was more successful than it might have been. But he travelled back across the Atlantic without getting to meet Nixon.

In the two years from 1970, the end of that visit, to December 1972 when the great eruption came after Palme's comparison with the Holocaust. Palme was mentioned a handful of times in the White House tapes. We know this because of the infamous Nixon Tapes. The president had installed a taping mechanism: five microphones under his desk, plus two mikes by the fireplace. Several of Nixon's phones were connected to other tape recorders. More than 15,000 conversations were recorded over two years, 1,530 hours' worth. It would be an exaggeration to say tiny Sweden took up much of Nixon's time. It would also be fair to say that, apart from Sweden, he was angry with many things. But it is also true that he showed little fondness for the progressive little country and its prime minister. On one occasion he asked about "that dirty film from Sweden" and what his aides could do about it, apparently in reference to I am Curious, Yellow, an art house film, a typical 60s film, with sex situations involving its politicised faux naïf feminist heroine. In one scene, Palme, appearing as himself, dressed, talked to an interviewer about socialism while playing with his son outside the family's suburban house. It is far from clear Palme knew what he was letting himself in for. The film became a cause celebre when showed in San Francisco, New York, Boston and other such receptive places. Its frank depictions of sex, which caused little stir in a Sweden caught up in its revolution of sexual permissiveness, caused a minor scandal with American Christians. So Nixon said once: "We have to do something about that dirty film from Sweden". Thorsell says, having listened to many tapes, that from the tapes it was also clear that Nixon was angry about the American deserters in Sweden and that he thought the North Vietnam was using Stockholm as its international propaganda base. (Meanwhile, State Department officials wrote a memo to the effect that that three cities in the world were unsafe for Americans: Peking, Hanoi and Stockholm.)

ONE OF the most notable incidents before the holocaust comparison that sent Washington ballistic in December 1972 concerned Olof Palme's behaviour at an environment conference held in Stockholm a few months before that. Completely forgotten now is Nixon's stated commitment to the environment in his first term, and he had sent his top advisers to Stockholm to try and make an impression. But Nixon was enraged by reports from his diplomats that Palme abused his role as chairman of the conference by going off topic with an attack on America in Vietnam. When Bob Haldeman, Nixon's chief of staff, came in they discussed the conference.

Nixon: "That conference in Stockholm. The only news from there is that the goddamn Swedish prime minister marched in and said American polluted the environment in Vietnam."

Haldeman: "State whacked them hard. Said they were shocked. The Swedes distorted the purposes of the conference."

Nixon: "We will find a way. Do we have an ambassador there when Holland leaves?"

Haldeman: "Not yet."

Nixon: "I don't… the ambassador…Let the Swedes..let's not think about them for a while."

Two days later Nixon was still angry about the conference and told his adviser, Al Haig, that State should make sure to "kick the Swedes hard". Haig said they had done so, and scared the Swedes. "They promised to avoid further discussions." A few days later Nixon raised the subject a third time and, when it was completely clear that Holland would be leaving Sweden, instructed his aides to ensure Sweden would not get another ambassador. Which it did not for another two years.

The longest talk about Sweden on the Nixon tapes was when the Pentagon papers were published by the New York Times. In terms of the debate it caused about national security secrets and whistle-blowers, the Pentagon papers story was the 1970s equivalent of the Assange or Snowden revelations. They were leaked by an official called Dan Ellsberg and dealt with the background of the war in Vietnam. Nixon and Kissinger tried to outdo each on in outrage against a press that prevented them from running a foreign policy.

At some point, Palme's name came up

Kissinger: "That goddamn Swedish prime minister has also made a statement. We just got this news telegram."

Nixon: "The Swedish prime minister?"

Kissinger: "He said this war was prepared through an act of betrayal. That the American government has undermined democracy and has to withdraw unconditionally from Vietnam."

Nixon's response is still secret. The following 22 seconds of tape have not been released by the Nixon archives to researchers "out of respect for America's relations with foreign states". One of the US researchers behind the Nixon tapes project said that a common reason for this classification is because Nixon said something rude about foreign politicians. Thage Peterson, a state secretary in Palme's government, one

Palme's closest ministers, claims in his memoirs this was the time that Nixon called Palme that "goddamn Swedish asshole." Peterson had asked Palme when he had heard it, and Palme had told Peterson that it came from a contact of Palme's inside the White House.

Such were the feelings about Sweden and Palme in the autumn and winter of 1972, when Palme made his holocaust speech.

The Christmas of 1972, for Richard Nixon and his family, were spent in Key Biscayne, Florida. It had been a hectic re-election campaign, and the President wanted peace and quiet. The day before Christmas Eve, Nixon was drinking cocktails and swimming in the pool. He watched football on TV.

Thousands of miles away, it was snowing heavily in Sweden. Palme was at home. In his functionalistic brick house in the Stockholm suburb of Vällingby, while Lisbet and the children were doing their Christmas preparations, sitting in his dressing gown, he was preparing his most uncompromising and controversial remarks ever on the Vietnam war. A few hours later the remarks detonated across the Atlantic.

Nixon received no visitors and took only two phone calls that day. One was from his doctor and the other was from Kissinger.

ON THE MORNING of the 23rd December, Palme had called up the Swedish national news agency, TT, in order to get his message out. A few hours later he read out the message, his voice shaking with anger and sadness. And in the afternoon, Rapport, the main evening news programme of the so-called "Red channel", TV2 of state television, came to interview him. Reuters cabled the news out across the world. And in the United States it received with a force in official circles in a way Palme cannot have foreseen.

The background to Palme's little speech was the launch of what has become known in history as the Christmas Bombings of Hanoi. The official name of the bombing campaign was Operation Linebacker II.

The operations involved round-the-clock bombings and used B-52 bombers in the largest such effort since the Second World War. Like much of Europe, Sweden was up in arms, and the Social Democrats' party secretary had the idea of getting a cross-party backing for a national signature collection campaign against the bombings. Even the conservatives, or moderates, the sole party that was usually allergic to any foreign policy proposal from the Social Democrats, went along with it, albeit with some reservations. The Swedish foreign minister made a strong statement before he left for his Christmas holidays. Palme, though, remained anxious and would not leave it at that. He wanted to send an even stronger signal. Later he told an American reporter he had written in his five minutes and only consulted a handful of people, including Erlander. It has been called a prose poem rather than a speech. He read it out in slow, mournful tones.

"One should refer to things by their accurate designation. What is happening right now in Vietnam is a form of torture. What they do is tormenting people. They torment a nation in order to humiliate it, compel them to subjugate with brute force. That is why the bombings are an infamy. Of such there are many in modern history. They are often linked to a name: Guernica, Oradour, Babi Yar, Katyn, Lidice, Sharpeville and Treblinka. In all those places violence was triumphant, but the judgment of history came down hard on those who were responsible. Now there is another name to add to the list: Hanoi, Christmas 1972."

Guernica referred to the bombing of the Basque town of that name in 1937 by Franco's forces, and is sometimes called the first air attack in history on a defenceless civilian population. Oradour was a village in southwestern France whose population of 644 was massacred by a unit of the Waffen SS over a few short hours. A church with women and children inside was set on fire, while the men of the village were shot in the legs, covered in petrol and burned alive. But the most wounding comparison was with Treblinka, the death camp in Poland where 800,000 Jews were reported to have died in gas chambers. The editors at Reuters knew exactly what the top line in the story was, and the news agency's telegram began with the words

"Sweden's prime minister Olof Palme said today that the bombings were ill deeds comparable to the Nazi massacres in the second world war."

The Washington Post only had a small item about Palme's protest. But the State Department was quicker off the mark. According to reports, when Kissinger heard the news, he was sick with anger. His family had fled Nazi Germany for America when he was a boy to escape Hitler's persecution of the Jews. Thirteen of Kissinger's relatives died in concentration camps.

In the morning of the 23rd, according to tapes Kissinger himself made of his calls, which were revealed only in 2004, he had received a news summary about the Christmas bombings. A hospital in Hanoi had been hit and many doctors and nurses had been killed. He received chiefs of the Pentagon who showed him maps of where the bombings had taken place as they discussed the next wave of targets. In the afternoon, the tapes showed that he was planning a trip to the theatre and dinner for the evening. A colleague rang to ask if he wanted to watch a Washington Redskins match on Christmas Eve, the next day. An hour after his call with Nixon, he was informed about Palme's speech and rang a colleague at the State Department.

Kissinger: "Bill, have you see that the Swedish prime minister has compared our bombings to the Nazis?"

Sullivan: "No. The bastard."

Kissinger: "I would like the Swedish ambassador called in by someone and given a really brutal dressing down. Who can do it?"

William Rogers was on vacation. The task went to his deputy, Alexis Johnson. A few hours later the State department rang the Swedish embassy and wanted to get hold of the ambassador, Hubert de Besche. He was out Christmas shopping. Once he had been told and made his way to the State Department, he was given the worst telling off in his life. One of the aides who had been involved in formulating the American response said they had been given orders to be "really nasty to the Swedish bastards".

JOHNSON SUGGESTED that the Swedish ambassador might wish to borrow a pen and paper and take down exactly what was said. He made sure to be clear that he was acting on the president's direct and personal orders, He said Palme's remarks linking it to the Nazi massacres were outrageous. He reminded the ambassador that the Swedes had never protested against Nazi crimes during the war but instead collaborated with the Germans. Since Sweden didn't value its relations with the States it was no point the Swedes sent their ambassador back to Washington after the Christmas holidays. There was no question of the American ambassador returning to Stockholm. The first secretary would also be staying behind in the United States. According to American archives, de Besche protested "lamely". In de Besche's own notes, stored in Swedish foreign ministry archives, he was a bit tougher than that, calling Nixon's bombing campaign outrageous.

De Besche's note back to Sweden on the evening of the 23rd caused a shock. Palme had clearly underestimated the likely American reaction. While the family put Christmas Eve celebrations on hold (Swedes celebrate Christmas Eve, not Christmas Day), he decided to pen another message to Kissinger, a peace offering.

"Mr President, let me say a few words regarding your message" In emollient tones, he went on to praise America, how many times in the past people around the world had looked to the States for moral authority. Palme talked about his deep gratitude to the country, his time at Kenyon. America's leadership in the fight for peace. Then he wrote about how the Vietnam war had created sadness and disappointment among millions of young people around the world.

"On this day when people gather to express their longing for peace I express my deepest wish to the President of the United States to cease these bombings."

On the evening of Christmas Eve, de Besche marched over to the State Department with Palme's bid to prevent a breach with America. It was in vain. The Americans didn't give a fig for Palme's new emollient message. Kissinger had flown to Palm Springs to celebrate the Christmas holidays with Frank Sinatra. And the State Department was virtually emptied of people who had departed for their holidays. The "peace offering" telegram was handled in the usual state department bureaucracy way and was placed in the files in the first week of January with the instruction: "Ad acta, no further action necessary."

In the days between Christmas and New Year, the Swedish embassy scrambled around for information. They found reasons to be concerned. One Swedish Embassy staffer had found documents in the Library of Congress suggesting a crisis of the magnitude that led to the withdrawal of an ambassador had happened only six times in US history. They were:

1.   November 1938 when the USA called its ambassador home from Nazi Germany after the Kristallnacht. He didn't return until after the war

2.   For six years during the second world war, the USA had no ambassador in Spain in protest at Franco's dictatorship

3.   When Janos Kadar came to power in Hungary 1956, on the back of the Soviet invasion, the ambassador was called home

4.   When Castro seized power in Cuba, the USA called its ambassador home from Havana

5.   In 1962 after a military coup in Peru, The USA recalled its ambassador

6.   A military coup in the Dominican Republic in 1963 also led to a recall

Palme was not exactly in flattering company: Hitler, Kadar, Franco, and Castro. Swedish opinion knew nothing of this, and when the peace deal on Vietnam was finally finalised in Paris in January 1973, and the bombing stopped, Swedish papers wrote about it as if the end of the Vietnam War was almost Palme's doing.

Dagens Nyheter's front page said, "The whole world celebrates Palme." Palme, though, spent January 1973 trying to rebuild links with the USA, using his trusted assistant Anders Ferm – sometimes called "Palme's Palme", with reference to the days when Palme himself was a trusted assistant – to explore third-party contacts in Paris who knew Kissinger. Eight months of not very successful manoeuvring followed. One big step forward came when Palme sacked his foreign minister, Krister Wickman, who made statements almost as direct on the war has Palme had, and replaced him with an old-school anti-communist from the right wing of the Social Democrat party. His name was Sven Andersson, and we will be encountering him again in the submarine affair. Andersson was a man to the Americans' taste. The US embassy in Stockholm noted that he was a "markedly positive to the United States".

Sven Andersson's appointment was an important step in the rapprochement, perhaps the most important. The Scandinavian actress Liv Ullmann was also brought on board to soften Kissinger's attitude. She was a big star in the States and Kissinger, that ladies' man, knew her well. And when American senators from the old "Swedish states" of Minnesota and Wisconsin began pressing for a resumption of relations, Kissinger accepted a visit from the senior remaining diplomat in

Stockholm. When Nixon, in early 1974, wanted to move around his ambassadors in Europe to clear the way for one of his big election donors to get the seat in Brussels, Nixon thought it worthwhile to open Stockholm again. A meeting between Palme and Nixon in 1975 seemed to mark the end of the freeze.

Nixon was soon gone, thanks to Watergate. Vietnam was soon to be yesterday's conflict, when the North won the war, as everyone predicted would happen after the United States pulled out. Operation Linebacker had made no difference.

Palme's engagement soon went beyond Vietnam.

The early to mid-1970s was a time of detente between the two superpowers, offering a good opportunity to a small country to be able to play an active role in world politics as Sweden did, countering the influence of the superpowers. America's reputation and self-confidence after the retreat from the embassy rooftop in Saigon, April 1975, were at an all-time low. There was space for Sweden to play a role and in Palme there was a man eager to play it.

In June 1975, he attended a women's conference in Mexico City where he held a powerful speech praising the Swedish model of women's emancipation. From Mexico he went to Venezuela and then – Cuba, a country which had earned the absolute, unrelenting hostility of the United States since the Cuban revolution toppled Batista and put the revolutionary Fidel Castro in charge.

The meeting with Castro was unforgettable for Palme. Both leaders were 48 years old when they met and came from similar upper-class backgrounds. And they had both since become radicals and leaders of their respective states.

Cuba was the only country in Latin America which received Swedish aid assistance.

Possibly the Cuban regime, which was not entirely happy with its relations with the Soviet Union, was hoping that good relations with Sweden would lead to better relations with other Social Democrat governments in Europe, in Scandinavia but chiefly in West Germany. Castro had sent an effusive telegram of congratulation to Palme on his election in 1969 - a big contrast to the very cool American greeting – and he pulled out the stops to make the Swedish visit a success. Many Swedes in the Swedish political climate of the mid-seventies saw Cuba as the great white hope of the region and a hopeful alternative to the military regimes with right-wing leaderships that dominated Latin and Central America. The Swedish delegation was a large one. Apart from Olof and Lisbet, the entourage included several ministers as well as the author Sven Lindkvist and the glamorous actress Bibi Andersson.

The heat was pressing when Castro received the Swedes at Cuba airport in the afternoon of June 28, 1975. The road to Havana was lined with thousands of people waving small Swedish flags and cheering "Palme Pal-me…."

HE WAS the first western leader to visit Castro, and Castro paid him a lot of attention. They talked intensively and uninterruptedly about all kinds of matters during the visit and the Cuban leader could often be seen pressing his finger into Palme's stomach while emphasizing a point. On Sunday, Palme and the other Swedes were driven to the military garrison at Moncada where the Cuban revolution had once started over twenty years before. Hundreds of thousands of people had gathered. When Palme started talking, a hush descended on the gathering. He spoke, in carefully rehearsed Spanish, for twenty minutes wearing a revolutionary red neckerchief, while sweating in the sun. He praised the enormous social advances that had taken place in Cuba and criticised the American blockade.

It was not exactly a huge defence of democracy but Palme perhaps reasoned that he wasn't able to place too harsh demands on revolutionary regimes that had recently liberated their countries. You had to look at the place they started from and be hopeful they were travelling in the right direction, as he once told a French journalist. It was the same reasoning that later motivated Palme's support for the Zimbabwean leader Robert Mugabe, who was invited to Sweden in 1977 with the Swedish foreign minister as host.

Palme wanted to build bridges between North and South (as he later wanted to build bridges between East and West). Back in Stockholm, he worked hard at getting a meeting arranged between Kissinger and Fidel Castro. It did not happen but it was an indication of his ambitions in international affairs. After his trip to Cuba, the leader of the conservatives, the Moderate Party, Gösta Bohman said it would have been better if Palme had stayed at home and looked after Sweden's inflation problems.

Palme, along with the socialist leaders of Austria and West Germany, forming a Germanic axis more of which later, did much to help democratic socialism flourish and succeed when Europe's remaining military dictatorships fell in 1974 and 75.

The Portuguese democratisation process is where he personally played the biggest role. On 25 April 1974, the Fascist regime in Portugal had been toppled by a group of liberal and radical army officers. People celebrated on the streets of Lisbon, putting carnations in the barrels of the regime soldiers' rifles; hence the "Carnation Revolution".

America and Britain were afraid that a radical leftist junta would seize power in the vacuum that resulted. But the Swedish Social Democrats were keen supporters of the Portuguese socialist party, the PSP, under Mario Soares. A few weeks after the coup the Social Democrat party secretary Sten Andersson went to Lisbon, where his car was surrounded menacingly by a large crowd belonging to members of a rival left-wing faction who wished the Swedes to transfer their support to them instead. But the Swedes stuck to Soares and Palme organised a conference in the summer of 1975 at the prime minister's summer resident at Harpsund in support of Portugal to which the whole European left had been invited from Harold Wilson to Francois Mitterand. US secretary of state Henry Kissinger contacted Palme and argued that the chaos in Portugal had created the conditions for a left communist revolution. His prediction was proved wrong, however, and within a few years Portugal had become a stable, if Social Democratic, society. Palme, and his allies in the Socialist International, especially Willy Brandt, chair of the West German SPD, arguably played an important part.

HERO OF THE LEFT, SCOURGE OF THE RIGHT

While many Swedes were proud and excited to be involved in the third world and democratisation efforts in southern Europe, because it turned their neutrality into something positive and superior, and washed away the tarnished legacy of neutrality in the second world war, the British and Americans were a bit cool. Guy Millard, the British ambassador between 1972 and 1974, in his valedictory dispatch, argued that foreign liberation issues as being some kind of substitute for the absence of domestic politics in Sweden:

"Swedish society lacks drama and challenge, and there is a certain frustration at the absence of any real political life and of effective opposition to the Social Democrats."

"The essentially consensus nature of Swedish politics leads to an ideological vacuum in which people look around for new causes and emotional outlets....it has a bearing on foreign policy. Swedish foreign policy is usually defined as one of active neutrality. It has developed a vocabulary of its own, expressive of its style. 'Non-alignment in peace, leading to neutrality in war.' 'Sweden's position as a small country.' 'The need to stand up and be counted'. 'Superpower hegemony.'"

Millard continued: "In turn, Greece, Chile and the Portuguese African territories have occupied the centre of the stage."

"Active neutrality means that Sweden does not forgo the right to have positions on international issues.

"The Swedish government considers it has the right and the duty to speak up for democratic principles and on behalf of smaller powers, and in doing so they are contributing not only to the maintenance of international values but Sweden's own safety. This is sincerely held but there are other motives at work. There is the need to relieve party feelings and pressures, and not an insignificant amount of nationalism. Swedes like to feel…they are qualified to speak as custodians of democracy, superior political virtue and humanitarianism."

Thus Millard. In a way, the expansion of Swedish moral influence abroad became an activity that could be described in almost martial terms. In the 17th and 18th centuries, Sweden had been a great power.

This was a new "Great Power" (storhetstid) period for Sweden, except now Swedes were travelling in peace – and their playground was the entire world. They were aid workers and government ministers, but they were spreading Swedish influence just as much as buccaneers and armies like Gustavus Adolphus and Charles XII once did, this time in the name of peaceful righteousness. And there was a large constituency to keep satisfied with tales of moral conquest. Sweden had perhaps one of the most powerful worker's movements in the world, argues Kjell Östberg in the paper Social Democracy after the Second World War. The main labour trade unions had 1.2 million members in 1989, out of a population of eight million. Unionisation rates were 90 percent, perhaps the highest rate in the world. The figure for the UK was 55%.

The Swedish workers' movement was a kind of parallel society in Palme's Sweden. Now, in 2018, it has almost vanished. But back then, if you were a member of one of the unions you were not only automatically joined to the Social Democrat party but could avail yourself of the workers' movement's many services. Workers could shop in the cooperative stores, be buried by the cooperative morticians. They could take their charter trips to Spain via the cooperative movement's travel agency. The workers' movement's children could join the Young Eagles movement, the Swedish Social Democrats' equivalent of the Soviet Communist party's Young Pioneers. They could take evening classes in all sorts of subjects at the workers' movement's education centres. There was strength in purpose, unity and numbers against the traditional, scattered, "bourgeois" Sweden.

And Palme was the maestro of the workers' movement, in a Sweden becoming increasingly democratic and thereby receptive to populist politics. He returned with tales of foreign lands. Mona Sahlin, party leader of the Social Democrats between 2006 and 2010, was, back in the 1970s, an attractive young woman from a working-class background, one of the many who fell in love with Palme, in a political sense. "I joined Palme before I joined the party," she always says in interviews. She liked his scruffy, sartorially nonchalant style, the casual swinging of his arms when he entered a room of Social Democrats. His intensely bright eyes showing curiosity for everything and everybody. He was so clearly different and intellectually superior, she thought. And the way that he treated everyone, black or white, as an equal. He made the working class proud of Sweden's humanitarianism and global good works.

PALME COULD attack the upper classes , on the defensive, in a crowd pleasing way. Biographer Henrik Berggren reckons that, during speeches in the Folk Parks, Palme's relentless attacks on the bourgeois bloc could partly have been brought about by his experiences of being bullied by upper-class boys at the expensive boarding school he had attended, Sigtuna. "As an adult, Palme often returned to the bullying and the misery [of his school days] when he discussed his youth. In part, it was to show that even an upper-class youth had attracted scars in the class war. But even if we use our childhood memories selectively it does not necessarily mean they are false. Palme's aggression towards right of centre politicians may have been to a degree for show, but even the most skilful actor fetches the feelings he expresses on stage from within." Palme was not good on TV, when he could come across as hectoring and demotic. His public persona could seldom resist poisonous, barbed remarks about the opposition.

He came across much better in face-to-face encounters. Palme loved the "ordinary people"; he made countless visits to schools, factories, offices; his subordinates always said he was willing to talk to anyone, especially people he did not feel challenged by. He treated the common man as an equal, believed he or she always had something to say. His secretary had had to drag him away from impromptu encounters with school youth, kitchen staff and even political discussions with prostitutes who loitered between the cabinet office and Palme's favourite restaurant near parliament, and whom he'd sometimes stop and talk while his advisers just wanted to get a bite to eat. According to his cabinet secretary, admittedly not an unbiased source, Palme was welcomed with open arms as he travelled from Social Democrat youth club to youth club. In these situations, he would talk long into the night about socialist ideology and was "much loved by young adults".

After Palme died, the writer Göran Tunström, a left-wing novelist, explained how his then 14-old-son had got Olof and Lisbet Palme, in tuxedo and evening dress, to wait in the foyer at a prize gala where Tunström had won an award. The boy phoned his "anarchist" group called "the pigs" to ask about their manifesto. The boy returned and talked to Palme, who saw the boy not as a child but "understood the world as a 14-year-old boy would". They talked intensely for five minutes and in the car the boy said that Palme had agreed to fix the "pigs" up with a place where they could hold their meetings. Two weeks later the phone rang: it was a prime minister's office. A meeting room had been organised.

Whenever Palme attended a Social Democrat meeting or dinner, he made sure to walk from table to table, chatting to each official, councillor and activist. He had a fantastic memory for names. His speeches, even his boilerplate speeches at local associations, were a balm and inspiration for the working class – especially to women over 40, who "went away better Social Democrats". He sometimes spoke poetically in a way you seldom heard in Swedish politics. Ending one party congress, he said:

"We shall meet again, comrades. We meet at Folkets Hus (House of the People), in the corner at the construction sites, at the break between 9 and 9.15, between the sandwich and the game of cards...a moment of politics. We shall meet in the stairwells with our political brochures. We shall meet at the factory gates at seven am on frozen mornings.

"We shall meet again, comrades, somewhere at that place where dreams and the everyday struggle meet...we shall meet again, comrades.".

One critic said Palme was a good speaker but a bad debater. He talked with emotion, which appealed to the converts, to the working class, but, in cross-party TV debates, seldom met his right-wing opponents' arguments at a consistent intellectual level, which infuriated them, and thus seldom convinced the opposition that needed to be convinced. Some of his high intelligence and knowledge ought to have behaved better, they felt.

His opponents, therefore, said he lowered the tone of Swedish democracy, that he was a demagogue, a kind of populist. Yet these criticisms seemed to make little impact on his enthusiasm for emotional speeches. He passed on the ideas he had absorbed and believed in, using poetry and metaphors sometimes even stolen from the children's books he read his children. The people's inspirer, the people's educator. One favourite poem, which symbolised the future he was building, was Sundbyberg by the poet Ragnar Thoursie, whose day job was an official for the state welfare board.

Sundbyberg is actually the name of a Stockholm suburb but the poem makes it sound as if it was some science fiction-inspired pioneer community Socialist man, inhabiting the edge of the universe. The poem opens something like this,

Man, not the moon, is the measure of everything. An open city without fortifications is what we are building together, its light shining up against the loneliness of space.

WITH KEY emotional solidarity words like "building together", Palme quoted it often in his speeches. The poems perhaps strengthened the sense that Sweden was not quite of this world, in the historical European present, but was a society somehow uniquely connected to the future, a pioneer of progressivism, which hoped to bring less advanced countries into its slipstream.

If he idealised the workers, his "little people" (småfolket), Palme found many businessmen boring and a bit wicked and the feelings were mutual, often. He felt they were uninterested in literature. Businessmen, for their part, could not trust his commitment to business, Some were driven into tax exile abroad. He offended big business leaders when he appeared to imply that capitalism treated children like "bags of rubbish". Palme was very prickly, very sensitive, about the rights of children.

THERE ARE almost no books covering modern Swedish military politics, either due to secrecy, or lack of interest, successful indoctrination from the left-wing teaching profession and journalism, perhaps all of these. The Swedish military was the giant elephant in the room of Swedish life. How many people know that, in some years, Sweden has been the world's largest per capita arms exporter? But we are aware from declassified British diplomatic papers that leading military chiefs complained incessantly to foreign diplomats about the decline in resources. The navy, in particular, was the last bastion of the old aristocratic culture of Sweden. They also complained of the new workers' rights and health and safety laws that made the military's lives harder. In the navy, there was a chronic shortage of medium rank officers. Repetition training often had to be cancelled. Air force chiefs complained that station life had been all been abolished. Pilots returned home at the end of the day, and with it went the squadron spirit. Twenty-four-hour use of simulators was prevented by Palme's health and safety regulations.

Their complaints were ceaseless. The 40 hour work week was rigidly adhered to in all the services which meant difficulties in carrying out service training. Army officers were weighed under with the burden of the day-to-day administrative tasks to meet the conditions demanded by the increasingly powerful servicemen's trade union. Swedish officers complained to their British counterparts that there was a new culture of political agitation among conscripts, long hair, socialist values and less discipline. At the time, defence budgets were being cut.

The proportion of research devoted to defence peaked at 50% already in 1960. The size of the defence research agency peaked in 1971, shortly after Palme's accession, at 1,500 staff, having grown exponentially after the war. According to the historian Niklas Stenlås, defence cuts brought about by the New Leftist climate, with the politicians rather than the military in charge of security decisions, combined with the expensive new Viggen aircraft, and meant cuts to the other two services – and fewer aircraft too, due to the high costs of development. The money spent in the 1950s on building up the world's fourth most extensive armed forces was now spent on kindergartens whose teachers, in the enraged right-wing mythology, were left-wing freaks who had embraced Palme's democratic educational dumbing down.

BREAK FROM GOVERNMENT: 1976-1982

After seven years in power, having won two elections, in 1970 and 1973, and changed Sweden quite a lot in a leftwards direction, Olof Palme was turfed out of office. In September, 1976 the non-socialist so-called Bourgeois bloc – the Centre Party, the Liberals and the Conservatives (also known as the Moderates) - won the general election. The news of the political earthquake made waves around the world and cheered conservatives everywhere. Margaret Thatcher, then Tory opposition leader, said triumphantly at the annual conservative conference in Brighton, "Across the world, from Australia to Sweden...socialism is on the way out."

The reference to Australia was the fact that Labor's Gough Whitlam had lost the election to the Liberal party in December 1975. The election had been prompted by Whitlam's controversial sacking by the governor general, Jim Kerr.

What resulted now in Sweden was a coalition government of the aforementioned Centre party, the Liberal party and the right-wing Conservative party. None had any government experience. The last non-Social Democrat government had been in 1932. Many civil servants were Social Democrat. Thorbjörn Fälldin, the Centre Party leader, was the new prime minister. He was a farmer by profession, proverbially slow when he talked. Palme never got on with Fälldin, and probably always underestimated him.

There was the famous election debate that arguably lost Palme the election. Palme had thought he had won because he was clearly the cleverer man until his advisers explained that Fälldin's slow delivery and homespun charisma looked much better on television, while Palme came across as hissing, partisan and too-clever-by-half. Fälldin attracted several categories of voter. His big thing was a resolute opposition to nuclear power. This earned him the support of the young, who had previously been drawn to Palme's radicalism. The "red wave" of the sixties had turned into a "green wave" of seventies. There was no Green party in Sweden. So Fälldin's agrarian centre party captured nascent ecological sentiment. Sweden had, thanks to Olof Palme, rapidly expanded the number of nuclear power stations since the first one started up in 1972.

Fälldin also attracted the rural voter suspicious of the technology optimism of Palme. He also exploited the theme of fears about "big brother" represented by busybody social workers and bureaucrats. Some intellectuals, not all of them conservative, bought into that narrative. The Astrid Lindgren tax scandal erupted in the same year of the election, and Fälldin was able to take advantage of that.

After becoming prime minister, Fälldin immediately reneged on his election promise in concession to his coalition partners, the Liberals and Moderates, who were pronuclear. He gave the go-ahead to the opening of a new nuclear power plant. His supporters were furious. The debate rumbled on. The Three Mile Island accident in Harrisburg, Pennsylvania, in 1979 prompted Palme, though pro-nuclear, to call for a referendum. Fälldin was happy to oblige. Held in 1980, the poll resulted in a victory for the second of three options: a slow phase-out of nuclear. However, the politicians never acted on the referendum result. Thirty years on, Sweden is as dependent on nuclear power as it was then.

Apart from squabbles over nuclear power between coalition partners, much of the new coalition's efforts were taken up with the economy. Meanwhile, Palme did not prioritise being the leader of the opposition. He focused his attention on travelling to the developing world as newly appointed vice president of the Socialist International.

The Socialist International, based in London, was reinvigorated with a Swede, Bernt Carlsson, as secretary and Palme's friend and leader of the German Social Democrats Willy Brandt as president. The movement expanded beyond Social Democratic parties in Europe into Africa, Latin America and Asia and portrayed itself as a Third Force between the two superpower blocs. Palme's responsibility was Africa; he made many visits to the frontline states, the states in white Apartheid South Africa's vicinity. The opposition newspapers made fun of the opposition leader's absences. "Palme pays a visit to Sweden," was one newspaper's jokey headline when Palme stopped by Stockholm.

A typical statement from Palme at around this time was that Apartheid was "a unique form of evil [and] the only form of tyranny which brands a person from birth on account of the colour of his skin". On behalf of his now opposition Social Democrats, he also criticised Swedish companies that had invested in South Africa. In a parliamentary debate in 1977 he had said "free human beings are more important than free movement of capital" and that Sweden instead of waiting for a UN decision should unilaterally impose an investment ban.

According to Pierre Schori, a close adviser to Palme and later a minister and senior diplomat, Palme's speech marked the beginning of "an unparalleled offensive" and a "crusade against racism never before undertaken by a party leader in the industrialised world".

Palme in 1977 and 1978 both privately and on behalf of the Socialist International argued for the region's liberation movements and economic sanctions against the Apartheid regime. In 1977, Palme was invited to the UN Security Council's anti-Apartheid debate; in May of that year he went to the UN-sponsored International Conference in Support of the Peoples of Zimbabwe and Namibia in Maputo, Mozambique; and in August the UN/OAU World Conference for Action against Apartheid in Lagos, Nigeria. He made the keynote speech at each event.

Finally, in early September 1977 Palme led a Socialist International (SI) mission to Angola, Zambia, Mozambique and Tanzania. During the trip, Palme and representatives from ten other affiliated parties, such as the German and Austrian social democrats, discussed the potential of sanctions against South Africa with the purpose of changing the regime. Palme noted in his diary that they had been well received everywhere and that there were high hopes concerning what the Socialist International could do to contribute to the liberation of Africa.

It was almost as if opposition leader Olof Palme had taken it upon him to be Sweden's travelling foreign minister, even though he wasn't in government. Fälldin didn't spend much time on foreign policy. The Liberals occupied the foreign ministry post, and when, in 1977, an aggressive anti-communist intellectual called Per Ahlmark was replaced by the left-liberal Ola Ullsten, who had worked his way up from a humble background, and was a former care assistant at a drying out clinic, foreign policy became almost as left wing as it had been under Palme, although carried out in a much, much less aggressive tone. In a way, Ullsten, officially, and Palme, unofficially, worked from the same page. It was Ullsten who got the opportunity initiated Sweden's first official sanctions against Apartheid South Africa; for instance, allowing Palme to build on a base of hostile acts against South Africa after his return to power in 1982.

THE BOURGEOIS coalition collapsed in 1978, then continued under a minority government, with Ullsten as prime minister. His foreign minister, Hans Blix, later achieved international fame as the UN's arms inspector at the second Iraq war in 2003. As a civil servant in 1962, Blix had helped renegotiate the Geneva conventions on war updated to a 20th century of terror bombing and guerrilla warfare. Blix became a leading international figure in trying to restrict new inhuman weapons, such as dum-dum bullets. He also successfully negotiated a protocol to ensure landmines were equipped with self-destruction mechanisms which guaranteed that landmines would not be around indefinitely.

The Bourgeois bloc won another election in 1979, by the skin of its teeth, or rather the expatriate tax exile vote, whose results came in after the election day – but bumbled through its second term, 1979-82 unconvincingly. The internal forces within the coalition were changing though.

Abroad, there were winds of change from the right. Fälldin's party, whose anti-nuclear voters were disillusioned, was the loser from the weakening of the "Green Wave" and the radicalisation of conservatism represented by Margaret Thatcher and Ronald Reagan, who lent style, language and ideas to the Swedish Conservatives. This third party in the bourgeois coalition, the Conservatives, also known as the Moderates, who had been regarded as a minority sect for the beleaguered rightists in the Palme years, advanced in the election of 1979, even though the premiership remained with Fälldin. The Moderates did even better in the election of 1982, overtaking the Centre to become the largest part of the Bourgeois bloc, while still remaining a distant second the Social Democrats. But their gains were largely at the expense of the other Bourgeois parties who, overall, lost: for 1982 was also Palme's year, the year he returned to government.

IF THE Moderates moved to the right in the early eighties they were not alone. Economically, Palme moved reluctantly towards the right too: under pressure from some Social Democrat economists he realised there had to be proper reforms of income taxes, which had turned tax evasion into an art form practised by many Swedes. In one poll, 84% of a representative sample of Swedish adults surveyed thought taxes too high, the percentage of those who believed the taxes ought to rise yet higher was so small it couldn't be measured There was one tax reform in 1981, enacted with cross bloc cooperation. But more was needed. By 1981, there was a new shadow finance minister, Kjell Olof Feldt, and his self-appointed job – as he says in his own memoirs – was to give a reality check to the party and to Olof Palme himself, whose generous socialist-style reforms of his previous period in office, in 1969-76, had proved so expensive for Sweden. Feldt's fiscally conservative views on the manifesto prevailed and this time, September 1982, after six years in the opposition wilderness and two election failures (1976 and 79), Palme was back in power.

After the 1982 elections, to deal with another problem with which the Social Democrats were associated (apart from those high taxes), the party's past bossy reputation for controlling people's lives, Palme appointed a minister for reducing bureaucracy "to humanise and democratise the public sector". The government devalued the krona by 16%, and started cutting expenses. It wasn't quite a Thatcher or Reagan style rollback of government. Reagan, after all, had said, in his inaugural address on 20 January 1981: "Government is not the solution to our problem; government is the problem." But it was a drastic change for Sweden nevertheless. Feldt said later, looking back on these years:

"The negative inheritance I received from my predecessor Gunnar Sträng (Minister of Finance 1955 - 1976) was a strongly progressive tax system with high marginal taxes. This was supposed to bring about a just and equal society. But I eventually came to the opinion that it simply didn't work out that way. Progressive taxes created instead a society of wranglers, cheaters, manipulations, false ambitions and new injustices. It took me at least a decade to get the party to see this."

Now assailed from the left, by the increasingly stroppy LO [Swedish TUC] trade union, which resented the reforms, Palme seemed a bit depressed at the change of course led by his finance minister and although he supported him to the hilt in public and in front of cabinet, he stood his ground in some areas. He resolutely opposed private solutions in day care homes. But he seemed to realise, without understanding all the details that Sweden needed to change, or at least his kind of high tax "functional socialism" had to be put on hold.

More reforms took place in early 1983: a five percent cut in state expenses, and no tax rises. At the same time inflation rose by 10% while he put a ceiling on index-linked rises. Medicine, widows' pensions, students' books, rent subsidies - all were reduced and made harder to get. Palme rowed back on a controversial plan from 1976 that had hung like an electoral albatross around the party's neck ever since. A scheme to give trade unions a growing financial stake in private companies, the so-called wage earner funds (löntagarfonder). This proposal was one of the things that had made people worry about whether his socialism was extreme. Palme symbolised the reform in the general public's eyes, even though in reality this particular legislation had been imposed on him by the unions.

His finance minister was against the funds, which had been placed before the Social Democrat leadership by an enthusiastic vote by Sweden's TUC, LO, back in 1976. The funds' enthusiastic trade union supporters eventually foresaw trade union officials running much of Sweden's industry, including export successes such as Volvo and IKEA. Feldt, who did not believe in them, said frankly in his memoirs that "they had been tried in Socialist Yugoslavia and already proved to be a failure there". In the end, the Swedish government did impose a version of the so-called wage-earner funds, in early 1983; but it was a weakened version. Some of the horses had already bolted: IKEA and several other privately owned companies had already left the country. Entrepreneurs with private companies, with a low level of capitalisation, were especially vulnerable to an early transfer of ownership to the trade unions, and people like IKEA boss Ingvar Kamprad were furious with Palme on a personal level. Feldt's watered down funds, mostly in name only, seemed to calm most businesses though. But IKEA never did return to Sweden; most of IKEA's operations, including the management of the majority of its stores, the design and manufacture of its furniture, and purchasing and supply functions, are overseen today by INGKA Holding, a private, for-profit Dutch company.

PALME'S LAST TERM: 1982-1986

In foreign policy, Palme had different targets in different parts of his life. It had been opposition to America in Vietnam of the sixties, democracy promotion in Spain and Portugal of the mid-seventies. In his period as leader of the opposition, 1977 to 1982, he had made himself the scourge of White South Africa.

Developments of the 1980s forced Palme to engage in northern Europe. International developments at the end of the seventies and beginning of the eighties, the elections of Ronald Reagan and Margaret Thatcher and the "New Cold War" with the stagnant Soviet Union that resulted, forced Palme, when back in power in 1982, to focus his attention on Sweden's geopolitical neighbourhood. The first half of the 1980s was a very tense period in international relations.

People old enough will remember the period perhaps best through memories of popular culture. Peace songs like Frankie's Two Tribes, or Culture Club's War Song, or Sting's Russians. The ABC television company film The Day After, which follows the lives and deaths of normal Kansas City families before and after a nuclear war, was seen by over 100 million Americans on its first showing, which is an all-time record for a TV audience. In Britain, the film Threads was an even gloomier effort on the consequences of total nuclear war on the civilian population of Sheffield. The latter half of the Threads film focuses on life after nuclear war for the few survivors, under the conditions of "nuclear winter" that is expected to occur for several years after a nuclear war, as the soot thrown into the atmosphere blocks the sun's rays and produces catastrophic earth cooling.

The Americans were placing out two new classes of nuclear medium-range missiles in Europe, Pershing and Cruise missiles. They were mobile and the Pershings could reach Moscow in eight minutes. The ostensible logic for their outplacement in West Germany, Italy, the UK, and the Benelux countries was to create a nuclear tripwire in the event of Soviet invasion. The Soviets were widely believed to have superior offensive forces, many first-rate tank divisions, with a plan to drive to the Rhine – maybe even the English Channel – in days. Because of intense awareness of the inferiority in conventional arms, NATO always preserved the right to first use of nuclear weapons as a mainstay of its defence doctrine.

But there were fears that, of the Soviets invaded, the Americans would not use the strategic nuclear counterstrike option, and risk obliteration of the homeland in a Soviet counterattack, just in order to save West Germany. Having nukes located in West Germany, in the direct line of Soviet advance, in danger of being over-run, would send a signal to the Soviets there was the full intention to use nukes defensively, and that therefore there was an American buy in into Europe's defences. They would deter a Soviet conventional attack and make a third world war less likely. That was the Washington think tank argument, used by US officials and defence academics with European diplomats at seminars.

But there was a flaw in that presumed that Soviet motives were basically aggressive and expansionary. In fact there was an argument that so-called euro missiles would make a third world war more likely since, because of the missiles' forward position, the Soviets apparently believed they were to be used in an aggressive decapitation attack against the Soviet leadership in Moscow. (In the same way, the Americans tried to decapitate Saddam Hussein with a cruise missile attack immediately before the Iraq war in 2003.)

Combined with Reagan's s belligerent rhetoric, it made the decrepit Soviet leadership all the more jittery – and maybe, in the logic of cold war retaliation, more likely to launch their "pre-emptive defence" first. So, did the euro missiles have the opposite effect than the one intended? In addition, the outplacement of the euro missiles was supposed to be accompanied by parallel disarmament negotiations between NATO and the Warsaw Pact ("the dual-track approach"), but in the early 1980s, they were going nowhere. Was Reagan even willing to negotiate – or was he some kind of End Times fanatic?

Even in Britain, America's closest ally, scepticism towards America and Reagan was common. In nearly every poll, there were pluralities or majorities, from 48 to 61%, against the placing of the missiles. A large number of Britons seemed to think a nuclear war was likely in the near future, reaching a peak of 49% in 1983, and the many blamed it on the policies of the Reagan administration. British opinion began to shift from a belief the Americans were committed to an arms deal to thinking they were not.

The West Germans were perhaps even more concerned than the British, polls showing similar levels of anxiety about nuclear war. Thousands of women formed "peace chains" linking the Soviet and American consulates in West Berlin. Professionals formed disarmament groups such as Doctors against Nuclear Arms, Artists for Peace, Teachers against Arms. Scientists for Peace. The German federation of trade unions, the DGB, with eight million members, staged a five-minute strike in October 1983 in factories around the country to symbolise the "five minutes to midnight" of the atomic disaster clock.

The women's camp at Greenham Common, an American airbase in Britain slated to receive the new missiles, became a sign of hope that public protest could be a powerful weapon for peace. For others, like the satirical magazine Private Eye, the "wimmin's camp" was a bit of a joke. Women, at times numbering in the hundreds, camped for months at a time in the mud and rain, outside the Berkshire airbase, living in bucolic surroundings of fields and hedgerows, but in tents surrounded by binliners bursting with rubbish.

One American reporter described the scene: "As I walked toward the main gate of the base, all I could see was low underbrush strewn with handmade peace signs and wreaths. Underfoot was a sea of mud. Wood smoke filled the air. A rough table was covered with half-opened cans and packages of food. More cans spilled out of doorless cupboards stacked against a tree. A woman tried to scrub a dish in dirty wash water. Black plastic trash barrels overflowed with garbage. Small tents dotted the scene. Sleeping bags were slung beneath plastic sheeting strung from ropes. It hardly seemed possible that such grime can have become one of the best-known political symbols in Europe."

CRITICS CALLED the Greenham Common women naïve exhibitionists, militant feminists, even communists. But they themselves claimed to be fighting the abolition of nuclear weapons so that their children could live in safety and peace. And they certainly had a sense of humour: one, Phyllis Bickerton, 61, who had ridden a bus for five hours from her home in Suffolk, told an American reporter: "It's this lunatic Reagan and his missiles that I worry about," she said On her left shoulder was a small button: "Ageing Hippies Against the Bomb".

The septuagenarian Ronald Reagan – who had come into power on a wave of anti-Soviet rhetoric in January 1981 – didn't mince words in his speeches aimed at a succession of physically sickly Soviet leaders.

Speaking to the House of Commons in June 1982, Reagan said he had a plan to leave "Marxism-Leninism on the ash heap of history". Given the fact that America had several thousand nuclear weapons guaranteeing instant obliteration of their targets pointed at the Soviet Union, the word "ash heap" was possibly unfortunately chosen. A few months after his Westminster speech, Reagan called the Soviet Union the "evil empire". In a speech to a congress of evangelical Christians in Florida, he added in theological tones.

"Yes, let us pray for the salvation of all of those who live in that totalitarian darkness—pray they will discover the joy of knowing God. But until they do, let us be aware that while they preach the supremacy of the state, declare its omnipotence over individual man, and predict its eventual domination of all peoples on the earth, they are the focus of evil in the modern world."

Soviet General Secretary Yuri Andropov responded by calling the US President insane and a liar.

There were several incidents. In September 1983, Soviet jet fighters shot down a Korean Airlines 747, KAL 007, which had strayed 300 miles into Soviet airspace, an apparently fatal mistaken navigation which may, or may not, actually have been deliberate. The South Koreans were allies of the Americans. Korean Intelligence was practically in the pockets of the CIA. Was KAL 007 actually on a spy mission? Writers such as investigative journalist Paul Foot and Oxford historian RW Johnson have argued that it was much like the incident involving another Korean Airlines jet, flight KAL 9502, which had turned around at the North Pole and headed straight into sensitive Soviet airspace, causing Soviet air defences to light up. That flight was forced down, and emergency landed on a frozen lake near the Finnish border. There were two fatalities. The survivors were flown out and the Soviets kept the plane

For the KAL 007 to have been an accidental misnavigation, argued Johnson, KAL's most experienced pilot, the "human robot", had to have ignored all his instruments for several hours. The accident theory couldn't explain why they misreported to Ground Control their location – actually inside Soviet territory – as being at the recognised official waypoints along the ocean route in international waters on several occasions

There are other difficulties: According to Johnson, the Korean pilot "fiddled his fuel papers to take on five extra tons of fuel; that he inexplicably left paying cargo behind at Anchorage. He also left behind notes in which he appears to have been planning the route he actually took (365 miles off his proper course)."

The death toll when the plane crashed into the ocean was 269. The Soviets stonewalled over the initial admission; President Reagan made propaganda hay over the incident, which he publicly condemned as an "act of barbarism" even though the Americans' own evidence was that the shootdown was an accident. An American RC 135 tanker was flying in international waters at around this time.

Foot and Johnson argue that the KAL flight was a provocative PSYOPs, psychological operation, aimed at testing Soviet air radar defences. And may have been carried out without Reagan's knowledge or authorisation. Foot says the cabinet around Reagan were a wild lot: They were "ushered by the old cowboy Reagan into the highest reaches of the most powerful government on earth. They came from the backwoods, from the Moral Majority, from the ranches of the Sunbelt, and from the phoney Institutes where the doctrines that the only good Russian is a dead Russian and that it is better to be dead than red are taught as religious dogma."

Perhaps the most critical incident in terms of being a nuclear war scare happened in the early morning of 26 September 1983 when Soviet air defence officer Stanislav Petrov was jolted upright by the sound of a klaxon. Petrov was a lieutenant colonel based at a nuclear installation called Serpukhov 15, south of Moscow. It was an early warning centre against American nuclear attack.

Petrov's screens were linked to Soviet monitoring satellites, and they were telling him an all-out US nuclear missile attack had been launched. They were coming in at three times the speed of sound and would be ready to obliterate Moscow in fifteen minutes. All the other operators were waiting for Petrov's decision. He had a telephone in one hand and his finger hovering over the start button. As he watched a screen with five more launches registered, Petrov had the fate of the world in his hands. However, he decided it was a malfunction and the Soviet missiles stayed in their silos. The false alarm, it was later discovered, was caused by the rare reflection of sunlight on high-altitude clouds at a certain angle which the Soviet satellite mistakenly read as heat exhaust from intercontinental nuclear missiles. According to peace groups later, the lieutenant colonel, who later retired on a modest pension, was deserving of wider recognition. At the time, though the world didn't realise how close it was to nuclear Armageddon.

Six weeks later there was a command post exercise held by NATO that simulated the period of escalation before a nuclear attack on the Soviet Union. Two years earlier, there had been closed meetings between KGB officials and the Politburo about the possibility of American nuclear attack. There was considerable Soviet paranoia about being, once again, as in WW2, taken by surprise by an attack from the West. Hitler's invasion Barbarossa in 1941, which achieved huge successes against a Soviet Union lulled by Hitler's assurances of peace, had left a permanent mark on a generation of Soviets who were now in senior politburo positions. Twenty million Russians had, after all, died in World War 2. Reagan's belligerence added to Soviet paranoia. So did the fact that Andropov was a man dying of kidney disease, with dark thoughts permanently on his mind, one imagines. The weekly politburo meetings of the old men that made up the Soviet leadership at the time took place at Andropov's hospital bedside.

THE KGB started running Operation RYAN, a Russian acronym for nuclear missile attack. KGB agents based in Soviet embassies in other countries were tasked with monitoring any nuclear war preparations coming from the West – utterly bizarre, in retrospect. For example, they were told to monitor the number of cars parked at the Pentagon and the UK Ministry of Defence as one sign of preparations for war. US flight activity, fake bombing attacks to Soviet radar capacities, kept the Soviets in a state of jitters. The Americans were demonstrating their powers by sending their planes towards Soviet territory and turning away at the last moment. When NATO seemed to be using never hitherto seen and highly complex cipher procedures for Able Archer, the Soviets feared the worst, that NATO was planning a real nuclear attack under the guise of a highly realistic exercise which moved through all the alert phases from Defcon 3 to Defcon 1. Fortunately, the exercise ended on 11 November 1983, before the deadline the Soviets imposed on themselves to move onto the next stage of alert.

American historian Ben Fisher argues that the PSYOPs launched by President Reagan when he took office were a significant cause of the war scare. He wrote: "Some Western observers dismissed the alert and the war scare as Soviet disinformation and scare tactics, while others viewed them as reflecting genuine fears. The latter view seems to have been closer to the truth.

Fisher also argued that Moscow's threat perceptions and Operation RYAN were influenced by memories of Hitler's 1941 surprise attack on the USSR

It was in this febrile atmosphere that Sweden, having commented superciliously on the world's affairs from the sidelines for much of the seventies, as East and West fought proxy conflicts in faraway Africa and Asia, now found itself on the frontline as the superpower conflict moved from proxy wars in the third world to a faceoff in Europe. Sweden, neutral, was in the middle, literally.

Palme worked hard to maintain a dialogue between the superpowers, and proposed disarmament as a way to reduce tensions. (He hadn't forgotten his first love, though: he proposed that the money saved could be used to provide more help to the third world. Arms for alms.) The peace movement in Scandinavia was just, if not more, powerful than it was in the UK and West Germany. Women for peace groups sprang up all over Scandinavia. There was a peace march from Copenhagen to Paris (where demonstrators met Palme, who happened to be visiting president Mitterand.) There was another march from Sweden to Minsk. A public appeal for a nuclear-free zone in Scandinavia received 2.7 million signatures across the region's five countries. Eleven out of 19 Norwegian counties adopted nuclear-free resolutions.

PALME WAS early on to the case of peace, even before Reagan's presidency began in January 1981. While still leader of the opposition, Palme had formed a peace commission in 1980 comprising senior officials and statesmen, usually retired from active politics, from both blocs, plus neutral countries. One member was former US secretary of state Cyrus Vance, another was former British foreign secretary and leader of the SDP David Owen. The group met about once a month in a different international city, including Hiroshima, where the first atomic bomb was dropped.

The underlying message of the Commission's report, published in June 1982, was that you could NOT win a nuclear war – and that both sides had to accept the idea of common security. It argued that no state could increase its security at the expense of another in the nuclear era – as the other could always respond by launching a nuclear attack.

So this was not like the conventional arms period, where the stronger side could indeed make itself feel safe by having the bigger military force. Instead, the quest for unilateral security could only lead to an increasing arms spiral and decreasing security between the two opponents. Enemies would have to learn to live together. It wasn't sentimental: that is just the way it was. Vance told a press conference: "In the 1980's, the concepts of dominant unilateral advantage and limited nuclear conflict are bankrupt. For security in the nuclear age means common security - a commitment to joint survival rather than the threat of mutual destruction." There was also a raft of concrete proposals such as curbing chemical weapons and banning tactical nuclear weapons. Much of it was not spectacularly original, but at a time when East and West were barely talking to other, it tried to be a constructive attempt at bridge building. No senior politicians, in the west at least, affected to notice the report. There was a polite review in the New York Times. As Milton Leitenberg wrote in The Bullet of Atomic Scientists, November 1983, the report was largely ignored.

Palme was undeterred. When he won the 1982 Swedish general election three months after the publication of his report, he announced his backing of a Nuclear Weapons Free zone in Scandinavia within sixty seconds of the opening of parliament. Of course, Scandinavia was nuclear-free in peacetime anyway. Part of the conditions of Norway's and Denmark's NATO membership was to have no NATO nukes, indeed no NATO troops, stationed on their soils in peacetime. The Soviets had six old Gulf submarines, nuclear armed, that could be moved in and out of the Baltic. There was a dangerous Soviet nuclear submarine bastion at Murmansk. On the Kola peninsula. If you included Murmansk in Scandinavia there was no way Scandinavia would be nuclear-free, since the nuclear missile subs were the Soviet Union's guarantee against a destructive first strike from the United States. They weren't going to bargain those away. If, on the other hand, Scandinavia did not include Murmansk and the Kola peninsula, Scandinavia was already, trivially nuclear free – in peacetime. In a crisis, Norway and Denmark might be under intense pressure to receive nuclear weapons, and it would be straightforward to move them in. And of course nuclear fall-out from the rest of Europe in a nuclear war would affect Scandinavia anyway.

A Nordic nuclear-free Zone might not have seemed to have much point to it – David Owen said in an interview that "it was mum's apple pie". Not serious, Palme's sop to domestic opinion.

If it was meant as a sop, Palme still managed to annoy the Americans. Richard Perle, a hawkish official in the Reagan administration, was critical of the Palme commission. Suppose a nuclear-free zone in Europe were established? The US would have to remove its nukes from Europe back across the Atlantic while the Russians needed only remove their nukes beyond the Urals, and could easily move them back into Europe. Palme's deal was asymmetrical.

On another occasion, Perle attacked Palme for wanting to remove the element that has preserved peace in Europe: nuclear weapons.

"It would be a catastrophe for NATO," Perle fumed. "The idea of 'common security' is an attack on the policy of deterrence that has preserved peace in Europe since the Second World war.

"Palme's resistance to this politics is irresponsible and can only weaken the West without making the slightest difference to Soviet politics. Palme ought to know. He hasn't had any success at making Soviet policy any more flexible."

It was a running theme: Palme was reckoned to treat the Soviets with too much respect. He was being used by the Soviets, who didn't listen to them. He had two Soviet members on his commission: Perle accused them of being actively connected to the Soviet government while Vance was not a member of the American government.

Actually, Perle was wrong. The two Soviet delegates were not part of the government. Georgy Arbatov, head of the USA Canada Institute, a Moscow think tank, wasn't even in the politburo's favour because of his reformist instincts. But the allegation was sticky.

That Palme was, by treating the Soviets as equal, a naif seemed to be borne out in the submarine intrusions

SWEDISH COASTAL WATERS experienced a significant number of mysterious submarine intrusions that could only – everyone thought - be the Soviet Union sizing Sweden up for invasion. The year before, October 1981, Soviet submarine, an old diesel sub built the 1950s, did up end up running aground on a Swedish reef, the famous Whiskey on the Rocks incident. The crew sat there, on the reef, in their sub, while Swedish fighter planes flew low and Swedish navy ships guarded it. Occasionally the captain would come and make rude signs at TV cameras in circling boats.

The Soviets insisted it was an accidental misnavigation and apologised; no one quite believed them. The incident received worldwide attention, The Times, wrote that the Soviet Union was the "bully of the Baltic": "The case of the Soviet submarine caught with its rudder down cannot be left where it is…One of the first lessons of the submarine incident is that there, as elsewhere, too much faith should not be put in Soviet professions of peaceful intentions"

THE SUBMARINE intrusions continued into 1982 and into Palme's term in office. With a difference: they never surfaced, despite considerable resources being put into submarine hunting. At Hårsfjärden, a bay south of Stockholm near Sweden's second most important naval base, a submarine, or several submarines seemed to taunt Swedish anti-submarine and patrol boat helicopters for a fortnight. For some reason, the navy chose to make it high profile. It opened a press centre and five hundred journalists from around the world turned up. They took it in turns to huddle on a local quayside and see the occasional depth charge being dropped from a helicopter or patrol boat. It kept Swedes glued to their television sets as the hunt was played live on their television screens. Anticlimactically, no submarine was brought up.

The New York Times, in two Stockholm dispatches, described Stockholm as a city whose leaden October skies drained the entire colour out of the buildings and the last leaves of autumn clung to the birch trees in the parks. The doings of JR Ewing in Dallas were much more interesting than speculation as to who was going to win the Nobel prizes. There was "alarm mixed with insatiable curiosity" about the Hårsfjärden incident. Daily press accounts made it seem as if world war three had started, but "the Navy had failed to uncover a single piece of evidence" only "hundreds of dead fish". The apparent failure to catch the submarine seemed to cause as "much relief as disappointment". "The Swedes last year had to release a Soviet submarine that ran aground off the southern coast and the failure so far to locate the new intruder has spared this neutralist nation the embarrassment of repeating that performance."

"To many Swedes it was if the Russian offenders were like the village drunk who gets locked up every Friday night but never spent enough time in jail to correct his ways". But many Swedes were deeply worried that Russian presence in Swedish waters would cause Sweden to be targeted by NATO's missiles. A commission consisting of MPs and military experts was appointed to examine the evidence and determine the submarine/submarines' national origin.

The commission was an opportunity for MPs to force Palme to drive a hard-line against the Soviets, about whom, in contrast to his excoriations of the United States over Vietnam and other issues had been scrupulously polite. The Moderates, who had been kept away from security issues by their coalition partners while in government from 1976 to 1982, had now, in opposition, had found a renewed confidence in right-wing monetarist solutions by the rise of the Right in the United States and Britain. And this had given them confidence in a Reagan - Thatcher approach to security policy.

And these challenges to the Social Democrat pacifist approach to security politics implied by the unstoppable intrusions gave a further boost to their fortunes, in that it supported to their pro-NATO security line. A young Moderate opposition MP, called Carl Bildt, 33, who had good personal contacts with several hawks in the Reagan administration, challenged Palme on the issue of the submarines. Bildt had been a friend of Washington since the early 1970s. In the same manner that the Americans trained future Swedish military leaders, they also had an eye out for young Swedish politicians of the future. Indeed, Palme, back in his day, had been "wooed" by America when he was given his scholarship to Kenyon College. His successor, Ingvar Carlsson, was also given a US scholarship. US diplomatic papers from the 1970s released by Wikileaks show that Carl Bildt, then in his early twenties, was viewed as an exceptionally promising young conservative with a bright future by the Bureau of Cultural and Social affairs.

As the Moderate party's defence spokesman, Bildt wrote articles in the Swedish national press saying Olof Palme was "soft on the Soviets" –

who were, after all, breaching Swedish sovereignty with their submarines - and that his evenhandedness in his peace initiatives was undermined by the Soviet Union. Bildt, who sat in the parliamentary commission to determine the origin of the submarines, was bitterly criticised by Palme for travelling to Washington to brief security contacts about the commission's conclusion.

In April 1983, the parliamentary commission produced its findings. The submarines were Soviet. Evidence was produced in an annexe which reporters weren't able to examine for themselves but related to acoustic and optical evidence.

This prompted Palme to make a noisy protest to the Soviet ambassador, Boris Pankin. Pankin, in his later memoirs, claimed Palme told him conciliatorily when handing over his harsh protest note: "I see it necessary to shout louder than anyone else so in that manner disarm the most persistent loudmouths." .

This marked a watershed. For 40 years more or less, the Social Democrats had had a monopoly on foreign policy, and their interpretations about Sweden's place in the world had completely dominated since the War. Now things were changing. Palme's angry parliamentary insults against the young Bildt led to the rest of the Moderate party closing ranks with him. The submarine intrusions became the platform for Bildt's expertise and authority. He eventually became party leader, and, in 1991, after the Cold War and after the death of Palme, prime minister.

Since Palme's peace plans depended on the Soviet Union as a fair-minded interlocutor, Palme continued to engage them. As Palme, as a man of action, believed in the virtues of personal diplomacy in his confidential talks with the Soviets. He did not trust his foreign ministry – which had leaked the embarrassing but not fatal fact that the formulations to his nuclear-free zone policy had originally come from a West German disarmament expert – so formed a back channel to Moscow through his UN ambassador. This too was leaked, by some diplomats hostile to Palme in the foreign ministry. There were those who thought the backchannel had been established to pass on more information to the USSR than just protest notes.

Rumours circulated that Palme was a spy or an apologist for the Soviet Union. However, the letter from his UN ambassador to the Soviets was read out on TV by Palme himself and seemed to show that Palme "talked tough" even in private. If the Soviets did not stop their intrusions, dead bodies would float on the water.

Even as the intrusions took their toll on Palme's credibility, he continued sending officials to talk to Moscow. Cabinet secretary Pierre Schori went in early 1983; another senior official in the economics department went to discuss Soviet Swedish trade. Palme no longer believed in the old diplomatic tricks of cutting contacts and freezing relations, he wanted to keep the dialogue going. At the Social Democrat party congress in 1983, Palme said: "We have to have the courage to look the superpower in the eye". In confidence, Palme told the other Swedish party leaders he couldn't understand that the Russians continued to act the way they did, especially as, in face-to-face talks, they swore they had nothing to do with the submarine intrusions. Were they lying to his face? Meanwhile, the intrusions continued, as if Palme's pleas to the Soviet leadership had no effect.

PALME LAST MONTHS: 1985-86

1984 was the year when Sweden was subjected to an unprecedented barrage of international criticism for its domestic policies. At times it was compared to East Germany. Was there some truth to it? If there was some truth to it, was there a reason why the wave of criticism happened right now? From time to time, from the sixties onward, for every three articles describing Sweden as a utopia, some curmudgeon would come along and criticise the Swedish control state. In 1953 Time magazine called Sweden a "despo socialist state" as we have seen. And 1976, for example, Time magazine headlined their article "Something souring in utopia". But now the odd article had become a flood of negative stories.

One Swedish university paper written decades later argues that the European and West German media onslaught against Sweden was part of the Cold War. Sweden was written up as a country that not only was engaging in dialogue with the East bloc – a kind of appeasement - but was also building up a Soviet-style social and political internal system. Sweden may not have been a perfect democracy, with zealous bureaucrats and a historically strong state living alongside the progressive social laissez-faire introduced by Palme and his generation. But a Soviet-style state it was clearly not.

So was it not a conscious effort by the West German press, in particular, to create and strengthen the image of Sweden as an Orwellian society, the purpose being that Sweden was to serve as a deterrent example for West Germans and the whole of Europe, and all related to the international political situation? If European countries engaged in dialogue with the USSR as Palme did, they too would become more like Sweden in its domestic policies: a DDR light.

The Swedish Foreign Ministry devoted much of its annual report on foreign coverage of the country on foreign journalists who had taken

Sverige as a symbol in its "1984 articles", The theme was Orwell's book and the purported resemblances to the present day in, of all countries, Sweden: The Swedish Foreign Ministry wrote: "Several prominent newspapers in Belgium, West Germany, Norway, France, Austria and Italy wrote strongly negative articles about the Swedish welfare state."

The anti-Swedish campaign, if it was that, lasted for about a year. Palme formulated a reply for Der Spiegel which was a robust defence of the high tax state: far from being oppressive, it offered freedoms and opportunities for the underprivileged. The criticism died away and an interesting thing happened.

The economy had improved. Negative news coverage of the effects of Margaret Thatcher's reforms on the British social fabric impacted negatively on the reputation of the Moderates' own economic reform plans, which Palme did not hesitate to exploit. He ran the 1985 election campaign with a vociferous anti neo-liberal approach, targeting the Swedish conservatives (ie Moderates), whom he said wanted to import the "dole queues and neoliberalism" of Margaret Thatcher's Britain to Sweden.

Neoliberalism, in its pure form, argued that the only thing the state should do is set up some ground rules, of which the most important is to hold down inflation. That is achieved through savings on public outgoings, a slimmed public sector and as low taxes as possible. Active stimulus programmes a la Keynes are seen as deadly poison. Big tax cuts are self-financing as people work more and thus pay more taxes. Regulations for banks, aviation, doctors and other commercial activities were to be abolished. Poor people's programmes are not solved by social insurance but by rich people doing so well out of capitalism that the poor get a share of the general welfare, the so-called trickle down theory.

Large organisations like trade unions are market disruptors and represent a dangerous corporatism whose importance ought to be reduced as much as possible. Finally, neoliberalism calls itself scientific. Not an ideology, but reflecting natural, universal economic truths. Sooner or later, alternative systems would collapse through their own contradictions. With a generational change, the Moderates had become more and more keen on the Neoliberal gospel.

In neoliberalism, especially in its rather stark Moderate variant, Palme had found a target he enjoyed reviving his energies for.

During the election campaign in August 1985, he told a high school of 900 pupils in a school at Angered, Sweden: "A society based on neoliberalism will be a cold one to live in. In such a society, people are each other's enemies. In such a society, the individual is forced to buy his security at the cost of others. Just look at countries where neoliberalism has been tried out. In these societies, morale has collapsed." It was clearly a reference to Britain and America.

The news agency reporter who covered the event said the school students sat along the walls and on the benches of the school's sports centre. "The pupils were so engaged it was enough to make any of their teachers jealous," commented the reporter. The pupils gave him powerful applause. Palme continued:

"The moderates went out with neoliberal slogans like 'new freedom' and 'invest in yourself' and they show pictures of successful people. Of course, there is nothing wrong with investing in oneself. But the neoliberals invest in the individual at the expense of the collective."

He added. "Today we have youth unemployment levels that are sweeping through Europe like the plague. In many places in England over half the young are without a job. That's free market forces for you," he said.

Palme had a good slogan: he played on the words of the anti-racist slogan imported from France "Ne touche pas ma pote" – don't touch my friend, with a flat palm symbol – and made up a joke Moderate party slogan instead. "Don't touch my income." He accused the moderates of suggesting tax proposals that would favour the rich and harm the poor.

Palme mixed his barnstorming anti neoliberal speeches by also emphasizing the inviolability of Sweden's neutrality.

"The Social Democrats are guardians of the country's neutrality and independence. The Social Democrats can never rest for one moment in that responsibility. We have had hard times in relation to the Soviet Union. We have to maintain our political rights against this superpower and never give a millimetre away of our rights. But at the same time we must never be drawn into a new cold war."

Despite the continuing anxiety about the submarine intrusions – which Palme must have felt, too - neutrality had always been a vote winner, a comfort blanket as much as the unreformed welfare state was – and Palme knew it.

They were both sources of the Swedish feeling of exceptionalism, in fact, expressions of a kind of special Swedish nationalism. That was why he pushed both issues. And the Social Democrats were a "safe pair of hands", representing a world many Swedes knew and felt familiar with. For vulnerable Swedes, the Moderates represented not the gusts of freedom into the stale people's home, but a chill wind of stark Cold War choices, getting closer to NATO and more hostile to the USSR; and Palme played up the systemic shift threat to the country represented by Carl Bildt and others in his party.

In trying to win the election, the opposition faced a further problem. The Moderate party leader Ulf Adelsohn – Bildt was just 35, and was tipped to be his successor - was no intellectual. He had an easygoing manner which was adequate enough for his former post as mayor of Stockholm but he had a credibility problem exemplified by his joke in front of journalists to bathe in the reactor pool at one of the nuclear power plants to show his support for atomic power.

All this came home to roost at the election, perhaps because the Moderates had overreached themselves with callow arguments about the superiority of the market in all situations (even though Palme, thanks to his finance minister Feldt had shifted to the left himself), they lost the 1985 election by a bigger margin than the one in 1982.

The autumn of 1985, after Palme's final election victory, was a tough period, though. Tax scandals, harassment by fringe right-wing groups, who blamed Palme for the world's ills with placards outside conferences he attended, failure over the Iran Iraq war, where he was a UN envoy – there was a lot on Palme's plate. Kjell Olof Feldt, his finance minister, recalls visiting him in his office: explaining some piece of policy, Palme picked up a musical instrument, a recorder, and started soundlessly playing on it, his fingers dancing over the holes as Feldt tried to explain a complex piece of policy.

When Neil Kinnock, the Labour Party's new leader, came to visit the dynamic young Welshman contrasted favourably with Palme, who behaved in a confused and gaga manner, according to one of Palme's aides. He was at the end of his tether. Now that much more is known about political warfare – was the harassment Palme received, or instance from the fringe right wing group, the EAP, with its book tables and extremely aggressive placards "Exterminate Palme with DDT" part of an organised campaign by foreign political or domestic busness interests? Conceivably, the Social Democrats' Sweden was a threat to some political forces in the world not because it was such a bad country, but because, basically, Sweden was such a good country.

THE MURDER INVESTIGATION: 1 Mar 1986 onwards

I was at boarding school in central London the morning after the killing, 1 March 1986. I remember it well. Most Swedes who were around those days I find have a flash memory of the assassination, just as Americans remember what they were doing when JFK was shot. We had Saturday school, and my roommate burst into our room with the gleeful expression that comes from telling extraordinary news, even if it is tragic news, with a copy of The Times: there he was, on the front page. I was not a political supporter of Olof Palme but I was genuinely shocked, nevertheless. He had been prime minister, with a break from 1976 to 1982, since the year I was born, 1969. A Sweden without him seemed unthinkable.

The murder happened, as we know, on the 28th February 1986, at 11.21 pm. The killer had shot him in the back with what was probably a Smith and Wesson Magnum .357, killing him instantly.

For Palme, it had been a busy month. In addition to his usual prime ministerial duties, he was up to his third world activism again. The big event in Stockholm in February 1986 was the Apartheid Days, and Palme made the keynote speech, giving a little support to his friends Oliver Tambo and other African National Congress leaders. But for once, he had a Friday night off. And the Friday itself was less hectic than usual.

In the morning of this fateful Friday, he played tennis with his old friend Harry Schein, chairman of Swedish state television. He beat him, which put him a good mood. He then went to change a suit in a shop. For the rest of the morning, he made phone calls and talked to journalists, diplomats and government officials.

At 11 am he met the Iraq ambassador to Sweden; as Palme was the mediator in the Iran-Iraq war, though too busy these days to actually visit the region itself. The war was horrific; no solution was in sight; it was launched by Saddam in 1980, chemical warfare was used and Iran was using suicide squads to clear minefields. The war ended in 1988. Then he spent an hour alone, between 12 and 1. It is not known what he did at that time, perhaps made or received some phone calls.

Some friends described him as being a bit agitated when he came down to the Riksdag (parliament) restaurant for lunch; Swedish cabinets have lunch together every day of the week when the Riksdag is in session. But afterwards he was in a good mood – until late afternoon, at least, when a photographer from a trade union magazine asked to take a photo of him looking out of his office room window and was declined.

"The thing is, you never know what is waiting out there," Palme said pensively.

As a cabinet minister in the 1960s, Palme had his home phone number in the regular phone directory and kept the spare door keys to their suburban house in a wooden clog under the stairs. By the time he had become prime minister, security precautions were a bit better but not hugely so. He did not like bodyguards at all. And sometimes went without them in the triangle bounded by his old town flat, the parliament, and the government chancellery. On this day, he dismissed his two regular detectives at lunchtime.

He made some phone calls from his office in the afternoon. At six pm, he headed back to his large apartment in Stockholm's mediaeval Old Town, just a few minutes' walk from parliament. There, his wife Lisbet, 54, was waiting for him; they discussed a vague plan they had had to see a movie that evening. Lisbet favoured a film about a boy growing up in rural Sweden in the Sputnik era, My Life as A Dog; but she was open to suggestions.

Palme rang his 24-year-old second son Mårten (pronounced Morten) and discovered that he, too, was going to see a film with his girlfriend. The film was the Brothers Mozart, a Swedish art-house movie. Palme said he and Lisbet might see them there; they hadn't decided. The Palme couple dined around 8 pm. In the half hour after that he took a couple of phone calls before they went out. At least two calls came from party colleagues, though there may have been more. They called for the bodyguards but did not succeed in getting hold of them.

When he took his last call, from former party secretary Sven Aspling, his wife was waiting by the door.

As they walked to the nearest metro station, a young couple claimed later, when interviewed by police, there was nothing unusual, except they were both laughing at a shared joke. Lisbet, though, had a subdued air. As the couple stood on the platform, one witness subsequently interviewed by the investigation was astonished by the prime minister's everyday and even disorganised appearance, with unpressed trousers. Palme's lack of personal organisation was not news to staff who worked closely with him.

Outside the Grand cinema, the couple were spotted by Mårten and his girlfriend; the queues were long and Lisbet scolded her husband's attempt to pull rank and walk to the front of the queue; so they obediently waited their turn: the ticket salesman managed to find two reserved seats that were not being taken. As it happened, they found seats close to the head of the white collar trade union. The trade union boss and Palme started talking about some political matters, but were interrupted by Lisbet as the lights faded. It was Palme's evening off. Work matters could wait. The Palmes shared a box of mint chocolates.

When the film was over, the Palme couple, their son and his girlfriend gathered outside on the pavement, as hundreds of people streamed past and around them. A lift from the trade union boss was refused.

Mårten wanted to go for tea and discuss the film; his father was enthusiastic about the offer, but Lisbet said she had a headache, and Mårten's girlfriend had to get up early for work. It was 11-05 PM. Palme jumped when the lights of a nearby shop went out; they briefly discussed how to get home. Although Lisbet had said she was tired, Palme suggested they start strolling south: even that they walk all the way home, even though it was a distance of nearly one and a half kilometres.

This was surprising, as not only was it cold but late on a Friday night, payday night, on one of Stockholm's most frequented thoroughfares, Sveavägen, where there might be quite a few dodgy or drunk people about. A note here about Sveavägen. Sveavägen literally means "Way of the Swedes" and along this parade route, lined for much of its length by trees, lay Sweden's largest publishing house. There were numerous shops, offices, and cinemas. Sweden's largest insurer - which had been founded by Palme's grandfather - and the Social Democrat party headquarters. As it happens there were not many pedestrians about.

The couples said their farewells and started walking south; there was an ice-cold wind and a thin layer of snow on the pavement. They walked down the western side of Sveavägen.

As they passed a grill kitchen, they crossed Sveavägen at a zebra crossing to the eastern side. Lisbet wanted to check out a gown in a clothes shop. Lisbet said later she didn't notice anything unusual: didn't notice if they were being followed.

In fact, for the last 30 metres of their journey to the assassination spot, they were. The man behind them was sauntering in the same southern direction, and was overtaken by the Palme couple. His name was Anders Björkman, an architect, aged 39, who had been shaken off by his companions from an office party held at a restaurant nearby, He wore a woollen hat lovingly knitted by his wife, and a large padded down jacket, and staggered around a little near a cash machine close to the assassination spot; the Palmes did not notice him as they strode past. For the last metres he followed them, a few metres behind, generally a bit out of it.

The time was 23.21.00. The prime minister had twenty seconds to live. An open metro station was located a few hundred metres away at Kungsgatan, a busy street of restaurants and clubs, and there were many people on the streets there. It would be too late if any assassin wanted to make a clean getaway. This was his last chance.

The Palme couple were just a metre away from a junction between Sveavägen and the quiet side street of Tunnelgatan....to the left was the eastern side of Tunnelgatan, narrow and pedestrianised. There was an artists' and painters' materials shop called Dekorima located on the corner with a slanted glass façade. The killer stood by the slanting façade, out of view of the couple.

As the Palmes strolled past the Tunnelgatan junction, the man moved out behind the couple…raised his magnum revolver, and fired twice from a distance of 20cm into the centre of his back. Palme fell at the first shot and dragged his wife down to the icy pavement with him. The second shot narrowly missed Lisbet as she twisted sideways. The bullet penetrated her coat and singed her back. It was a matter of millimetres. She was very lucky.

THE KILLER stood swaying slightly, looming over the body and the wife. Clearly deciding against firing off a third bullet to deal definitively with Lisbet, he quickly ran east down Tunnelgatan, past a stack of building cabins, up the long, steep, flight of outdoor stairs and was out of sight. This was a quieter, more residential area, a contrast to the traffic canyon of Sveavägen. Here was a network of streets it was easy to lose any pursuers in. One witness gave chase up the stairs but it was to no avail: the killer had disappeared.

The police arrived within minutes. First a Volvo police car, then a police van, then another police van, and four cops from one van raced in the direction of the assassin's escape. First one, then another, ambulance, arrived. Pedestrians had already hastened to the scene, their breath exhalations lit up by the police van headlights as they jostled to give their names and numbers. Palme's body was lifted into one of the ambulances and Lisbet jumped nimbly into the back. The vehicle sped off to the nearest hospital. It was no use. He was already dead.

The cops who gave chase by foot found nothing and returned. Within an hour, a few kilometres away at Rosenbad, the government chancellery, government ministers gathered, nervous, blinking, shocked, worried that that the killer might be part of an assassination squad, and that they might be next: that maybe the killers were lurking outside the chancellery, too. (Protection there was, in fact, abysmal.) After they had unanimously appointed Ingvar Carlsson, a long-time friend of Palme, and his deputy prime minister, as successor, the national news agency put out a message on all the international news wires that Sweden had a new government.

Already, at the junction where the killing had taken place. A small crowd of Friday night revellers, mostly young, had begun to gather. The police had roped off an area with tape, but there was now little activity after the ambulance with Palme's body and police cars had driven off.

One reporter from the Aftonbladet newspaper who turned up said at 0030 said it was eerily, strangely calm. A single red rose, which happened to be the symbol of the Social Democrats, had been thrown into the snow, next to the pool of dried blood. Some young people wept. Others looked stunned. The police response might have seemed efficient enough on the night if you were an observer on the scene – as I just described. But in fact, what the police actually did, how much or rather how little, became a huge source of controversy later. The police did not rope off the assassination spot properly, did not close off the inner city.

There were only a few policemen involved in the murder chase on the night. Most dispatchers at the alarm centre were engaged in other, routine, crimes, even when it became was clear there had been a murder of a prime minister. There was a delay in the issuing of an alarm to national police forces, and so on.

The oddities in the Palme murder investigation began almost straight away. Stockholm's police chief Hans Holmér had taken charge. It was true he was within his rights to do so. On the other hand, he had very limited experience of real murder investigations. He might have passed off the hunt to an experienced investigator in the national crime squad. The 56-year-old Holmer was an interesting character. The son of a top athlete, and part-time thriller writer. His enemies accused him of being a womaniser, a liar and someone who drove his company car while drunk. But women liked him, and he gave reassuring, articulate press conferences. He seemed to be tough, charismatic, in control, and to those who think he was somehow involved in a cover-up about the murder, somehow demonic

He claimed to be out of town on the night. He said he was in Borlänge, in northern Sweden, for the annual ski race called Vasaloppet. He sped back to Stockholm early next morning and took charge, wearing his sports clothes. Once at the Stockholm police house, he took control of it and never let his charismatic grip go for the year he ran the investigation, backed by a government which felt comforted by his stated Social Democrat party sympathies. For sure, an infinitely more technically qualified man, Arne Irvell, head of the Stockholm murder investigation squad, was one of several experienced detectives who was sidelined from the investigation. Irvell found out about the assassination while having his morning cereal, and the call from Holmer which he might have expected never came.

Like the assassinated prime minister, Holmer was charming, strong-willed, a man of action, but, not far beneath the surface, strangely androgynous, sensitive and vulnerable.

As he approached his first press conference, Holmer thought he would look forward to dealing with the media. He had good descriptive powers and the role-playing with journalists stimulated him. There were several press conferences in the first few days, and indeed it turned out well. In the TV footage there he was, a tall, casually dressed man with a slightly cracked voice, a man who exuded self-confidence. The newspapers drooled about a Swedish Clint Eastwood and the country's women like what they saw and heard.

After fielding tough press conferences from tense journalists, looking for answers and reassurance, he was deluged with flowers and home-baked cakes from the public who thought he put on confident performances. However, his investigative work soon became routine, he told an interviewer later. Life in the windowless room where dozens of policemen were working on sorting clues was like living in a submarine. Every day, the same people, same hamburgers.

The first suspect was Victor Gunnarson, a 33-year-old supply teacher with an extensive social life who was happy to talk about his hatred of Palme on every possible occasion.

In the first few days, he stood out in the flood of tips because of his hatred of Palme, according to Holmer. He aired his views both in his social life and in the classroom. He was in the area where the murder took place and behaved so oddly that passers-by noted it. He was hauled in for interrogation on 6 March 1986, then let go. He was questioned again on 8 March on orders of the prosecutor. He was released shortly after the funeral. After that, Holmer focused on the Kurdish trail, after interpreting a bugged telephone conversation between two PKK activists as being about the assassination of Olof Palme. The whole affair, which took up most of the police's investigative resources in the important first year after the murder, collapsed after dawn raids on PKK activists' homes in Stockholm in January 1987. Most commentators now believe this was a complete red herring of a trail. Holmer resigned. The question was why Holmer was allowed to stay in his post as long as he did. Maybe because the government wanted it that way.

THERE WAS a report written by Richard Reeves, a New York Times correspondent, who did a large story on the state of the investigation on the first anniversary of the murder, March 1987. He spoke to a senior Swedish government official, who told him: "We know at this point that there is less than a 10 percent chance to solve the murder. That is not our problem. Our problem is what the people of Sweden believe happened and how they deal with that." It was more important to "resolve the murder" than to "solve the murder". Perhaps what this official was stating was that the PKK were "safe" candidates for the assassination. According to Gunnar Wall, a journalist and expert on all the twists and turns of the Palme murder, arresting and deporting a bunch of people who were bad guys anyway would save Sweden the inconvenience of a trial, it would produce closure of the drama of the murder - even if the PKK were not actually the murderers. But why exactly would solving the murder, truly and properly, not be worth the Swedish government's trouble? What was the Swedish government so afraid of?

THE SUSPECT WHO WOULDN'T GO AWAY

In March 1987, Swedish state television showed a Soviet drama documentary with the straightforward title "Why was Olof Palme murdered" at the hour of 11.30pm on TV1 station. No certain conclusions were made, based on no firm evidence, but only indications that the killing could ultimately be laid at the feet of the CIA. Georgi Zubkov, the scriptwriter of the documentary and Soviet television's chief foreign policy commentator, explained in the film how, when Palme was given an honorary doctorate from his old college, Kenyon, in Ohio, he was met with placards saying "Go Home Palme" or "Go to Vietnam".

"America never concealed its hostility to Palme and never forgave him for his engagement in Vietnam. President Lyndon Baines Johnson blamed Palme for anti-Americanism," Zubkov commented. He added: "The murderer's name will never be known." Palme was high up on the death list of the Chilean junta. From there it was possible to draw connections to Palme's international activities, which were a barrier to America's interventions in Central America.

Such remarks had not escaped the American embassy in Stockholm which, before the documentary was shown, sent two officials to visit the boss of Sweden's TV1 station, Olle Berglund, and remind him that they were teaching anti-American propaganda.

The film was originally due to go out on 27 February 1987, the near anniversary of Palme's murder, but the Americans persuaded him to delay the broadcast by a week, so that the film wouldn't be seen as a kind of Swedish endorsement of the thesis in the Soviet programme. The Swedes later lodged a protest with the US State Department, complaining about American interference in domestic affairs.

Jörn Svensson, a communist MP, had, a few months earlier, told the Swedish parliament the assassins were probably from the CIA. His chain of reasoning went as follows:

It was an incredibly odd detail that the assailant knew about the Palmes' cinema visit and just as strange that he was aware that Palme was unaccompanied by bodyguards. Svensson dismissed continuous monitoring of the Palmes' outside door. It would take enormous energy and time and above all risk the chances of being spotted. The likelihood was that Palme was bugged or that there was an insider inside the structure who could pass on information in some other way. Svensson told a debate with the minister of Justice Sten Wickbom – following on from a pamphlet he wrote – that the murder was probably carried out by a western intelligence agency.

Svensson said: No one could seriously argue the killing was carried out because of a private reckoning or because of generalised feelings of hatred. It must have been because of Palme's role as a disarmament politician and representative of Swedish neutrality policy that made him a threat and that was why had to be taken out. The Palme commission's proposals about disarmaments must have been seen as catastrophic for the "current American administration, central interests inside the military establishment, higher circles in NATO forces plus some of the smaller states in the western sphere". The threatening thing about the Palme commission's proposals was the suggestions for a nuclear-free zone, reduction of the level of medium range and intermediate range weapons and control over the nuclear fuel cycle. Palme was also influential with public opinion in several NATO countries, notably in the Netherlands and West Germany, which might lead to an altered strategy for NATO in Europe, which would be uncomfortable for the USA. It was Palme's support for a certain stream of opinion within the alliance which threatened to give the overarching American state interest a very serious setback. It made central parts of the political development in Europe uncertain from an American perspective. If there had been Social Democrat and Labour election victories in the UK and West Germany, NATO might have faced with a wholly new future.

The conclusion was that the real motive for the murder lay with the American administration, plus governments related to America in a subaltern relation. Spelled out: Israel, South Africa, Turkey. To kill a prime minister was a project that required extensive organisational resources and experience was his reasoning.

South Africa, Chile, Turkey, Israel were countries that had carried out political murders in the past, but they had too little capability to engage in advanced murder conspiracies outside their own sphere. On the other hand, the CIA had twice tried to kill Fidel Castro, while the American military had openly engaged in a murder attempt on Libya's head of state, Qaddafi. The CIA was involved in a coup that included an attempted murder on Cyprus's president Makarios. The carrying out of a murder of a prime minister in a neutral country required arrogance you just wouldn't find outside a superpower.

But Svensson did not believe that the CIA agents themselves carried out the actual murder; rather it was mercenaries or commandos inside the European right-wing movement. The cold-blooded behaviour of the killer suggested a professional killer. The strange thing about the murder was that it happened after a spontaneous visit to the cinema which showed the killer must have had inside information about Palme's comings and goings. Even that pointed in the direction of an intelligence agency with big resources behind it.

Jörn Svensson hoped that the debate about the background to the murder would rise above "the gossip level".

"Does anyone really believe that a madman would turn up?" or "Would we have to live with the security police's ridiculous disinformation about Kurdish scapegoats?" he said, concluding his speech. The next day, responding to a journalist query, the US embassy refused to issue a comment.

The investigation, from a public's and journalists' perspective, continued to keep a very low profile for a long time, leaving the field free to speculators, reporters and private investigators. But on 4 March 1988, the bureau chief of the National Police Board, Ulf Karlsson, told the press that "we don't see an immediate solution, but a long-term and rather dull daily routine work which is going and will continue to go on for a while yet". He said: "I am optimistic that we will sooner or later get a solution." Karlsson had been in charge of the investigation since Holmer's departure a year earlier. There had been no new suspects, little coverage in the media. He then announced he was climbing down and handing over to a new team, to police superintendent Hans Ölvebiu. The police investigation, which had been spread over four different departments, was now to be concentrated in one unit. Thirty-five men were engaged in the inquiry, down from 300 in the first weeks when Holmer had been in charge. There had been 15 or 20,000 leads in the beginning; that had shrunk, many had been looked at and dismissed. Much, said Karlsson, was now manageable.

They had carried out isotope tests on the bullets: the police were now convinced it was the same bullets as fired at the Palmes. Whether the police had also found a plausible weapon he did not wish to speculate. He refused to what trails were hot, and added "there are ten or so trails that are interesting to work on", without further comments.

A BOOK WAS published in the spring of 1988 that would seem to give some support for a Jörn Svensson-type theory. Published by a writer under the pseudonym of Mikael Rosqvist, it described 1980s Stockholm as a playground for spies, agents and intelligence officers – just as, in the Second World War, it had been a nest of spies. The Swedish security agency sat in the middle of the spider's web and exchanged information with most western intelligence agencies. Palme, said the author, had tried to stop this information exchange, without much success, the author added. Boris Pankin, the scholarly Soviet ambassador, was, in reality, a KGB general. There was also a detailed description of the CIA in Sweden. A quarter of US Stockholm embassy staff were CIA. The officials mostly worked with acquiring information openly. However, there was a period when the CIA bugged Olof Palme. There was a special surveillance patrol. Palme avoided talking about sensitive subjects on the phone. The book added though that relations now were good.

The new post-Holmer police leadership, however, had lost interest in planned murders, whether intelligence agencies or terrorist groups. The PKK was out. The CIA was never looked at. There was a new team of prosecutors, and a new police chief in charge, the 43-year-old Hans Ölvebro, a reliable policeman from a provincial post. Their aim was to anchor the "murder to Sveavägen" – as the first group of prosecutors had asked Holmer to do, and he had failed to provide. The working theory was that there must have been a "Grandman", someone who had spotted the Palmes before they want to the Grand cinema, fetched a gun, waited for the couple outside the Grand cinema and followed them to the street corner where he finally pulled the trigger. The Grandman hypothesis would avoid the need for a team to have carried out the murder, and so averted the need for a conspiracy. The police were now looking at that figure Jörn Svensson thought scarcely likely. The lone spontaneous killer, lunatic, who had happened upon the unaccompanied couple, seen a chance to kill the man, gone to fetch a weapon and killed Palme when the couple were walking home.

In December 1988 the new investigators arrested an unemployed alcoholic and drug addict called Christer Pettersson, 42 years old. The fact he was a heavy drinker was to make him a perfect villain for the Swedes, who have a distinctly ambivalent relation to alcohol, as any foreign visitor who wants to buy a bottle of wine at the weekend finds out. The state liquor stores have restricted opening hours.

PERHAPS NO figure in Sweden of the late eighties and early nineties was to dominate the public's attention in this era as this character, Christer Pettersson. He was, and remains, a household name. Basically, he was Sweden's equivalent of Lee Harvey Oswald. The same question loomed over Pettersson's guilt – or not – as over the former US marine whom the Warren Committee had declared guilty in 1964. (As nearly everyone knows, Oswald was killed by the nightclub owner Jack Ruby in prison while in custody; so his case was never tested in court. Judging by polls, a majority of the US population is said to believe the official story, of Oswald the lone killer, is a lie.)

The subject of countless tabloid stories and TV reconstructions, Pettersson's name became part of the daily currency of exchanges in popular and political culture. The story of his guilt, or non-guilt, was to become a running serial. Every tabloid newspaper interview with a new witness who purported to know something about new Pettersson's life, background or whereabouts on the night added a new twist. Their destruction of the value of witnesses by journalists briefing them before the police had a chance was very harmful for the investigation.

Journalists, and the general public, just could not get enough. Was he the killer or was he innocent, framed, to cover up for other possibilities? Later, as a free man, Pettersson would sit, sphinx-like in his slicked-back hair and thug's leather jacket in TV discussion programmes, while the other guests tiptoed around his presence, treated him with exaggerated respect. He was prone to violent outbursts in front of the TV cameras, which made for good ratings. Were these explosions of violence the kind of behaviour that preceded his most heinous act of regicide? Almost terrifyingly thrilling to watch. Or was here as a caged beast, a man from the underclass who had been falsely convicted before his release on appeal? Was it just a piece of television theatre agreed on by Pettersson and the TV host before the show began? Sometimes he seemed to confess. But it wasn't quite clear. His pronouncements were always shrouded in ambiguity. And he got paid for every TV appearance, in fact, rather sordidly, and made a living out of "confessing". To some commentators, he was like a circus animal, paid to perform. It paid for his drug habit. He was often intoxicated before the live TV cameras. It was tabloid TV of the best – or rather, worst – sort. And he was manna for the kind of television chat programme that definitely would not have appeared on the more purist educational TV schedules of the Palme era.

So what was he really up to that night, 28 February 1986? It has been definitely established that Pettersson was in town on the evening of 28 February scoring amphetamines. His drug dealer, a nightclub owner called Sigge Cedergren, lived in central Stockholm. In fact, Sigge's flat overlooked the Grand cinema, on the opposite side of the road, and drug addicts sometimes used the foyer themselves on cold winter nights waiting for Sigge to return from a nightclub he owned a kilometre or so away. They would wait for the light to flick on in Sigge's kitchen on the third floor so they could go and buzz on his doorbell and get their supplies.

Pettersson looked like a thug through-and-through, a hard man with a hard face, but he had actually come from the middle class and had a high IQ, 130. His father had been an accountant, his mother had been loving but weak, and he had grown up in a middle-class suburb in the 1950s. But he had been on a quite spectacular downwards class journey since his teens. There were early indications of severe psychiatric problems. He had managed to hold down a couple of manual jobs for short periods but always been fired after being caught stealing. Out of work, he had resorted to petty criminality and male prostitution. He had in fact killed before, in 1971. Got into an argument with a young man who bumped into him during the Christmas rush, saw "the red mist", pulled out the old military bayonet he always carried and stabbed him.

He was convicted of manslaughter and sentenced to psychiatric care. When set free, after a shamefully short period inside, he embarked on a criminal career that included numerous robberies, assaults - but no further killings. So, in early 1986, Pettersson was out of jail for the N-th time, living in a government-funded flat in the highrise northern suburb of Rotebro. The name Rotebro is well known to Stockholmers, as it is a train stop en route to Stockholm's airport, Arlanda. Built as part of the "million programme" in the sixties to house people from rural Sweden flocking to the capital for the new factory jobs of the boom years, Rotebro's social housing highrises visible from the station do not exactly encourage people to get off.

Pettersson had a routine, and 28 February 1986 was probably not very different from any other day. It involved ambling down to Systembolaget, the state liquor store, to buy a bottle of vodka he could fit in his jacket pocket. Then his routine involved sitting on the shopping centre benches, or someone's flat, drinking and talking to friends, people who carried clinking plastic bags, and often crutches wherever they went. He could have stayed in boring old Rotebro that fateful evening, 28 February 1986, and his life would have turned out differently. But he had made a promise to a friend to score drugs, amphetamines, for the two of them. It was a cold evening. How did he feel? Perhaps he was woozy from drink, and slightly regretted his promise - but he had to make "something" of the day. Or perhaps he had timed it and was surfing on the wave of positive emotions. The amphetamine rush would – perhaps he expected – nicely round off the evening.

We know for sure Pettersson took the train to the centre of Stockholm to score drugs from his dealer, Sigge Cedergren, living within a short distance of the Grand Cinema.

Had the killer seen Palme enter the cinema and then had the impulse in him to kill the prime minister? Having dropped the PKK trail, and determined that Palme had not been followed or bugged at home (that was what the police claimed, anyway), so the murder could not have been planned, that became the police investigation's working hypothesis from mid-1988. Now they only needed to find a suitable candidate. What rough characters had been in the area at the time of the murder? The police trawled their underworld contacts and looked over old interrogations. The criminal crowd surrounding Sigge was an obvious place to start.

Pettersson had first been heard over two years earlier, in May 1986. In a brief telephone interview he admitted he had spent part of the evening at Sigge's club, Oxen, or the Ox, which was a few streets away from the murder scene. He left his flat in Rotebro early evening and hung about the Ox till eleven. There he had met his friend and drug dealer Sigge, who owned the Ox club.

AFTER MEETING Sigge, Pettersson told police, when quizzed in 1986, that he had walked back to the Central Station, taken the commuter train north out of Stockholm and then got back to his flat at midnight. There, a drug addict friend, Ulf Spinnars, was waiting for him. Ulf was staying the night – sleeping on the floor of Pettersson's kitchen – because Pettersson had promised earlier that evening to score amphetamines for the two of them. On waking up at eight in the morning, Pettersson had opened a daily newspaper and seen the tragic news of Palme's death. He had cried because he was a "Social Democrat" and "great fan" of the prime minister. Because of Pettersson's return at midnight, Ulf was able to give Pettersson an alibi that precluded Pettersson's responsibility for the murder.. The police, satisfied with that story, and Ulf's confirmation, left him alone. That was back in 1986. They were not all that interested. That was under Holmer's period of leadership. Holmer was busy chasing Kurds and directed nearly all police efforts in that direction.

Two and a half years later, late 1988, under the new team, the police started bugging Pettersson. They had shaken the criminal tree again and his name had come up among Stockholm's underworld fraternity as a possible candidate for a murder. The bugging of Pettersson didn't produce anything incriminating. He talked ramblingly to his girlfriends about his cat and sometimes read aloud from the Bible too. On this basis, the police hauled him in. In late 1988, they also reinterviewed Ulf, who appeared to have changed his mind about what had happened nearly three years earlier. Pettersson had come home later than Ulf had initially claimed. He had got back to Rotebro at one in the morning, not midnight as previously claimed. The murder took place at 11.21pm. It takes 45 minutes to get to Rotebro from the centre of Stockholm by suburban train. The police were overjoyed. Thanks to Ulf's "change of mind", Pettersson no longer had an alibi.

When Pettersson was taken into the Police House for questioning in December 1988 (the police came out to Rotebro and collected him by car), he was confronted by two witnesses, Mårten Palme, Palme's son, who had been at the cinema on the night with his parents and said farewell on the street outside, and Lars Eriksson, a 28-year-old air traffic controller who had waited in the driving seat of a car parked outside the Grand, waiting to pick up his parents. The police had interviewed a number among the hundreds in and around the cinema that evening and Eriksson was one of them. Eriksson had seen an unpleasant character pace back and forth in front of the cinema entrance. This had prompted him to lock the car from inside.

Both Eriksson and Mårten Palme identified Pettersson from a line-up of about a dozen people in the police house, on the day of Pettersson's arrest. Most of the others were policemen in civilian clothes. Those testimonies meant little on their own. Pettersson might easily have been loitering around the cinema without being in any way involved in any murder.

However, Lisbet Palme was brought in and also pointed out Pettersson from the 12 man line-up as the man she saw at the killing scene 300 metres further south from the cinema, at the Tunnelgatan Sveavägen junction. His is the face of the killer, she said. She remembered it clearly. Her testimony was, and is, the absolutely central statement in the whole prosecution of Pettersson. This was enough to put Pettersson in custody.

Months passed as the police gathered more evidence. Pettersson remained in custody. That is standard Swedish procedure. You are allowed to be in custody theoretically indefinitely, if the police think they have a strong case you are suspect and want more evidence, As long as they resubmit their application every two weeks to a court that you under suspicion. When the evidence the police gather is, they feel insufficient, they can just drop the prosecution. On this occasion, they felt they had a case. The trial began after Pettersson had been custody for six months. In July 1989, before a packed court, Pettersson was sentenced to life for the murder of Olof Palme. The case immediately went to appeal.

Was Pettersson the killer? The prosecution case rested on the following scenario: it was an unlucky coincidence for the Palme couple, a chance encounter with a crazed addict. That, loitering before or after visiting Sigge's club, and while hanging around waiting for his dealer, Sigge, who lived near the cinema, Pettersson spotted the Palmes at 9 pm heading into the Grand cinema. Palme, as the leading figure in Swedish public life, was a man for whom he harboured a deep hatred, on account of his general failure in life. Pettersson then went to fetch a revolver from somewhere, waited for them to emerge at 11 pm, tailed them to the murder scene 300 metres south, fired off two shots and then escaped unscathed up the Brunkeberg ridge steps.

It was a spontaneous, unpremeditated murder.

WHAT SPOKE against this theory? For one, witness testimonies, apart from Lisbet's, failed to identify Pettersson at the scene of the crime. That, among the 200 people that came out of the Grand cinema after the end of the movie, police were only able to find, by the time of the trial, two, Mårten Palme and Lars Erik Eriksson, to testify and identify Pettersson. That was factor in Pettersson's favour when Pettersson's conviction went to appeal. Another was that Pettersson was experienced in the use of knives. The "Bayonet Man" was his youthful moniker for his favourite robbery accessory, and which he had used, but Pettersson had never been seen handling a gun. Where would he have got the gun from – just like that – in the two hours between "spotting" the Palmes going into the Grand cinema and emerging after the end of the film? Another reason for scepticism: There was no obvious motive. Pettersson was not obviously political. He had no history of stalking the prime minister or sending him letters. There had been no altercation between the victim and Pettersson of the kind that might have provoked a spontaneous attack. The killer's dark clothes – knee length black coat, possible black roll-down cap – matched neither the clothes Pettersson habitually wore – a blue quilted nylon jacket that covered the bum - nor the clothes of the man pointed out near the Grand cinema as being Pettersson.

Twenty-four people – pedestrians, people in cars - were in the vicinity when the murder took place. None but Lisbet was able to identify Pettersson's face. Luck – or skill of disguise and restraint on the murderer's part? Restraint was not one of the characteristics associated with Pettersson, who was a volatile, impulsive and aggressive character, known to shove cameras back in news photographers' faces when being snapped.

Lisbet's identification of Pettersson at the murder scene was the crucial bit of evidence. However, there was nothing technical, like fingerprints or a weapon, to tie him to the killing. So his defence set about discrediting her testimony. Some of Lisbet's descriptions of the killer in the many sessions with the police before she was confronted with Pettersson were uncannily descriptive of the astonished Anders Björkman, the worse-for-wear architect who had walked a couple of steps behind the couple when he was shot. Was it Björkman's alarmed, frozen figure she saw staring at her when she looked up from her husband's fallen body, to call for help – rather than the killer's, who hadn't hung around?

Her clothes descriptions of the killer in her early witness testimonies to the police fitted Björkman's.

So why was she so sure she had seen him? According to Pettersson's defence lawyers, her pointing out of Pettersson in the line-up could then be explained away by the fact that the police had primed her, pre line-up, by saying the suspect looked like an alcoholic. Pettersson did, in fact, look different, more run down, than the other candidates who, as said, were all policeman drafted in from other parts of the Police House. A Swedish criminology academic had tested the line-up by showing photos of the confrontation to a group of college students in Seattle, where he was lecturing temporarily. The students knew nothing about the Palme case and the lecturer tested them. When he told them nothing but the fact that one of the twelve had killed Palme, one in twelve picked out Pettersson. The same statistic as if he had been selected at random. Then the lecturer gave the students one more piece of information, the same information Lisbet was given: the killer was an alcohol addict. Three-quarters of the students picked out Pettersson when statistically only a twelfth of them would. Pettersson obviously looked the "alcoholic".

It was true Lisbet was "sure" it was Pettersson she had seen. On the other hand, wrongful identifications do happen. Mistaken witness testimony is the leading source of miscarriages of justice, in both the UK and USA, academic studies have shown. In many cases, the witnesses were as totally convinced of their righteousness as Lisbet was. In many cases of mistaken identification, innocent men have been sentenced to long jail terms until DNA advances exonerated them. Police schools now teach that it is imperative that the police don't give any tip-offs that could pollute the chances of a successful identification in a witness line-up. And be aware that witnesses can get things; being convinced makes no difference. In this case, the Swedish police disregarded that.

Also – it was two and a half years between the murder and the witness line-up. Memories fade. It was a dark night. It happened quickly. The killer was fast. Lisbet was hysterical. How reliable was her pointing out in the witness line-up, really?

The lawyers for Pettersson's defence argued it was a terrible concatenation of confusion, public pressure for a result and poor police procedure that got Pettersson convicted, the defence in the appeal case argued. Finally, Ulf, away from the influence of his police interrogators, changed his story back, in open court. Pettersson's return time was now back to midnight, giving him an alibi again. Ulf told the court he had been put under enormous pressure from police interrogators and they had dangled the £5m (50 million kronor) reward for revealing information leading to Palme's killer in front of him, many times. Police corruption in other words. All this was enough to secure Pettersson's release on appeal, in 1989. One reason he was convicted in the first place, it was said later, was that the Swedish criminal justice system involved a mixture of laymen and professional jurists as the jury in the lower courts, but only professionally qualified judges as jurors in the appeal courts. The laymen, who are appointed on a political basis, had convicted Pettersson on the basis of their emotions against the wishes of the professionals in the lower court, who wanted Pettersson freed but were outvoted. The laymen wanted closure to the trauma and most were Social Democrats. Since they dominated parliament, Swedish law says Social Democrats must dominate the juries. But since the whole jury at the appeal level consisted of professional judges, they as such saw more clearly the legal weaknesses of the prosecution case and freed him.

After Pettersson's freedom, other factors emerged in his favour: Some of those who read all the interview transcripts of the entire investigation, "förundersökningen", available from the government stationers for a high price, found worrying the progress from uncertainty and confusion to certainty, the pressures and shaping of testimonies by police, and the winnowing out of witnesses who did not support the thesis. Although the transcripts were available to any member of the public, the photocopying costs for anyone so interested amounted to thousands of kronor, so few got that far. One who did read it, the writer and novelist PO Enquist, on commission for an evening newspaper, has penned one of the most thoughtful critiques of the murder. His whole host of doubts was aired in a very long newspaper column. One of the many things he questioned was the timing. If Pettersson's defence had raised this in the original trial, he might not even have been convicted in the first place.

The prosecutor's theory was that Pettersson took the 2346 commuter train from the central station. It was five minutes late, that is, the train left at 2351.The assassination happened at 23.21. Pettersson had, including the delay, half an hour to get to the central station. No reconstruction was ever made, even by the defence. The quickest possible route, theoretically, went east/south and double backing west. The killer headed east initially. However, he was spotted at a distance heading east even after the point at which he should have started double backing in order to make it to the train on time.

A simple calculation of time. The killer was heading east, in the wrong direction – away from the station. He could not have made it on the last train.

In any case, it was bizarre that not a single Stockholmer, on a night like this, saw the lunatic Pettersson, with his terrifying gaze and limping gait, this typical criminal character, in his sweaty twenty-minute flight from the crime scene to the central station. (Pettersson, as said, claimed he left central Stockholm earlier.)

OTHER OBSERVERS also picked holes in the prosecution's original case. A TV company had a bright idea to subject Pettersson to a polygraph test. He passed. He was asked on live television, "Did you kill Palme?" He got a generous fee for this, of course. Although some experts question polygraph tests' 100% scientific veracity, you could argue that Pettersson, free at that point, and, if guilty, would not have risked his liberty by the likelihood of failing the test. But he passed the test – and in a most convincing way too, said the expert attending. His nervous system and pulse reacted in such a way to suggest he was very strongly telling the truth when he denied any connection to the murder and had no idea who did it. West Germany's leading polygraph administrator, a scientist with decades of experience of using polygraphs in criminal cases.

And here was another important finding. Evidence emerged, from journalistic digging after Pettersson was set free, that witnesses had seen observations of fit men in their twenties wearing down jackets with walkie-talkies (This was years before the first mobile phones came into general use) in the vicinity of the areas where the Palme couple were walking that evening. People who had noticed this contacted an investigative news analysis programme that appeared on state radio. They said they had been completely ignored by the Palme investigators. The cops did not seem to care about their stories.

In time a pattern emerged. A dozen witnesses had seen men with walkie-talkies just in the vicinity of Palme's home in the old town. There were also a few observations near the murder scene before and after the assassination. Of course, there was scope for error, wrote journalist Lars Borgnäs – a journalist for Swedish television who made some groundbreaking documentaries on "alternative theses" - later when analysing the murder. Some of the sightings might well have been mistaken. But none of them were given any rational explanation.

In one instance, there was a person who had seen a man with a walkie-talkie standing along on a parallel street to Västerlånggatan, near the Palme couple's home, about an hour before the Palmes set out for the cinema. The man looked like a cop in civilian clothes, the man told his companions. The police showed no interest in this observation.

In another instance, there was the middle-aged woman who had seen two men with walkie-talkies standing inside Gamla Stan (old town) metro station immediately before the couple arrived to catch a metro to the Grand Cinema. One of them looked like a "security police kind of guy", she thought. The explanation that the police eventually came up with, that the men were two transport cops, proved not to check out. The men remain, as of today, unidentified.

There was a woman living at Drottninggatan street just two blocks from the murder scene who saw, through her window, a single man sitting in a car and talking on a walkie-talkie a few blocks from the murder scene some minutes before the film was due to end. He said "I can see them" and sped off. Even here, the police's official explanation, that it was a security guard from a commercial company, turned out to be false. The security guard denied he had ever been there and the details the witness had noticed about the car excluded the possibility the car could be from the security firm. The man was never found.

Yet another walkie-talkie sighting. There was a middle-aged man in the company of his wife who had left a bingo hall 150 metres from the murder scene just a minute before the murder. They then saw a fit young military looking man coming, half jogging, from the direction of the murder, speaking into a walkie-talkie. The police asked the witness whether the stranger had a foreign appearance. He denied this and said he looked Nordic. He was not even asked to show, in situ, where he had made his observation.

IN ALL THESE and several other cases the witnesses were reasonable, trustworthy people who could give detailed descriptions of what they had seen. f they were part of the murder plan, then the murder was clearly not a random killing by a crazed, lone drunk like Pettersson. Unfortunately, the official investigation simply denied the existence of these walkie-talkie observations. Mind ghosts, the prosecution said. But they were convincing and numerous. If these men had honest motives – if, for instance, as some suggested, that they were undercover policemen, on another job like drugs surveillance in central Stockholm – why hadn't this activity been made public to scotch the pesky conspiracy theories that arose? But no explanation for these walkie-talkie observations ever emerged. In fact, their existence was frequently denied. Ingemar Krusell, the deputy chief of the investigation, wrote the main protocol for Christer Pettersson prosecution in 1989. There he stated that there was "no evidence that the Palme couple were under observation."

This was repeated in a book – a kind of standard text for Pettersson-is-guilty believers - he wrote about the Palme murder in 1998 where he constructed a case for Pettersson's guilt. At least two recent books on the Palme murder lean on Krusell's book to argue Pettersson was guilty.

However, I emailed Krusell in 2011 to ask some questions about the assassination. (I had an introduction from a common writer friend.) He wrote back and said, sure go ahead with some questions. I asked whether he still held the view there were no walkie-talkie sightings as he had in his book from 1998. I never had another reply from him.

After his release from prison in December 1989, free on appeal, Pettersson celebrated with an orgy of drinking on his compensation money from the state. He had been in custody for six months; in prison for another six months. The shrewd writer PO Enquist argued Pettersson actually enjoyed the whole circus:

"Pettersson had a good year inside. He came in from loneliness to the warmth that surrounds a regicide. Since he was innocent he probably had no problems with his conscience, either. I am working on the principle that he was innocent. If he was guilty it certainly is not demonstrated by this gigantic, grotesque and in every way depressing trial as mirrored in the investigative material."

"So he had had a good year. It was the big year of his life: his year as a 'killer'. Now he is out, and he will probably drink himself to death."

Written in 1991, Enquist's words were prophetic. In 2004, Pettersson did die, from a fall after leaving a hospital, where he had been taken in after a drinking bout. Enquist reasoned, from reading the full interrogations with all of Stockholm's underworld types, that it was the drug dealer Sigge, fed up with always being nagged and threatened by Pettersson to give him free amphetamines who, together with the police, led the police on to the Pettersson trail. And that some of his sidekicks gave false witness testimony at the trial. From all the material I have read, that rings true. One cannot, of course, be 100% sure...

After being forced to let go of Pettersson, in late 1989, when he was released on appeal, the police were back to square one. And there, 25 years on, after a few trips to South Africa and a second, failed attempt to get Pettersson, they still remain. There has been an unwillingness or an inability to make another theory, with other assailants, stand up to the level where it could be taken to a prosecution. Some policemen in the "Palme room" wanted to work all out on alternative theories, but the murder investigation bosses were mentally stuck on Pettersson, and that limited efforts in other areas. It was as if focusing on the familiar Stockholm petty crime underworld, thinking of the Palme murder as just another crime, was something the Stockholm crime police were used to, and continued with that. There is evidence to suggest that the police were blocked by the Swedish government even from looking at the CIA trail. After Pettersson was released, the deputy chief of the investigation declared defiantly. "The courts may have freed him. But in a police sense, the murder is solved." In other words, Pettersson may have been released. But the police "know" it is him., only it could not be proved beyond reasonable doubt in a legal environment.

Many Swedes agree with the police, despite the indications that Pettersson is innocent. After all, since no one else has been put to trial, it must have been him, right? The ins and outs of the trial were complicated. Police never presented any serious alternative theories after his release, so his name stuck in the public's awareness. The Swedish public's trust in the authorities is very high compared to other countries. A lot of people find Lisbet's pointing out of Pettersson the fact that decided the case for them. Ingvar Carlsson, Palme's successor as prime minister, in connection with the Palme murder's 25th anniversary, in 2011, told Swedish radio he was "absolutely convinced Christer Pettersson murdered Olof Palme."

Earlier he had been cautious about commenting on the assassination because he did not want to interfere with the legal situation. There was a theoretical possibility Pettersson might be brought to trial again, if they found a murder weapon that somehow could be linked to him – finding this was the Holy Grail for the diminishing number of policemen on the case. But in 2004 Pettersson, who had carried on living a park bench drinking existence, died, so now he felt free to speak out, "I know Lisbet extremely well, and she has a fantastic gift of observation," said Carlsson. Is this statement to be trusted? On another, much earlier occasion, he had also admitted. "It is probably best for Sweden if it was a lone, drunken killer and not a planned murder." Did he genuinely believe that Pettersson had done it, or was it a strategic remark, for the fear that the true story of the assassination of Olof Palme would be so much worse from the point of view of the interests of the Swedish nation and state?

OTHER THEORIES

Since the police were still stuck on Pettersson, alternative solutions came from journalists and private investigators. They took neglected witnesses, people who had seen something strange on the night. They re-examined work dismissed by the police, since police cover-up, as said, was one of the earliest conspiracy theories. The truth no doubt was out there somewhere. Some of the alternative theorists were respectable journalists, but most of them contributed to the confusion. If you vacuumed the area within two kilometres of the Sveavägen Tunnelgatan junction at 11 pm on a Friday night in a big city like Stockholm, you will

get a whole gallery of characters. Throw a number of plausible oddballs
into the mix – 130 have confessed to the murder so far – and you get a lot
of a stories. A confusing number of stories, which may help the murderer.
False trails, frustrations, false conspiracy theories mixed up – maybe –
with the real story, but can't tell the bad trails from the good trails in this,
the most extensive and quantitatively substantial of the world's murder
mysteries. Yet it could be addictive to follow this large, metastasised,
spaghetti ball of a story.

Lars Borgnäs, who followed up the initial walkie-talkie trails for
Swedish Radio and then for Swedish state television, SVT, has been the
leading campaigner with credibility for an alternative theory. With
immense patience, he has made a number of programmes and written
books over the course of 20 years that pick apart the Christer Pettersson
trail and argues for other alternatives, He is better than most. Gunnar
Wall, an investigative journalist from Uppsala, is another extremely lucid
sceptic of the Pettersson trail, author of several books on the subject.

They are at one end of the scale, and then there are the crackpots,
lunatics. One day I go along to ABF House, the workers' education
movement centre, in Sveavägen, right next to the churchyard where
Palme was buried, two doors along on the other side from the Grand
Cinema. Here, once a year, the freelance Palme theorisers for many years
coordinated with each other in an annual conference, fuelling the flames
of conspiracy, in these finely panelled rooms named after the great
figures of Social Democracy, Branting, Erlander, where they would
confer. They would take breaks in the corridors, and lean back against
neatly painted walls, next to South American political murals, black and
white photos of solid Swedish agitators in simpler times. These days the
passion among the private investigators has faded away, the chief
organiser has died, and the Palme researchers – often retired middle-class
men whose wives were probably happy to have them out of the house -
become discredited or bored. You can read a lot of their stuff on the net,
on web pages written in old code. Ten or 15 years ago they would
probably have brought their thick manuscripts to these annual meetings.
Some of them were very active and very imaginative. Others were
agnostic, just along for the experience, and more or less normal. It was
the extremists who attracted my attention initially.

One evening in February 2014, I walk around the centre, briefly
attending a meeting devoted to the inequalities in the Stockholm housing
situation – where the egalitarian Palme era was favourably referenced -
and have a coffee in the kebab restaurant next door, I check my notes of
these guys' internet work. If I understand it correctly, one theory
involved the arms manufacturer Bofors, nuclear power and cocaine.

Another theorist also believed Palme was homosexual.
Homosexuality is a recurring claim and that, unlike other parts of planet
conspiracy, is not completely outlandish. I too have heard rumours that

Palme was gay or bisexual and that there exist photographs of him, taken by another of his girlfriends, Eva Rudling, dressed in women's clothes.

FROM WHAT I heard, the lively conspiracy meetings towards the end – I think they ended in the early 2000s – got a bit out of hand. The theories got wilder and wilder. Yet another, rather outlandish, theory was not only was Palme shot by his son, but that Palme was complicit in this. In other words, he planned and staged his own death, with his family pulling the trigger. Six months before the assassination, the great Russian filmmaker Andrei Tarkovsky, in fact, shot his nuclear apocalypse scene for his final film the Sacrifice at Tunnelgatan. (It was made in Sweden, Tarkovsky having been exiled from his homeland.) You can see the famous steps in the film, amid the devastation of wrecked cars and furniture. This was no coincidence! said some conspiracy theorists. Palme and Tarkovsky knew each other (which was true); Tarkovsky had pleaded with the Swedish premier to get his son out of the Soviet Union (which was also true). So they had struck a deal…I get your son out. You film the place where I will be killed six months later. By my son and wife.

You could see the psychological need for this among some of the elderly "private investigators". The more time they spent on the case, the more important it was to make the solution more and more extraordinary. Senility could not be discounted.

Journalists have had a lot of fun at the outré Palme researchers' expense.

A journalist called Robert Aschberg used to hang out with these Palme researchers and has described amusingly and almost affectionately one occasion when Christer Pettersson turned up. Eight of them sat down for lunch and Aschberg described the kinds of debates that were taking place. One private investigator denied the bullets came from a 357. It was just a red herring. Pettersson meanwhile drank two rums and cokes The private investigators asked Pettersson who he thought the killer was. "The P2," suggested Pettersson. The private investigators listened devoutly. P2 was the Italian lodge closely connected to the mafia as well the top of the Christian Democrat party in Italy. Pettersson ordered a new rum and cola while the youngest present asked whether Palme liked Pamela Anderson. Pettersson said no. Pettersson then told an unfunny sex joke and explained he took amphetamines to get horny.

Another private investigator said the whole thing was a Dreyfus affair. The Palme researchers didn't quite understand Pettersson's dirty jokes interwoven with lines of philosophy or tales of Life Inside. They were interested in the details of the murder but Pettersson was not really in the mood. He was more interested in talking about card games. Whist, Poker, Chicago.

They all talked about their pet theories. But nothing quite jelled thought Aschberg. The whole lunch developed into a kind of Ionesco play. Some told complicated theories, others told jokes about penises.

"I have only killed one person," said Pettersson. "That was at the beginning of the seventies." That was the reference to the bayonet killing. The investigators asked how much Pettersson could drink and Pettersson said a bottle of vodka straight down in one from the Systembolaget, the state liquor store. Then they all took turns to be photographed next to him, after a few pulls at his fringe with a steel comb. Then he ambled off to the subway.

As the above anecdote shows, the public tended to take the Palme researchers not quite seriously, often treated as idiots, occasionally with indulgent affection. One of the best reviewed Swedish cinema films of 2012 features one of Sweden's best-known action TV detectives from the 1980s and 90s, called Hassel, a kind of macho Miami vice cop - as the same cop, (and same actor, 20 years older) now retired, lonely and extremely depressed. He plays a very different role from the action man of the original series. It is an ironic commentary on Sweden's best-known detective, in a different style, with a different director, not really a sequel. There is no crime to solve. It's a fake documentary purporting to show Hassel's life after retirement. His career as a freelance investigator devoted to the Palme murder, a privatspanare.

Hassel attends hobby association meetings with uncombed hair and a shabby jacket, then attends regular meetings with privatspanare (played by actors since this was a fiction film), and the film climaxes in a detailed and rather poignant re-enactment in the snow at Sveavägen on the anniversary of the murder, complete with witnesses, played by other obsessives in Hassel's group. All accurately, as far as I could tell. The leader of the group coordinating the movements with a stopwatch of his witnesses in exact accordance with what actually took place, with someone's battered old Volvo estate a stand-in for the ambulance. It was funny to see these old men, on a dark and snowy night shuffling from one position in the snow to the next, acting out the roles of those who were out on the town on the actual night in 1986. The actual witnesses having shown no interest in reappearing for TV anniversaries or anything else.

It was really a film about old men and loneliness in 21st century Sweden, with little plot and no resolution, shot grainily in the faux documentary style, a deliberate contrast to the garish car chase movie action of the original Hassel. The film's subtitle was "Hassel's last job." The young film school graduate said he wanted to make a postmodern style "anti-cop chase film".

The false documentary also featured a real private investigator, ex-Dagens Nyheter journalist Sven Aner, 92 years old, in a cameo role. Aner is not quite as on the ball as Borgnäs and or two others, but he did write one or two important books immediately after the murder. He continues to write books, which are not quite up to the early standards. But his broader thesis is exactly that of Borgnäs. The trouble is, when he mutters it in the Hassel film, out of context and mocked, he comes across as a lunatic. And I, what do I, think?

THE SOLUTION?

Let us go back to the last political term of Palme, and particularly the last year, of Palme's life, and go into more detail about the number of political affairs he was subjected to, and what amounts to almost a hate campaign in the media from certain sectors of Swedish society traditionally hostile to leftist Social Democracy. Information has come to light that puts the tough time he had into context, and allows us to formulate a hypothesis.

When you seek to destroy your opponent, in the history of western covert operations in enemy countries, after the war, assassination is only the last step, sometimes. Psychological and political warfare operations might be tried first, using brought journalists, to discredit an opponent so they might lose the next democratic election. Manipulation of the political process, through leaning on senior figures in the political system, is next. If that fails, an internal coup, from party members or the military is the step after that. Only then might an assassination be contemplated.

According to American writer and intelligence historian William Blum, the CIA has tried to overthrow, successfully or unsuccessfully, 50 governments since the war. Most of them in the third world. But even the maverick Australian leftist Gough Whitlam was pressured by the CIA for a foreign policy that was not a million miles away from Palme's: reining in the country's own secret services' collaboration with the CIA; calling for the diplomatic recognition of North Vietnam.

Some of the evidence in Blum's book is highly circumstantial. You could also look at sources with a sceptical eye: for instance, his account of subversion by the CIA of the Jamaican Labour party leader Michael Manley in the seventies seems to derive principally from one (admittedly serious-minded) long article by two investigative journalists in (the admittedly occasionally aspirationally serious) Penthouse magazine.

In the regime changes that Blum provides the details for, often the instigator is some domestic faction – typically the military, sometimes powerful people in business, so that it is not clear whether the CIA is a bystander, passive supporter of events, or driving force. As is inevitable when researching the clandestine, the historian's work is a question of joining the dots between firm facts, bridging it with guesswork and assumption. All history is detective work, and much more of an art form than maybe even historians admit to laymen. Research into intelligence activities all the more so.

But let us set aside Blum's book for the moment. To stick to certainties, and avoid allegations that is one a speculator or conspiracy theorist, one need only stick to coup events the CIA itself has admitted to.

THE AGENCY went through a great period of scrutiny and self-examination in the 1970s, in the wake of the sense of self-doubt that gripped the United States after the moral debacles of Watergate and the Vietnam War. The Church hearings – led by Senator Frank Church - in US Congress followed a number of reports in the media from investigative reporters and were meant as a kind of democratic political reckoning with the agency's clandestine activities between the start of the cold war and the seventies. CIA officers were questioned under oath and the CIA's own documentation and papers were turned upside down. The biggest controversies were assassinations or alleged assassination attempts. Looked at were rumours of CIA assassination plots against Patrice Lumumba of the Congo, Rafael Trujillo of the Dominican Republic, the Diem brothers in Vietnam and Fidel Castro. After strenuous questioning on the record of CIA officials, the Senate committee found:

"that the U.S. initiated plots to assassinate Fidel Castro and Patrice Lumumba. In the other cases, either U.S. involvement was indirect or evidence was too inconclusive to issue a finding. In Lumumba's case, the Committee asserted that the U.S. was not involved in his death, despite earlier plotting. The Committee was unable to state with certainty whether any plots were authorized by U.S. Presidents."

In the case of Lumumba, the firebrand leftist leader of newly independent Congo in 1960, two CIA agents were asked by superiors to assassinate Lumumba, the Church committee could reveal. Poisons were sent to Congo and some exploratory steps were taken toward gaining access to Lumumba. However, in early 1961, Lumumba was killed by Congolese rivals, so the US was not involved in the killing.

In the case of Castro, US intelligence personnel plotted to kill Castro over a course of five years, the Church committee's investigation found. "American underworld figures and Cubans hostile to Castro were used in all these plots, and were provided encouragement and material support by the United States." All these plots failed, obviously, as Fidel Castro died in his bed aged 90 last year.

In other cases, for instance, Ngo Dinh Diem, leader of the US-backed Republic of South Vietnam, who, was killed on 2 November 1963 in the course of a South Vietnamese generals' coup there was "no evidence US officials favoured an assassination". However, the United States government "supported the coup". It seems "Diem's assassination was not part of the generals' pre-coup planning but was instead a spontaneous act during the coup and was carried out without the US government's support or involvement".

But if the CIA's involvement in assassinations on a scale that some intelligence historians imply is not supported by the Church Committee – which is likely to be on the cautious side, admittedly – killings only represent, as said, the very small apotheosis of the full range of destabilisation activities aimed at hostile regimes.

For instance, in Chile, the Church committee writes that the CIA mounted a huge political warfare campaign to discredit and eventually unseat Salvador Allende – even though the agency never tried to go as far as assassinate him:

"Covert United States involvement in Chile in the decade between 1963 and 1973 was extensive and continuous. The Central Intelligence Agency spent three million dollars in an effort to influence the outcome of the 1964 Chilean presidential elections. Eight million dollars was spent, covertly, in the three years between 1970 and the military coup in September 1973, with over three million dollars expended in the fiscal year 1972 alone."

The Church committee's final report continues:

"What did covert CIA money buy in Chile? It financed activities covering a broad spectrum, from simple propaganda manipulation of the press to large-scale support for Chilean political parties, from public opinion polls to direct attempts to foment a military coup. The scope of 'normal' activities of the CIA Station in Santiago included placement of Station-dictated material in the Chilean media through propaganda assets, direct support of publications, and efforts to oppose communist and left-wing influence in student, peasant and labour organizations – in addition to these 'routine' activities, the CIA Station in Santiago was several times called upon to undertake large, specific projects."

"Moreover, the bare figures are more likely to understate than to exaggerate the extent of U.S. covert action." The CIA's own historians later complemented the Church report with their own monograph, available on the CIA's own website, cia.gov, in which the agency readily admits to the Chile operations. "In the 1960s and the early 1970s, as part of the US Government policy to try to influence events in Chile, the CIA undertook specific covert action projects in Chile. Those hereby acknowledged are described below. The overriding objective—firmly rooted in the policy of the period—was to discredit Marxist-leaning political leaders, especially Dr Salvador Allende, and to strengthen and encourage their civilian and military opponents to prevent them from assuming power."

The agency funded three separate military groups to get rid of Allende, and armed one of them. One of the groups then went on to assassinate General Schneider, a moderate military commander of the Chilean armed forces, who wanted to play by the rulebook.

"The US Government and the CIA were aware of and agreed with Chilean officers' assessment that the abduction of General Rene Schneider, the Chilean Army's Commander in September 1970, was an essential step in any coup plan. We have found no information, however, that the coup plotters' or CIA's intention was that the general be killed in any abduction effort. Schneider was a strong supporter of the Chilean Constitution and a major stumbling block for military officers seeking to carry out a coup to prevent Allende from being inaugurated."

The Church committee was not exhaustive. The Committee only covered CIA covert action from 1945 to 1974, and probably not even all of these.

Groups of academics at the National Security archive project at George Washington University have used freedom of information requests to build up pictures of CIA covert actions in other places around the world since the Church Committee Hearings. Writers and journalists such as Bob Woodward of the Washington Post and Tim Weiner of the New York Times have also filled in some gaps about the CIA's actions since 1974 in books like Veil and the Legacy of Ashes, based on interviews with former officers and examination of CIA archives. (Much classified material remains, though.)

Just to take an example, the coup against the president of Brazil, Joao Goulart, in 1964.

Peter Kornbluh, a director at the National Security Archives in Washington, and a historian and author, writes in 2014 that the speculation about whether to overthrow the democratically elected Social Democrat Brazilian president began back in 1962, two years before the coup which eventually took place.

TRANSCRIPTIONS OF the White House's secret tape recording system reveal, as Kornbluh uncovers, how Kennedy became increasingly hostile to the presence of "Anti-American" radicals in Brazilian president Goulart's government and looked to give help to the Brazilian military to overthrow him. At White House meetings on July 30, 1962, and on March 8 and October 7, 1963, tapes record how US officials discussed how to force Goulart to purge leftists or he would be removed from power in a US-backed coup.

On July 30, 1962, US ambassador Lincoln Gordon told the president: "I think one of our important jobs is to strengthen the spine of the military." "We may very well want them [the Brazilian military] to take over at the end of the year if they can," Kennedy's political aid Robert Goodwin suggested, on tape.

The National Security Council, presided over by President Kennedy, met at the end of 1962 and concluded that, while a coup should be held under consideration, the opponents of Goulard currently lacked the will to overthrow him. For the moment, peaceful attempts to modify Goulart's political orientation should be continued, the council recommended.

However that sentiment began to shift after JFK's brother Robert was dispatched to Brazil and was unimpressed by Goulart, complaining of "signs of Communist or extreme left-wing nationalists' infiltration into civilian government positions."

The ambassador to Brazil wrote a long, top-secret memo saying that, unless Goulart would change his ways, US should work "to prepare the most promising possible environment for his replacement by a more desirable regime".

The transcripts of Robert Kennedy's meetings with the president show him to be the most forceful about operations against Brazil. He asked the president to "personally" clarify to Goulart that he "can't have the communists and put them in important positions and make speeches criticizing the United States and at the same time get 225-250 million dollars from the United States. He can't have it both ways."

Meanwhile, in Brazil, there were growing plots from the right wing against the president, Kennedy wondered aloud whether the CIA would have to depose the President directly. "Do you see a situation where we might be—find it desirable to intervene militarily ourselves?"

They settled for help to the local military.

Ambassador Lyndsey Gordon apparently feared a Communist revolution, and to help the rumoured coup along he argued for the US to take measures "soonest to prepare for a clandestine delivery of arms of non-US origin, to be made available to [coup leader] Castello Branco supporters in Sao Paulo."

In a cable declassified in 2004, Gordon recommended that these weapons be "pre-positioned prior any outbreak of violence," to be used by paramilitary units and "friendly military against hostile military if necessary." To maintain deniability over the US role, Gordon recommended the arms be delivered via "unmarked submarine to be off-loaded at night in isolated shore spots in the state of Sao Paulo south of Santos."

According to Gordon's diplomatic cables, the CIA had already carried out covert operations "to help strengthen resistance forces" in Brazil, including underhand support for pro-Democracy street rallies and help for anti-Communist sentiment among trade unions and church groups.

In another memo, National Security Advisor McGeorge Bundy told a meeting of high-level officials three days before the coup, "is such that we should not be worrying that the [Brazilian] military will react; we should be worrying that the military will not react."

The picture we have of what happened next is limited by the fact covert actions of CIA agents in Brazil at that time of the coup remain "deeply classified" fifty years later, Kornbluh complained in 2014. But we can hypothesise the US did likely have some involvement, based on these discussions and preparations before the dates covered by deep classification..

We have seen that the CIA was able to destabilise powerful Latin American middle-income countries led, in Brazil's case, by a Social Democrat, same as Palme's party. What about cover ops in Europe? This is much more sensitive, there is even less publicly available material. Some writers on the CIA, though, have found evidence of how the CIA funded some newspapers and political parties on the continent to avoid Communism succeeded in countries such as Italy. Blum argues that, for instance, the Greek junta's coup in 1967 had CIA fingerprints, and there were covert operations into the 1970s in other European countries under the codename Gladio. There is a frustrating lack of detail about what went against these US allies. Such absorbing material as exists remains almost certainly also in deep classification. (If it hasn't been burned) We would have to go the other route: look at indications, make guesses, from other sources of evidence.

GRO HARLEM Brundtland, the onetime prime minister of Norway, is a senior witness to the stresses Palme was living under in his last year. Berggren, his biographer, has also written that, in the summer of 1985, the "many years at the centre of politics, and the tough attacks, had left their mark on Palme". "In the final TV debate before the 1985 election, the Swedish people were able to see a tired and grey prime minister...his ability to focus and push away unpleasant matters also seems to have abandoned him. Journalists who interviewed him might suddenly find him looking out of the window, completely absorbed in other thoughts."

Another biographer, Kjell Östberg, was told by Lisbeth Palme that she was woken up by her husband one night. He had just had a bad dream. The plane he was travelling in was about to crash and he had to get out into the wing to fix the fault. One of his cabinet ministers told Östberg that "Palme's tolerance reserves were completely exhausted. That was my first impression when I came into government." One source of difficulty was the young Carl Bildt, challenging Palme about the intrusions of "Soviet submarines" and accusing Palme of being weak on security and appeasing of the Soviet Union. Göransson said: "Everyone in government – to a man – said: 'Ignore him'. Palme replied: 'No, we have to..;

He perked up though, when, in the company of his girlfriend, Cambridge academic and peace campaigner Emma Rothschild, then in her thirties, who had a flat in Stockholm just a few blocks away from Lisbet's and Olof's flat in the old town, he animatedly discussed the merits – and mostly demerits – of Reagan, Thatcher and Neoliberalism. He was tired of the daily grind of politics. He was still interested in engaging in the debate of ideas.

But he was also a frightened man, frightened by the enemies that his position as prime minister had created as never before. In the past, he had never strayed from controversy; indeed, had relished it. In his youth, political courage and the joy of battle had always been hallmarks. So this marked a change.

Brundtland, opposition leader in Norway in the mid-1980s, was a close friend and political ally of Olof Palme, and esteemed member of his peace commission.

She noticed the fear in the man on a flight to New Delhi from Frankfurt. The work on his peace commission continued. He had less energy to devote to it than while in opposition, but still, a few times a year, he flew to far-flung places to debate with the other statesmen on the future of peace. His work had arguably become less relevant now that Reagan and Gorbachev were talking to each other. Still, he continued searching for solutions to peace. Gorbachev's arrival in power had led to one of the senior members of his commission, Georgi Arbatov, being welcomed in from the cold. Georgi Arbatov having been a bit of a pariah in the Brezhnev and Andropov years; now the Moscow think tank intellectual was serving as a useful conduit for Palme's – and other European doves' - ideas into Gorbachev's circles,

THAT LAST conversation stuck in the Norwegian's mind. It was January 1986, just a few weeks before his murder.

Brundtland and Palme discussed the pressures of office, as she recalls in her eponymous memoirs. "We talked about threats, from the right, not least in Sweden, which created an environment of total hostility aimed at Social Democracy and its leader Olof Palme."

You saw the same trends in Norway, she wrote, but it was much stronger in Sweden. The polarisation was much stronger. Carl Bildt, Olof Palme himself, contributed through their debating style to a tone of debate which pushed in that direction. She added:

"We were also aware that this was an international movement. There were forces working across national borders who aimed their hatred at Scandinavian Social Democracy."

"On one occasion, the Palme commission met in Chicago where a group of people had gathered in front of the hotel with hate-filled placards aimed at Olof Palme. His name was for them equivalent to World Communism. Olof said he also had other experiences of this kind that made him anxious. He had for some time noticed certain repeated faces appearing in different places in Sweden and sometimes abroad when he held speeches at large gatherings. Sometimes his assistants knew who they were, others they didn't and he couldn't deny it…if it made him feel better he tried to push it away from himself"

Brundtland wrote: "I saw the fear in his eyes, and I never forgot it."

Probably many of the domestic the political attacks against Palme – well documented in mainstream literature and newspaper coverage at the time - fed off each other, created an internal momentum, but was there, in addition, an external source, an actuator? A memo sent to a journalist which later found its way into the public domain. It is undoubtedly genuine in that the writer, a retired intelligence operative called Ulf Lingärde, wrote it, and believed what he wrote. He argued that leading figures in Swedish industry, intelligence and military – including the signals intelligence service – formed a loose network against the threat of communism. (Recall that the CIA, in Latin America, liked to work through local, often military, critics of national leaders that displeased the US government.)

IN A LONG, chatty letter, rambling and comprehensive, with a surfeit of unverifiable details about intelligence networks existing in various parts of Swedish society, he stated something explosive.

There was an organisation comprising elements of the right that had formed to oust Palme. It started because of worries that an official inside the Swedish foreign ministry was a Soviet spy, and so this committee for psychological defence published a thinly disguised book of fiction that pointed this fellow out as a spy. The turning point was when one member of the network, a professor of East bloc studies at a Swedish university, became convinced Palme was a spy, based on examination of Palme's work for his peace commission and reports of various Soviet intelligence activities in Sweden. Several leading members of the network – intelligence chiefs, military commanders, business leaders - coalesced and gave themselves a name called "the Freedom Movement".

Lingärde is long dead. He died relatively young, at 58, but no evidence has come to light that he died of anything but natural causes. One yearns to ask questions about the letter: there are too many details peripheral to the substance of the claim, too little on the central elements. How much did he know, and how much did it was plausible secret information about the organisation of the Swedish intelligence services added to speculation about the murder? There exists a transcript in the Palme commission – which looked into police work on the killing in 1999 and found it wanting – where Lingärde talks around the same subject, makes similar claims. Did such a movement exist, and did it, in turn, have a relationship with an intelligence agency abroad, likely one in the West? How responsible was it for the media attacks on Palme, which spread into a generalised atmosphere of hostility towards the man, in little magazine, the finer dining room tables in the land, even in schoolyards. Creating an intellectual atmosphere is a central part of propaganda. We will recall that the US government funded propaganda targets in Latin America as a means of unseating by buying off local journalists.

Feelings of hostility were common in officers' messes and police stations. A small circulation magazine called Contra contained right-wing propaganda against the Soviet Union. It was a popular read among officers. One of its covers from 1984 included a picture of Palme on the cover as a devil's caricature framed by a cut-out target pattern, The picture was "circulated among the right wing as an enjoyable summer pastime idea, perfect for owners of dart sets, air rifles, service pistols and others." The point about service pistols was the reference to the fact that many of Contra's readers were in the military.

Articles in the magazine said he was "Moscow's henchman" and called him a traitor. A cartoon in another issue had Palme covering his eyes, sitting on a small island surrounded by submarine periscopes. The message: Palme was blind to Soviet activities. The organisation sold dart boards by mail order with Palme's portrait on it, so that officers and policeman could get an outlet for their dislike on coffee breaks in the mess. An organisation popular with officers, but also oddballs, was called the European Workers' party, the EAP, a fringe sect funded by an eccentric US millionaire called Lyndon LaRouche. One Washington Post article from 1985 said the group had some supporters within the CIA in Washington.

It published a monthly magazine where Palme could be described thus. "The Swedish people are ruled by a lunatic, a mentally disturbed murderer who appears out of the dark, frozen winter's evening and advances on his victim with an axe".

The organisation, apparently well-funded, was able to spread its messages through newspapers and civic organisations and appeared at Palme's public meetings with their book table. They used to stand outside his block of flats in the old town and Palme and his wife often used their staff to try and look for new ways of walking to work so he wouldn't be harassed by them, writes one of Palme's biographers, Kjell Östberg.

The submarine intrusions doubtless played a part. Every time the Navy failed in yet another hunt, the impotence in the Swedish response seemed to impel the military type and Russophobes to look for someone to blame. Palme was a convenient target.

But Palme's reputation was also damaged by a regular sequence of "political affairs" between 1982 and 1985, in the mainstream media, so much more extensive than Contra's reach, all orchestrated by one man, a conservative journalist who later became Carl Bildt's head of information. Lars Christiansson was described as a "politician who pretended to be a journalist" by colleagues.

Christiansson's campaigns were all aimed at damaging the credibility of Palme's foreign policy by implying he was soft on the Soviet Union. The implication could be that he was working for the Soviets. As such, there are also parallels in Sweden's own history:

We talked in the first chapters of the two Swedens: pacifist leftist Sweden, and conservative aristocratic Sweden, where Russophobia was rampant. Palme had, in a sense crossed from the latter group to the former group. By talking with the Soviet Union, he offended some of the deepest beliefs of what remained of the upper class and military sector of Swedish society, the sectors which had wanted to side with the Kaiser in

WW1 and the Nazis in WW2 to go on the unprovoked attack against Russia.

THE FIRST of Lars Christiansson's campaigns against Palme was the Ferm affair in 1983, when Palme was accused of creating a back channel with the Soviets to assure them that his diplomatic protest following the Hårsfjarden submarine intrusion was not meant to be taken seriously. Lars Christiansson first broke the story in Svenska Dagbladet. The evidence was a letter he was supposed to have sent to Arbatov, via his UN ambassador. The scandal rumbled on, and eventually Palme was forced to read the letter on live television, revealing that the interpretation of events that he had maintained all along to the media– that the letter continued nothing in private which Palme had not already communicated in public, that Palme promised very robust responses if the Soviets continued intruding. Östberg argues that Palme closed the scandal by improving his position in the opinion polls.

THE SECOND scandal, in 1985, involved discussions at a dinner party involving Palme's foreign minister, Lennart Bodström, and five reporters. The substance of the conversation at the dinner party was that Bodström did not think the evidence for the Navy's belief the submarines were Soviet held water. He also argued for a realistic position in foreign affairs. Different countries had different regimes, and you had to deal with them as they were, not as you would wish them to be.

As such, he was just arguing the standard realist position in politics, practised diplomats of all ages every day, but it went against the Reagan administration's delegitimisation efforts of the Soviet regime, as well as the Swedish right's desires to treat the Soviet Union as a pariah.

Five of the reporters got together to write similar articles, breaching the off the record rule. Christiansson organised it: one reporter stood outside the cabal, and published a record of Bodström's conversation that was much less incriminating of Bodström's credibility than the other five. Palme was forced to step in and defend his inexperienced but honest foreign minister, but that did not prevent the parliament from holding a vote of no confidence in the foreign minister, almost unheard of in Swedish history. Bodström survived, but, again, it gave the impression Palme was on the defensive for a nuclear disarmament policy based on mutual commitment of the superpowers to common security, which itself was based on the idea of treating the Soviet Union as a rational, if non-democratic, partner.

A third attack on Palme took place in the autumn of 1985, when Christiansson rounded up a number of navy officers who had been chasing submarines, without success. He interviewed them and got them to say things like they did not trust Palme. It was followed by a number of articles in the Swedish press from navy officers where it was speculated whether Sweden was a dictatorship, following a meme that was current at a time and discussed in earlier chapters.

Palme responded by making his strongest ever speech in favour of absolute neutrality, at the Foreign Affairs Institute in Stockholm on 12 December 1985. It must have been a red rag to the bull to the pro-NATO, intensely russophobe, elements of the Swedish military.

Christiansson's biggest coup against Palme was the Harvard affair. In 1984, Palme had given a speech at the venerable American university's school of international affairs. He declined a fee but when the university offered his son a year's scholarship he accepted that. When his tax return came in, he did not declare it as income, which meant that, according to the tax office, he enjoyed a benefit on which he did not pay tax. It was Bildt – Christiansson's later employer, Palme's nemesis - who was tipped off by an old school friend, who was now working at Harvard. The Moderates sat on the information, then found an outlet. A friendly journalist was tipped off and was able to ask Palme during a live radio interview. Palme was enraged at being ambushed. His failure to declare the benefit went through the courts and contributed to Palme's depression in the autumn of 1985. He was cleared after his death.

Were these attacks on Palme – funnelled through Christiansson – planned by the psychological operations part of the shady network of industrialists and military men that Lingärde talked about? If it was a coordinated intelligence operation to do Palme down, was it solely domestic or was there was an international angle? I heard from at least one journalist, Anders Hasselbohm, that Christiansson, Bildt's right-hand man, was a CIA asset.

The suggestion that the West may have wanted to do Palme down is strengthened by the revelation, in research in the 1990s and 2000s that at least some of the many submarine intrusions in the eighties were by NATO submarines. There is plenty of speculation that Swedish senior naval officers knew about the true origins of some of these submarines, playing at being Soviet. In an interview for German television in 2014, Admiral James Lyons, top naval admiral for the US Navy with responsibility for northern Europe in the 1980s, said that the Swedish navy was holding the US/British navy's coats.

In 2000, Caspar Weinberger, former US defence secretary, and Keith Speed, a former British naval minister, told Swedish television that these were training operations, designed to test Swedish submarine defence capabilities against the Warsaw Pact and it was done with the authorisation of the Swedes. This was news to the prime minister. Ingvar Carlsson had no idea. He certainly hadn't given permission. He said that, if the Swedish navy was going behind its government's back, this was a very serious matter indeed. Aftonbladet called Swedish navy officers "traitors". After all, the definition is someone who works with a foreign power against one's own government.

The Swedish navy did a hasty inquiry and found that, no, there hadn't been any secret exercises of the kind Weinberger and Speed spoke about. Bildt phoned Weinberger. According to Bildt, who was quoted in the Swedish media at face value, Weinberger said he had been "seriously misinterpreted." Yeah right.

But Weinberger's very clear testimony is there for all to see on online Swedish TV archives. And when I spoke to Sir Keith for an article for a British newspaper on the covert submarine operations, he essentially confirmed what he had said to Swedish television. British submarines were regularly in Swedish waters. He said that Margaret Thatcher authorised every single operation – so there was political backing on the British side, but whether the Swedish military informed their government was their problem. He also said, "Everyone is trying to cover their backs." Sir Keith did not specify to me the operations which the British were involved in, or how common they were. But sterling forensic work by the research professor Ola Tunander convinces me and many others that the submarines at Hårsfjärden, the important first hunt, were British or American. The origin of the many other submarine hunts, half a dozen big ones over the next decade, remains an entirely open question but I have heard from other reliable sources that every single one of these political destabilization campaigns was British or American - and definitely not Soviet.

MUCH OF THE evidence pointing in a western direction seems to have been removed from archives by Swedish naval officials, but certain technical indications relating to the supply voltage of disturbances to brief encrypted radio messages, as well as the description of a transponder left behind on the bottom of the sea, the dimensions of keel tracks, indicate NATO submarines. One journalist, Anders Hasselbohm, spoke to several Norwegian NATO sources who confirmed that the submarines there were from the US and the UK. According to Tunander, one or two of the Western submarines were damaged, possibly by accident.

Navy minister Speed and Weinberger said they were training operations – both of NATO and Swedish capabilities. It makes perfect sense, to both sides' mutual benefit, since they have different tactical routines.

However, could NATO have been blind to the fact, even if the "training missions" were not psychological operations in intention, they had psychological effects in consequence, in that they made the political life of the prime minister of a supposedly friendly neutral state, Sweden, much harder? It begs the question. Who, if anyone, was manipulating whom? Was the Swedish military using the NATO training exercises and transforming them into psychological damage exercises which, combined with the various "affairs" put Palme under intense domestic political pressure, unbeknownst to Western governments? Or were the West the very knowing instigators against Palme, and the Swedish navy went along. Or is there another answer?

It is worth knowing that Reagan's administration carried out a whole range of covert operations and psychological political warfare aimed at the Soviet Union, and her allies, aimed at regime change in the Soviet Union. This is not a secret – there have been many books about it since the end of the Cold War, even though few among the western general public seem aware, since most people adult at the time stopped their interest in the Cold War with the Cold war's end. They are stuck in the Cold War's mindset, unaware that history writing has moved on, with a publication of a slew of books detailing US covert efforts in the 1980s. Books like Veil, by Bob Woodward, or the Legacy of Ashes, by Tim Weiner.

Reagan's CIA chief, the maverick Bill Casey, funded Afghan rebels, got the Saudis to pump cheap oil, called in cheap loans to eastern Europe, causing payment problems in these Soviet satellites which the Soviets were forced to cover. In one operation, he even got the CIA to ensure that a Canadian engineering company exported faulty microchips to the Soviet Union. When installed in Soviet oil pumps, they worked for the first million cycles, then malfunctioned. The Urengoi pipeline explosion was apparently one of the largest explosions ever seen – and put the export of one of the Soviet Union's chief hard currency earners out of commission for quite some time.

It begs, of course, the question. Why? Why would the US/UK, through its submarine operaion, part training, part reputation destroying psyops of Palme's peace commission, take the risk of discovery, which would have huge repercussions for the NATO alliance's reputation? Was Palme's peace-making really such a danger to NATO's and the Reagan administration's hawks? It is true that in the archives concerning Scandinavia that are available, which go up to 1981, that is, the year before Hårsfjärden, British and American officials expressed great concern about the neutralist tendencies of Danish and Norwegian ministers, and even worried about the likely return of Palme to power the next year. Even if Palme was seen as running the Soviets errands' in splitting NATO by selling the attractions of neutrality and dividing NATO over nuclear issues, covert operations still seem disproportionate. However, there were forces in Sweden, though, that were emotionally fully capable of doing Palme harm.

THE WRITER Lars Borgnäs interviewed one Swedish intelligence service official who talked of attending a coup attempt talk at the police house in the town of Norrköping weeks before Palme's assassination. I remember meeting one self-proclaimed leader of an opposition movement, one Alf Enerström, a doctor, who claimed to have been in a position to be able to raise a resistance army which could take over the Riksdag and seize the offices of Swedish television. It was a snowy three days in 1994, my first encounter with the murder. He was referring to the situation in 1985, early 1986. His support couldn't be verified at the time, but other sources have related accounts of how he was able to raise large sums of money, from private volunteers – officers, upper-class housewives - who felt that Sweden was going in the wrong direction, and who were in anguish over the fact that Palme, against all odds, had won the election of 1985 by painting the bourgeois coalition as Trojan horses for Thatcherite-style neoliberalism. Enerström possessed the Palme dartboard and claimed to hate the man, whom he blamed on the forced removal into foster care of his 13-year-old son. This may have been an abuse of power by the mighty Swedish social services. On the other hand, he did come across as a bit disturbed, albeit financially and socially successful. Maybe it was because Palme dominated politics and life in the seventies and eighties Sweden that he became seen as the ultimate cause of the misfortunes on their lives of many unhappy Swedes. He became a symbol, and a hate figure, for many Swedish people with problems. If powerful or organised enough, of course, they might also create networks against him. Enerström said with a passion he hated Palme, but hadn't killed him.

Which brings us to the assassination. There is nothing to link the submarine intrusions to the murder directly. That is, there is no evidence – as yet – that the same group of people planned the western submarine intrusions then went ahead and plotted the death of Olof Palme. As in: When they did not sufficiently derail Palme – after all, he was re-elected just months before his murder, plan B had to be put in place. That is not to say that this was not what actually happened – only that there is no evidence for it.

Another hypothesis is that the submarine intrusions had an indirect effect on the murder. That Palme was killed by someone else, perhaps a local small-scale conspiracy of people experienced in arms, perhaps lower-ranking policemen. (This happens to be the hypothesis of one Sweden's most famous crime experts, the academic and crime TV expert Leif GW Persson). It might be that the submarine intrusions had an indirect – unintentional? - effect of causing the assassination. The assassin/s case against Palme included his failure to deal with the submarine question. An angry policeman? A small grouping of people in the intelligence services pissed off with Palme's "appeasement" and "pro-Russian attitudes"?

Set that aside for a moment. Let us hold that possibility open of a Swedish engagement – whether organised at a high level or a small grouping - possibly with some CIA aspect, and begin at another end.

Palme's enemies extended beyond Sweden and the North Atlantic. For much of his career, he had been active in the third world.

In 1996, Eugene De Kock, the South African Apartheid government's top hitman, let casually drop during his trial for life for 89 counts of murder that a colleague of his, Craig Willamson, was responsible for the murder of Olof Palme. De Kock's case was one of a series of trials and hearings, known in the media collectively as "South Africa's Nuremberg", dealing with the legacy of Apartheid and its covert war against various opponents of the white regime.

De Kock, a rumpled, overweight, short-sighted figure, who had already spent a long time in custody, made the claim at the end of his testimony "dropping his bombshell almost as an afterthought", as one reporter put it. He had earlier outlined a whole host of covert operations such as the "black on black" violence in 1994, largely orchestrated by the white security forces. De Kock had masterminded bombings of the South African Council of Churches, the Congress of South African trade unions in Johannesburg as well as the bombings of the ANC's offices in London in 1982.

The colleague implicated was special operative Craig Williamson, who had worked with de Kock for many years. Williamson immediately issued a statement denying De Kock's statement.

"Why do you only tell us now?" Judge Willem van der Merwe, asked with bemusement.

"It slipped my mind before," replied de Kock.

Palme had many fingers in many pies. He was a brave man. As we have seen already, Swedish engagement in the frontline states of South Africa was continuous and committed from the early 1960s, started by liberals and the Swedish church, but gratefully picked up Palme, disturbed as he had been about racial inequalities in the United States in the 1950s. The South Africans were a satisfying enemy: A Germanic culture, like Sweden's, pursuing clearly racialist policies, like those Nazis whom the Swedes never had a chance to fight.

After losing the election of 1976 and taking on the vice chairmanship of the Socialist international, Palme travelled to Africa and saw weak and vulnerable people, saw the newly independent frontline black states struggling to contain mighty South Africa. Countries had an absolute right to self-determination. Palme was idealistic and humanitarian of course, but it also brought international lustre to Sweden: a sort of moral imperialism, if you like; after the shabby experiences of the second world war and the long period of geopolitical inactivity before that.

Instead of subordinate to capitalist racialist South Africa, the free frontline states were going to be little African versions of successful Social Democracy. Perhaps, if apartheid were toppled, South Africa would follow.

Journalists and priests travelling in the fifties and sixties set the scene before Palme's entry on the political stage by writing angry reports about Apartheid South Africa. Most other African countries were gaining their independence from the French and British colonial empires. But the Portuguese empire, in Angola, Guinea Bissau, Sao Tome and Mozambique, was a holdout. So was Southern Rhodesia, which had a large white settler community and, rather than allowing itself to be decolonised in the fashion of the rest of the British African empire, declared unilateral independence under the White regime of Ian Smith, a farmer and former RAF fighter pilot. These holdouts also consequently became targets for Swedish activism, via the black liberation movements in these countries.

One small contribution to the decline in relations with South Africa itself, which had been good during the early Erlander era, was the sex scandal involving one of Sweden's most famous young female novelists, Sarah Lidman, who was exposed as having had sex with the black leader of the ANC youth organisation when on a visit. Interracial sex was, of course, illegal in Apartheid South Africa. The tabloids in both countries had a field day, from different perspectives: the Swedes were shocked that she faced a potential ten-year prison sentence. The South Africa media revelled in Swedish sinfulness. In the end, she was expelled. But the negative coverage continued; two large Swedish supermarket chains instituted consumer boycotts against South African products.

A charm offensive whereby the Swedish and other Nordic foreign ministers were invited to South Africa to see "what it was really like" was rudely rebutted by the Scandinavian foreign ministries. The South African UN delegation's attempts to compare the situation of the Lapps in northern Sweden to the one of blacks in South Africa fell somewhat flat, even though you could argue there was some merit to their case: the Lapps have been disadvantaged under Swedish control, and it is a much underexplored area. Swedish historians have not rushed to write about it. Not for the first time, an outside nation came up against Sweden's Teflon image. Sweden, the perfect democracy.

AN INDICATION of real change in policy towards Southern Africa came when Palme made a sulphurous speech about every oppressed nation's right to freedom from oppression. We have encountered this kind of manoeuvre before., aimed at the US over Vietnam. It took place in 1965 while Palme was deputising for the foreign minister during the latter's summer holiday. As we have seen earlier, the speech was held at the Brotherhood movement's annual congress. The Brotherhood movement is the Christian wing of the Social Democrat party. The speech was mainly aimed at the Americans who were then in Vietnam, but it could also be taken as an attack on white South African misrule over blacks. The Swedish church had always been incredibly engaged in the rights of Africans. Palme had done the groundwork for the speech by making friends with black underground leaders in Southern Africa.

He had acquainted himself with African liberation movement leaders, such as Oliver Tambo (ANC), Mugabe and Aghostino Neto. (Of the MPLA, the freedom movement of Mozambique).

Several times in the early sixties they had met on Workers' Day (1 May) marches in Stockholm, though sometimes they gathered in Palme's suburban home rather than at a central Stockholm restaurant, to avoid getting the attention of the British and American embassies. Then, in 1969, Palme, who had just got into power, started financing the liberation movements directly. Over the years, the movements came to include SWAPO, the South West Africa People's Organisation. MPLA, the People's Movement of the Liberation of Angola. FRELIMO, the Mozambique Liberation Front. Then, ZANU and ZAPU, the Zimbabwe African National Union, and Zimbabwe African People's Union, the latter Robert Mugabe's organisation. Finally the ANC, the African National Congress, whose goal was the biggest prize of all, a democratic black majority ruled South Africa

Sweden's best friend in Southern Africa was a country that was already independent. Tanzania, the country furthest from South Africa in the region, had a leader sympathetic to Swedish style socialism, the benevolent autocrat Julius Nyerere. The capital Dar Es Salaam was to be an informal capital of the liberation movements.

The liberation movements that Sweden supported were rather left wing, and were aligned with the Soviet Union. The countries usually had right-wing liberation movements, like UNITA and FNLA in Angola, or later RENAMO in Mozambique; they had an anti-Communist stance. But the Swedes ostentatiously refrained from supporting these, since they had South African (and American) backing.

Palme and his people always said they opposed Communism and wanted to give Africans a real choice: he did not want to the left wing liberation movements to be captured by Soviet ideology and go down the wrong development route. He wanted to cast his protection over them. Whatever his motives, it put Sweden at opposing sides from the Americans and British. Holden Roberto, the leader of the FNLA, the rightist liberation front in Angola backed by the British and the Americans, complained: "There was, in fact, a very strong involvement in favour of the MPLA. Even a certain aggressiveness towards FNLA when we came to Sweden. I personally saw this at the Ministry of Foreign Affairs. There was an aggressiveness by the Secretary of State at the time. He was deeply committed to the MPLA. Really committed!"

It also opened Palme up to criticism, both domestically and abroad, that Palme supported movements that were undemocratic and violent, regarded in some quarters as terrorists.

Of course, the Americans had the same problem with the movements they backed, but they never had the saintly pretences of the Scandinavians. The Swedish backed ANC in South Africa had an armed wing, which carried out bombings in South African cities in the 1980s. It wasn't that large numbers of people died, but Sweden was the most generous financial supporter of the ANC. And Sweden came big and early to the game. Sweden was the first – and for many years the only – industrialised country to extend direct official aid to the other African liberation movements. Later the Norwegians came on board. Officially, the Nordics never supported war, but only humanitarian spending, but if the spending in rebel groups was not ring-fenced, and could not be verified in any way, who was to know if the money was spent on arms or medicine? And the Nordic money flowed into the same pot as Soviet funds.

Much of the Swedish assistance was paid through official channels. But at least one Swedish run organisation appears to have had a slush fund that was used to support guerrilla activities. It was the educational organisation International University Exchange Fund, based in Geneva, co-funded by the other Scandinavian countries, but primarily run by a maverick Swedish official called Lars Göran Eriksson who was close to several officials in Sweden who themselves were very close to Palme. The IUEF was a direct successor to the ISC, the international student union Palme had helped form in the 1940s. The ISC had been closed down in 1967, after revelations in a US news magazine that it had been funded with CIA money, as we saw earlier. The IUEF rose in its wake and the headquarters moved from Leiden to Geneva.

The exact degree of Palme's knowledge of the IUEF's covert anti-apartheid activities have not been established, but we will recall Palme's involvement in intelligence work and that he was well acquainted with student organisations used as vehicles for subversion since he himself had opposed the Soviet-subverted International Union of Students in the forties. His creation of the ISC was in direct opposition to this.

Officially, the IUEF funded student exchanges and scholarships, but a proportion of the money was apparently diverted by Eriksson to a fund in Vaduz, Lichtenstein, called Southern Futures. "Lars Göran Eriksson used to report to the donors: 'Look, on certain confidential projects all I can tell you is that when the money leaves IUEF's account, you have to accept that for auditing purposes it has been spent'," as one insider later said. "He would take the money out of IUEF and put it into Southern Futures Vaduz and, of course, he could then do what he liked with Southern Futures Vaduz".

Eriksson was well paid and apparently not corrupt, but he would hand a lot of money in cash when liberation leaders like SWAPO leader Sam Nujoma came to visit Geneva. The money was given freely when activists asked for expensive air tickets for this or that non-existent conference. They did not spend the money on air tickets but their own activities. Lars Göran Eriksson justified it by the fact that you had to live in the real world. "Sitting late at night, having some schnapps and coffee, he would say: 'This is politics. This is the real world. We do not all live on refugee scholarships and little farms that make handicrafts. These people are fighting a liberation struggle. They have to pay hotel bills and so on.'"

Inevitably, perhaps, the IUEF was infiltrated by South African intelligence agencies. Enter Craig Williamson (b 1947), sometimes called

South Africa's superspy, an employee of BOSS, the South African Bureau of State Security.

The smooth-talking English South African Williamson, who had attended South Africa's equivalent of Eton, St John's, had been recruited by South African police after school. At his school, one of those elite institutions attended by the relatively liberal English-speaking upper middle class, Williamson was described as a racist and a bully. Far from academic, he had a practical intelligence and was known as a doer. At university he started working as their informant and agent when he progressed through the ranks of South African radical student life in the early 1970s, working his way up to the post of deputy chairman of the very anti-apartheid National Union of South African Students, NUSAS.

WILLIAMSON MANAGED to avoid any suspicions by handling all the "essential but boring account keeping and avoiding the intellectual cut and thrust of student life". When he spoke it was "forcefully, convincingly and usually related to the all too often neglected practical side of student affairs," says one South African political writer. After a few drinks, he had a bouncy bonhomie and was once arrested for drunk driving after a fistfight with a waiter. But generally he kept out of controversies: he was the effective loyalist (apparently) who kept his head below the office parapet.

On a trip to Europe in his capacity as deputy chair and treasurer of the South African student union, he met and made friends with Eriksson. Williamson was travelling with the president-elect, a young man of impeccable and genuine anti-apartheid credentials, who made less of an impression on ANC exiles, eager for news from home, than Williamson did. This fellow, one Mike Stent, was well aware of the possibility of meeting South African regime spies and agents provocateurs, and so was very cautious and withdrawn in his contacts with European exiles. Williamson, of course, had no such qualms, and his enthusiasm impressed senior ANC figures, including treasurer Thomas Nkobi, who assessed him over tea, and apparently approved.

A year later Williamson and Eriksson met in Botswana where Williamson told Eriksson that, as a student radical, he was in danger of his life from the South African security services and needed Eriksson's protection. It was a cover story: The little-suspecting Eriksson bought it, though, and employed him in Geneva is a staff member, first as an information officer but later as Eriksson's second-in-command. In this capacity, Williamson often travelled to Stockholm, where he made himself at home in the Swedish Social Democrat headquarters located at Sveavägen 44, opposite the Grand Cinema, as it happens. Eriksson's "partners in crime" in Sweden's secret war against the Apartheid regime, the officials Pierre Schori and Mats Hellström, who later had very senior positions in the Social Democrat party, looked after him. Williamson also apparently met Palme on several occasions.

From this position, by talking to the Swedes, having infiltrated the Social Democrat headquarters, Williamson was able to map out the ANC's strategy against the South African apartheid state. Information he duly passed on to his superiors at the South African secret service. Back in Geneva, he was entrusted with an ever greater proportion of the IUEF's disbursement activities, but he diverted some of this money to build up a training facility outside Johannesburg for South African intelligence service called Daisy Farm. He also funded, on behalf of the IUEF, the anti-apartheid South African News Agency and sent its reporters to cover ANC conferences and funding trips. By debriefing the reporters, who were genuine anti-apartheid activists, this secret covert agent for the South African regime got a pretty good idea of what anti-regime black activists were up to. This too he passed on to his superiors. There were some doubts about Williamson's bona fides, especially from the South African Council of churches. But Williamson had been cleared at the highest levels. ANC's treasurer general Thomas Nkobi trusted him, as did ANC president Thabo Mbeki.

It has been speculated that the death of anti-Apartheid activist Steven Biko was down to Williamson's exploiting information flows between the IUEF and Palme in Stockholm. After finding out about secret arrangements for a meeting in September 1977 between Palme and Biko was leaked to Williamson's South African bosses, it is speculated that this prompted them to act.

BIKO WAS arrested at a roadblock in the Eastern Cape in South Africa in August 1977, in breach of his curfew, a few weeks before he had the secret meeting arranged in Botswana with Tambo and Palme. The police took him and he did not emerge alive from police custody. A South African magistrate miraculously found no policeman to blame. Thousands attended the Black Consciousness Movement activist's funeral; thanks to the hit song Biko by pop singer Peter Gabriel, and later the Hollywood film Cry Freedom, Stephen Biko has become an international symbol of black oppression in South Africa. So what is the story? Was Biko really murdered because he was going to meet Palme? The reasoning goes like this; the Black consciousness movement was powerful inside South Africa; combined with the ANC it would have been even stronger. Both movements threatened to take on a strong military tone. Tambo, ANC leader in exile, was also due to attend the secret Botswana meeting with Palme.

According to Williamson, interviewed much later by Swedish journalist Tor Sellström, the South African authorities dreaded not only an alliance between two powerful black African activist movements, but the fact they had a Swedish connection, which would weaken the South African claim that the country was being besieged by a worldwide communist conspiracy with tentacles into the African liberation movements. Sweden could not be painted as communist; Palme well knew this. Terry Bell, a South African journalist, explains how one Swedish official had requested from Eriksson information about possible military training for Black Consciousness volunteers, via Swedish contacts in Algeria. "Minutes relating to these plans were intercepted by Williamson, and copies were sent at once to Coetzee [his superior] in South Africa. Those minutes amounted to a death warrant for Biko."

Several people around Williamson suspected him for years of being a spy. His boss, IUEF chief Eriksson, who drank heavily, would have none of it. But an article in the London Observer newspaper in 1980 from a South African intelligence service defector, about the regime's foreign intelligence activities, led to Williamson breaking cover, fearing his story was about to be exposed also. South African intelligence chief Dirk Coetzee turned up in Geneva and threatened Eriksson: let Williamson exfiltrate himself quietly, and no one would know; the Swedes would be saved embarrassment. If Eriksson would not comply, action would be taken against senior Social Democrat politicians. Instead, Eriksson scarpered back to Stockholm and the scandal became public. The IUEF was closed down; its student scholarships transferred to the administration of other charity funds. And Williamson returned to South Africa, where he became something of a star in the media. He was South Africa's superspy, who had rumbled Sweden's "spy ring" against South Africa, the IUEF, according to a series of articles in the Johannesburg Sunday Times, where the imagination was given free rein, and Sweden very much in the focus as the villain.

Williamson was promoted to higher – or lower – things, from spying on unfriendly Swedish run organisations to organising burglaries, bombings and, ultimately, hit jobs on opponents of the apartheid regime. He worked with commandos, or special forces operatives, in a project known as Long Reach. "Long Reach" meant that the South Africans were able reach far beyond the nation's borders when striking out at the enemies of Apartheid. In March 1982, a 10 pound bomb blew up the ANC's London headquarters; police sealed off the street in Islington for the whole day. We know this because Williamson confessed to all these activities, along with a number of other secret policemen, at Truth and Reconciliation Commission hearings organised by the post-apartheid government in 2000; he sought amnesty for them, saying he was just a servant of the regime; in return for which he told the truth. But did he and his hit men kill Olof Palme?

Williamson was certainly capable of assassination. Two women activists had died in separate letter bomb attacks organised by Williamson, Ruth First and Jeanette Schoon.

Ruth First was a friend of Olof Palme, an academic and author of a study on the history of Namibia. She was also married to the (white) head of the South African communist party, Joe Slovo, a close ally of the ANC. They were living in exile in Maputo, the capital of Mozambique.

Williamson arranged for a letter bomb to be sent to Slovo; it was Ruth who opened it. Two years later he had a letter bomb addressed to the exiled anti-apartheid activist Marius Schoon in Angola. However, the letter was opened by Schoon's wife Jeanette, while holding their six-year-old daughter Katryn on 28 June 1984. When Marius returned home, she found his wife and daughter splattered across the walls of their home, while their two-year-old son Fritz was found walking around the home, unharmed, though he was later to suffer from epilepsy. The murder was particularly appalling because, in his "escape" from South Africa ten years earlier, Williamson, posing as the anti-apartheid student activist, had actually been sheltered in the Schoon's family home in Botswana, where he got to know Jeanette quite well. Did Williamson go ahead and plan the assassination of Olof Palme as De Kock claimed?

The Swedes were aiming at regime change in South Africa and were funding, indeed were the main financial supporters of the ANC at a time when it was carrying out terrorist attacks in South Africa.

During annual aid negotiations with the ANC in 1980, Swedish officials stated that Swedish foreign policy in South Africa is "dedicated to bringing about political change in Namibia and South Africa." The money was transferred to a bank account held by the ANC in London. From there, ANC couriers took over, distributing the money to the various causes. The Swedish government insisted though in negotiations with ANC officials in March 1981, "so that the assistance to the ANC avoids being called into question", "the Swedish government must at all times be in a position to confirm that the money is exclusively humanitarian". The ANC's representatives agreed. However, a year later, the Swedish authorities found "significant shortcomings" in the way the money spent was accounted for in the ANC's spending reports.

Later, in 1997, talking to journalist Tor Sellström, the sometime director general of the Swedish Aid agency SIDA, Carl Tham, said that "we had no indication of misuse" but also added: "We are not saying it did not happen". Based on extensive research for his report for the Nordic Africa Institute, Sellström writes that "although Swedish funds certainly benefited the liberation movement's armed wing, the Apartheid government was never in a position to present evidence that official Swedish support was diverted to military activities."

And how was one to separate military and civilian spending? The ANC did carry out some military activities, through its armed wing, MK, of which the best known was the Church Street attack, in Pretoria, in 1983, when a bomb was detonated near South African air force headquarters, resulting in 19 dead and over 200 injured. Over the next few years, a series of bombings took place in urban areas took place that killed, if not a large number of people, then the odd person here or there. In the 1985 Amanzimtoti bomb on the Natal south coast, five people were killed when a bomb was detonated in a rubbish bin at a shopping centre.

THE SOUTH AFRICAN government couldn't let such behaviour go unpunished. In the late seventies, its security services had struck in death squad cross-border raids at ANC activists in the frontline states. The UDI regime in southern Africa had just stepped down and newly formed Zimbabwe, with Sweden friend Robert Mugabe at the head, had taken its place. There were South African death squad attacks in Matola outside Maputo, Mozambique, in 1981, Maseru in December 1982 and Gaborone, Botswana, in June 1985. In January 1978, Bafana Duma, the ANC's boss in Swaziland, lost an arm and suffered serious facial injuries from an explosive device placed inside a post office box in Manzini. Four years later the movement's acting boss Petrus Nyawose was killed along with his wife in a car explosion outside their flat in Manzini.

The ANC's top official in Zimbabwe, Joe Gqabi, died in July 1981 in Harare. Ruth First died a year later in Maputo. These figures were replaced by less experienced officials, less able to carry out the ANC's work. The ANC's headquarters in Islington, London, was bombed in 1982, as said. While the leftist FRELIMO government, which had been supported by the Swedes in the past and, now, since Portugal's departure, sat in government, was in sympathy with the ANC, by 1983-84, it was finding it necessary to come to terms with South Africa by signing an agreement of "non-aggression and good neighbourliness", known as the Nkomati accord, which would severely limit the ANC's activities in the country.

Palme was involved in resisting the South Africans as much as he could. He rejected a South African proposal – an olive branch, if you like – to have joint ventures between South African and Swedish companies to develop the Mozambican economy. Instead he severely reprimanded the Mozambican president Machel at a meeting of the Socialist International in Arusha in September 1984 for signing the Nkomati accords, as a kind of letting the side down, a compromise with Apartheid.

Palme authorised Swedish diplomats to take ANC activists under attack from cross-border South African death squad raids under their wing. In mid-1985, the South African government started putting pressure on ANC activists and their families based in the tiny mountain kingdom of Lesotho, a country completely surrounded by South Africa. South African foreign minister Pik Botha – who incidentally knew Sweden well, having been stationed there as a diplomat in the late fifties – presented a list to the Lesotho government of activists he wanted deported from the country. This was not easy, since Lesotho airways had no connections to any country outside South Africa, and the small Fokker passenger plane donated by the Swedish government had not yet entered service. The climate was tense, since rumours abounded that the South Africans would mount military raids into Lesotho if the ANC members were not resettled.

The problem seemed settled when, using Swedish funds, the ANC's regional headquarters in Lusaka, Zambia, chartered a Boeing 707 from Zambia Airways. As it flew over South African territory, it was asked to land. The Zambian pilots returned to Lesotho. Some tense days followed among the passengers on the ground. Eventually, the plane took off again and flew over South Africa without its passengers. The Swedish charge d'affaires reported the panicky climate among the 140 stranded activists. The Fokker aircraft delivered by Sweden to Lesotho airways only had a capacity of 40, but eventually it was used to ferry the ANC members in groups across to Zambia, using Finnish aircrew. The final flight was stopped by Pretoria which accused the Lesotho government of allowing ANC "terrorists" to leave the country to take up further training elsewhere.

Finally, the South Africans did carry out an attack: a commando squad led by Eugene de Kock – the man who fingered Williamson as Palme's assassin, and more of whom later – attacked two houses in Maseru, killing 6 ANC members and three Lesotho citizens. Anxiety remained high. So that Limpho Hani - the wife of the second in command of the armed wing of the ANC, Chris Hani – moved in with her children to the Swedish charge d'affaire's residence. More ANC activists were transferred in January 1986, and with this South Africa was satisfied; It ended its temporary embargo and the border gates with the tiny country were opened at the end of January 1986.

In Botswana, too, Sweden was active – again in opposition to South African interests. In November 1981, the South African commando squad known as Vlakplaas raided a house in the Botswanan capital Gaborone and killed ANC member Joyce Dipale, who was a friend of the Swedish aid agency SIDA's local representative Sten Rylander and his wife Berit. Another woman, Lilian Keagle, who was shot at point-blank range, survived the attack and, with three bullets lodged in her back and bleeding heavily, managed to make her way to the residence of her Swedish diplomat friends. They took her to the local hospital and it was arranged for her to fly to Canada for further surgery.

The United States could be quite critical of Swedish engagement in southern Africa during this period. In fact, says Sellström, it would be fair to say the UK – and US – were on a diplomatic collision course with Sweden. When the US embassy found out that the Oliver Tambo was due to pay yet another of his many visits to Sweden, in May 1984, US embassy second secretary Jimmy Kolker delivered a thinly veiled protest to the Swedish government when he said: "We cannot have a relationship of any sort with an organisation dedicated to terrorism and cross-border violence. One that uses a foolish Marxist optic for defining reality and proclaims the US as the main villain of the piece. If we are defined as the enemy we will defend ourselves. If the ANC remains dedicated to destructive violence, polarisation and Marxist clichés, it will reinforce its isolation and irrelevance. And we will draw the necessary conclusions."

The South African government was also growing increasingly angry. The exact details of Swedish assistance for the ANC remained confidential, the general political thrust and Sweden's general sympathies were extremely well known. In November 1985, the South African embassy in Stockholm submitted an extremely critical note. "The South African government regards the fact that the ANC is allowed to maintain an office and to further its aims with the approval of the Swedish government as being irreconcilable with its well-known opposition to terrorism." Under the leadership of exiled South African communist party chief and ANC ally Joe Slovo, which the diplomatic paper alleged was an agent of the KGB, the ANC was accused – the South Africans said - of building links with the PLO and the Baader Meinhof Gang.

"There was little doubt that the ANC is a revolutionary organisation aimed at destabilising the entire southern African subcontinent as part of its global drive against Western influence." The ANC not only posed a threat to the people of the Southern Africa but to people in other areas of the world, concluded Pretoria's representative.

Back in Sweden, engagement against Apartheid was reaching a new climax. In November 1985, there was the ANC gala in Gothenburg, a sort of Swedish response to Live Aid, Bob Geldof's star-studded rock concert against starvation and poverty, which had taken place in July. It was a much more politicised event than Live Aid at Wembley, which had featured artists like Queen, Madonna, Bruce Springsteen and Phil Collins. It was no less passionate. The ANC gala featured Sweden's leading pop artists; for example, the top-selling Bjorn Afzelius, whose folk songs sung in Swedish are drenched in a kind of naïve revolutionary romanticism and whose maudlin, sentimental work as much as any artistic statement summarises the Palme era for a whole generation of Swedes over the age of 45. (Afzelius was hated by the critics, who complained about his bleeding heart songs about shining stars and gentle breezes; his short-sleeved paisley shirts and his habit of shouting "Arriba!" before launching into politicised folk rock. A beanpole of a man, with hippy hair and the spectacled charisma of, let us say a high school Maths teacher, his biographers posthumously revealed an enormous appetite for brief liaisons.)

The international affairs secretary of the ANC, though Johnny Makatina, and Barbara Masakela, the ANC's arts supremo, were both present at the concert and invited on stage and joined in an ad hoc rendition of the movement's song of thanks. When Olof Palme – who had come down from Stockholm especially - was called on to the stage he made a speech recalling his first political act as a young man in 1948: donating blood for South African blacks. He said that if the youth of the world wished to get rid of Apartheid, it would disappear. He also announced the decision of the Swedish government to increase the ANC's annual budget by 5 million kronor.

The musicians, technicians, promoters and everyone else gave their services for nothing; a double album of the concert appeared within two weeks, and then 10 million kronor in record sale proceeds eventually made their way to the ANC's London account. The album - an intense exercise in nostalgia for a generation of Swedes – was still selling well in the late nineties.

Three months after the musical gala, Sweden hosted another event against Apartheid. On 21 February 1986, a week before Palme's assassination, the People's Parliament Against Apartheid took place in Stockholm. Nine hundred participants and 700 institutions from all across Sweden were there. All the Swedish political party youth organisations, women's organisations, trade unions, and solidarity groups with Southern Africa all attended. It was the biggest international solidarity event ever hosted in Scandinavia. The UN secretary-general, Javier Perez de Cuellar, sent a message of support, and many of the great African leaders were there: Zambian president Kenneth Kaunda. Olof Palme, Oliver Tambo, Joseph Garba of the UN Anti-Apartheid committee, and the British bishop Trevor Huddleston of the British anti-Apartheid movement, all made speeches. Launching the opening session, Palme made his most sulphurous ever speech, summarising his white hatred of the apartheid regime down the decades, from his blood donation in the forties through First of May speeches alongside black leaders.

Extracts from his speech included lines like the following: "What we are witnessing now in South Africa is a vicious circle of increased violence in defence of a system that is already doomed...The white people must be aware of their interests in negotiating a peaceful solution, while such a solution is still at all possible...

"By declaring our support for the struggle of the black population and by helping to isolate the Apartheid regime, we must give up to our responsibility for bringing the repulsive system to an end."

Apartheid did indeed end, but it was to take another eight years. Palme's life ended much sooner than that: he died just a week later.

Within days of the murder, Hans Holmer, the head of the Palme investigation, was receiving tips that the South Africann apartheid regime agents could potentially be candidates for the killing – from for instance Pär Westberg, the Swedish left-wing writer and novelist who had brought the iniquities of apartheid to the wider public's attention in the sixties and who knew several of the African leaders.

TWO DAYS after the murder, Karl Bäck, the head of the Swedish civil defence association, and a former Aftonbladet correspondent in London, was contacted by a former contact in Britain with links to MI6. He said that, according to his sources, those responsible for the murder were to be found in the South African intelligence community. A couple of Swedish policemen were also involved. Karl Bäck couldn't get through to the Palme investigators on the phone so he recorded the tip-off onto an audio tape and posted it the local office of SÄPO, the security police, located in his hometown of Uppsala.

The South African trail did not become a major issue for years, though. The early tips never made an impact, or in some cases never even reached the police, as the investigators pursued other favourite trails, from the Kurds to Christer Pettersson. For instance, SÄPO never reported having received Karl Bäck's tape about South African involvement.

As the Palme murder investigation continued into a new decade, significant changes were afoot in the world. In 1989, Communism loosened its grip on Eastern Europe. In 1991, the Soviet Union ceased to exist and became a democracy. In 1994, South Africa experienced the end of Apartheid. Nelson Mandela was now president, and the henchmen of the old regime started to tell their stories. In the autumn of 1996, Colonel Eugene de Kock, former boss of the Vlakplaas commando/assassination squads, a much decorated "war hero" who had been involved in several cross-border death squad attacks against the ANC in the eighties, and had also participated in the bombing of the ANC headquarters in London in 1982, made his claim, as we have seen, that the South Africans had killed Olof Palme.

De Kock had been accused of 129 crimes, including many murders, and was fighting for his life. De Kock, dubbed "prime evil" by the South African tabloid press, was desperately trying to cast aside suggestions from his former superiors that he was a rogue policeman. By implicating former presidents in his orders to assassinate, he was trying to spread the blame by saying he was only acting on the state's orders: doing his job. De Kock also mentioned that Palme had been killed by South African death squads, and that had been organised by Craig Williamson. Williamson and De Kock went back a long way. One was South Africa's "super spy", master of infiltration and, later, letter bomb assassinations. The other the leader of its death squads, which had carried out cross borders hunts for ANC activists in Botswana and other places. They had worked together before. Together they had bombed ANC headquarters in London in 1982.

The news that De Kock, the South African regime's chief assassin, said his agents had killed Palme, exploded in Sweden and Jan Danielsson, prosecutor, and Hans Ölvebro, the head of the Palme investigation, went down to South Africa to investigate. According to some sources, they asked perfunctory questions and were not very interested in what the South Africans had to say: Ölvebro didn't even take notes. It seems they were still fixated on Pettersson, were convinced of his guilt, and were only going through the motions because of media pressure in Sweden.

Following his claim in court that Craig Williamson and a few other people associated with operation Long Reach had been behind the murder of Olof Palme, De Kock was interviewed by Danielsson and Ölvebro the day after their arrival in South Africa, 11 October 1996.

However, the Swedish investigators did not manage to interview a crucial another special police operative who had briefed De Kock. Nor did they talk to Peter Casselton, a South African agent who had worked with both Williamson and De Kock on the London bombings of ANC headquarters and who visited the Swedish embassy in Pretoria in the same month as the Swedish police were in South Africa, claiming that Williamson, this proven letter bomb killer who also knew Sweden well, was a participant in Palme's murders.

BUT THE Swedish police duo did take the opportunity to head to Angola to interview Craig Williamson. On 18 October 1996, the Swedes conducted a three-hour questioning session with Williamson in Angola, where for three weeks Williamson had been detailed because of "visa problems". Since the early nineties, he had worked in the diamond and rare wood products export business. Williamson told the Swedes he had been head of one section of the security police from 1980-85. At the beginning of 1986, he had been given the job of chief of international operations by the Directorate of Covert Collection's chief.

Craig Williamson denied Casselton's and De Kock's claims that he had anything to do with the murder. He said had not been in Stockholm since 1978, when he worked for the IUEF, and he did not know any Swedish police officers. Williamson was aware of the rumours that circulated about him being involved in the murder: he said Eugene de Kock was resentful of him because Williamson had succeeded in the new South Africa and Eugene de Kock had not.

Because, or despite, their conversations with Williamson et al, Danielsson and Ölvebro were going very cool on the trail. They declined to seek out a second interview with De Kock. Ölvebro said he only had second-hand information; now the Swedes were looking for firsthand information and concrete evidence. They did not meet up with Casselton on their return to South Africa from Angola. In a press conference to Swedish journalists held in Cape Town, just before leaving for Sweden, Danielsson said the South Africa trail had become a "cuckoo in the nest" because it took so much of the Palme investigation's resources.

The big challenge now was to sift out the best bits of the large quantity of information that has come to them, Danielsson said. "We have all this time been in danger of being dragged into the massive changes now taking place in South Africa that concern all the crimes of the Apartheid era," said Ölvebro. But it was also this process that promised potential further openings. At the same time as they had been to South Africa, intensive police work had been taking place in Stockholm in parallel, with substantial resources from the National Criminal squad harnessed to provide them with background information about South Africa. Interpol had been contacted to provide information from other police authorities around the world. They had also sent back a lot of material in South Africa but which they hadn't had the opportunity to process. They therefore refused to be drawn on any conclusions. That said, Danielsson let slip that there were other, more interesting, trails in the Palme murder.

Six months later it was clear that the South Africa trail had lost steam. The prosecutors and police had organised the material and been able to dismiss a couple of false leads. There were other areas that could show promise but where they were making no progress. Danielsson, when speaking to reporters, seemed to entertain the vague hope that something would come out in the Truth and Reconciliation Commission amnesty applications, some of which had not yet been processed. Some secret agents might come out of the woodwork and give a valuable lead.

It was strange that the Swedish police hadn't been more curious about Peter Casselton. Casselton was Williamson's European man, the London-based intelligence chief, or middleman, in the 1980s. A Rhodesian with a British passport, a journalist who knew him described him, when starting out in life, as "blue-eyed young pilot and warrior for Ian Smith's thousand-year Reich."

Casselton was part of the team that had bombed ANC's Penton street headquarters in Islington in 1982, along with De Kock, Williamson and a few others. But he was the only one of the team not to have received the South African Police Star for outstanding service – the other members of the team, including De Kock and Williamson, did. As the agent in the field, they hadn't wanted to blow Casselton's cover. Two years later, however, he was caught burgling the headquarters of the Pan African Congress in Willesden, North London, and sentenced to four years in jail.

When Casselton came out of prison, he found he had been dropped by South African intelligence. A bitter man, he went into a series of casual freelance jobs, worked as a bush pilot, delivering supplies to the South African backed liberation movements UNITA and RENAMO. (Which, we will recall, were at war with the Swedish-backed left-wing regimes Frelimo and MPLA).

He also delivered drugs to rebel fighters in Somalia and rhino horn to the Chinese embassy in Nairobi. But after the end of Apartheid he found himself without a job, only a host of secrets in his head about Apartheid's dirty tricks, and he began drinking, holed up at Vlakplaas, the South African secret police's former training centre, and spent a lot of time with De Kock, who counted him as one of his few friends. According to a testimonial by De Kock, as stated by SABC, the South African broadcasting corporation, Williamson wanted to kill Casselton. By the autumn of 1996, when Casselton was interviewed by South African television, he claimed to be working as an aircraft engineer in Beira, Mozambique, fixing old planes – not making much of a living. However, he pledged on the programme that he would give a full testimony about all the dirty laundry of South African operations to the Truth and Reconciliation Commission in the spring of 1997. Would he be expanding on the story about the Palme assassination allegation he had told the Swedish ambassador to Pretoria when he walked into the Swedish embassy to "clear a few things up" in October 1996?

We will never know. In February 1997, Peter Casselton was badly hurt and went to hospital when a truck he was repairing at a friend called Paul Venter, in Pretoria, apparently "started" by itself and pushed Casselton into the wall. Venter's wife Cherry told the Swedish Expressen newspaper that "there were a lot of loose cables under the bonnet and the truck seemed to start when these cables touched each other." A former security police friend said that he was "kept alive by machines and had a minimal chance to live." The next day, Casselton was dead.

Was it really an accident? Casselton had shown every intention he was about to blow the whistle. The various books about Apartheid-era death squad activities showed ingenious different ways to kill traitors or opponents, masking it as accidents. For instance, at the Motherwell bombing in 1989, the South African security services "turned" four black African ANC activists and got them to infiltrate an ANC student movement who were planning some training activities with a view to carrying out a future attack. The police got their double agents to give the 20 students hand grenades which the security police had primed to explode as soon as they pulled the pin, rather than after some seconds.

It worked spectacularly. In the explosions that followed, 13 of the black students were killed instantly. Seven survived but were severely injured. To add insult to injury, the seven survivors were arrested on charges of terrorism and unlawful possession of hand grenades. The state investigator, Francois Steenkamp, who conducted the police investigation of the incident, knew exactly what had happened and why the grenades had gone off prematurely but kept quiet about it for twelve years. Another dirty trick involved four black police recruits for the apartheid regime who were suspected ANC double agents who were sent on a mission in a booby-trapped police car that was detonated by remote control by De Kock. All the men were blown apart instantly.

The dirty tricks of the Apartheid regime that climaxed in the 1980s, the letter bombs, assassinations, cross-border raids into the neighbouring states, are published in detail in the Truth and Reconciliation commission's reports in 1998.

Separately, whether or not Casselton's death was an accident, a slew of reports coming in after the police had got back from South Africa indicated that Craig Williamson was in Stockholm on the week of the murder. With the proviso that a decade had passed before the sightings were reported to police after the media reports about Williamson and co – and that science shows how fallible witness memories can be – here are the testimonies: John Lysaker was the desk manager at the Birger Jarl hotel near SIDA, the Swedish international development agency. The hotel is a few blocks away from the Grand Cinema, as it happens, and near Social Democrat party headquarters. Lysaker, 64 in 1996, had worked for 20 years at the Birger Jarl hotel, 1974 to 1994, and had become an expert on faces, as one does. On Sunday afternoon 2 March 1996, 40 hours after the murder, he was on duty at the hotel. The obese and bearded Williamson stood hanging around the reception, and Lysaker reacted to and memorised his appearance. A reporter asked the retired receptionist in 1996: Are you sure it was Williamson you saw?

There is no doubt about it, Lysaker replied. Williamson gave him a look of contempt; Lysaker had another customer to attend to and when he looked up he was gone.

ANOTHER SIGHTING was made the morning after the murder a woman was flying from Stockholm to Gothenburg. Next to her sat Craig Williamson, she said. She recognised him from the media coverage now that the South Africa trail was hot. "I am completely sure. It couldn't have been anyone else." He was wearing his outdoor clothes throughout the journey. He stared in front of him and didn't utter a word. Then there was the witness testimony of Henry Nyberg who saw three men outside the Palme couple's home in the old town. The men hung around Västerlånggatan street during the entire week from morning to late afternoon. After the murder, they disappeared. When he opened the Expressen newspaper, he was shocked. "My God. That was one of the men I saw outside Palme's flat." Finally, Jan Danielsson, before he set out for South Africa, told a television news station broadcast.

"That Williamson was in Sweden that week is something I can confirm. We know he was in Sweden. But he wasn't at Sveavägen if that is what you mean," he said to the TV reporter.

Danielsson did not respond to calls for clarification when the tabloid newspaper rang up to get a confirmation of the quote he made to the TV channel.

I have not heard Danielsson explain why he came to know Williamson was in Stockholm. It may have been that they hadn't given much thought to it. They evidently continued to believe – or chose to officially believe - in the Christer Pettersson trail.

After they had returned from their South Africa trip and digested the material, they did nothing further in their direction, Swedish Palme investigators focused all their energies in the next 18 months, through 1997, on trying to get enough evidence to put Pettersson on trial again, which is possible under Swedish law, provided new evidence appears. The supreme court rejected their application for a retrial; the witnesses who came forth and said they had seen Pettersson near the murder scene did so after too long a period for their claimed memories to be reliable. Had they not, after all, been affected by media coverage? Some of the new witness testimonies contradicted one another.

The murder investigation continued at a lower key over the next few years, briefly interrupted by Pettersson's death in 2004. His health had been failing: his promise to swear off alcohol had not been kept. In 2014, a few policemen are still at it. Many among the general public, but also politicians and journalists, apparently still believe it is Pettersson. However, Sweden's leading criminologist, who hosts a weekly crime programme, has said he doesn't think it is Pettersson.

So, back to the South Africa trail? Why stop there? Let us examine the whole anti-communist network. Several commentators have argued that the West's intelligence agencies were all part of the same family, all devoted to defeating Communism. There were considerable sympathies in the CIA, in MI5 and MI6, for the apartheid regime's battle against the "communist" ANC. For instance, in the BBC documentary on Palme's murder in 2014, Neil Aspinall, who burgled the ANC in 1982 at Casselton's and Williamson's request, was picked up by MI5. They told him that when he burgled the ANC's offices in London, they should pass the stuff on to them; he would get it back within 24 hours. It seems that British security agencies were looking the other way on South African dirty tricks against their political opponents on UK soil, and benefiting from it.

DUNCAN CAMPBELL, a well-known investigative journalist, who was writing about the activities of mercenaries, with a background in the special forces, a lot of this period, wrote an article for the New Statesman in 1988 where he said that, within weeks of the murder, he had been approached by three independent UK-based mercenaries who all had the same story to tell.

Swedish businessmen, with Finns and Germans also involved, possibly with links to a South African group, had approached arms dealers and mercenaries in London to find a suitable hitman. They were looking for an assassin to kill Olof Palme. These mercenaries had said no, but passed on their information to MI6. So MI6 knew of the threats to Palme's life.

Did they act on it, did they warn the Swedish prime minister and those around them. Or were they themselves complicit in some way? There is no evidence for this – yet. Is the lesser crime of failure to act on a warning sign not itself a kind of complicity, though? But what seems certain is that British and American intelligence had their own gripes about Palme. His activities played over so many fields. As we have seen, in Europe, his involvement and promotion of nuclear-free zones and disarmament politics, which had considerable support from European public opinion, but stood in complete opposition to the Anglo-Americans' aggressive prosecution of the Cold War against the Soviet Union, had caused concerns. There were anxieties about the way NATO's integrity was threatened by the peace movements, of which Palme was a leading figure.

CIA/MI6, side by side with Swedish business and a South African "Group" – were they all involved the murder of Olof Palme? In the absence of evidence, it is just speculation. Anyway, involvement and involvement: these things have gradations. It varies from active commissioning, while maintaining plausible deniability, to general support, to the foreknowledge of it while not actively working against it. Williamson and the South Africans may have been the active force; we also know that Williamson worked together with American interests in Africa. They were on the same side, when supporting, for instance, the right-wing African guerrilla movements UNITA (in Angola) and RENAMO (in Mozambique.) Both of which were at war with the movements (and then governments) Palme and the Swedes supported, namely the MPLA (in Angola) and Frelimo (in Mozambique).

Palme was not only the biggest financial supporter of the ANC, but the biggest financial supporter of the Nicaraguan Sandinistas, a left-wing socialist regime. As this was America's backyard, it was particularly neuralgic for the Americans. Ronald Reagan had accused the Sandinistas, who were not God's Children, perhaps, but whom Palme saw as his typical benign third world socialist reformers, of "eliminating human rights and imposing a Marxist totalitarian regime on Nicaragua." Reagan backed this up with massive covert support for a right-wing guerrilla movement, the Contras. According to Pierre Schori, the senior official in the Swedish foreign ministry, 1985 was a crisis year in Swedish American relations.

In 1984, Palme had been the first and only statesman from the West to visit Nicaragua. In a speech to the young Swedish Socialists in 1985, Palme said that "military manoeuvres and great power threats never could promote freedom and democracy" The crusade against communism in Nicaragua was nothing less than a plunder crusade against poor self-owning peasants and brutal rapes of women who were in fact children.

The State Department dismissed Palme's remark as "One-sided and provocative."

Six months later Palme was dead.

BIRCHAN, THE WOULD BE ASSASSIN

I met a retired mercenary and former intelligence officer in Sweden, of Yugoslav origin, who said he had been approached by a man whom he says came from the CIA in the autumn of 1985 with a mission to kill Palme. Was this the same grouping that was shopping around in mercenary circles in London for a killer at around the same time, as reported by Duncan Campbell? Were there two conspiracies to kill Palme, one from South Africa/Sweden and one from the CIA? More likely it was just the one, using different cover stories.

Ivan Birchan, a man of about sixty, picked me up at Stockholm's central station; He was portly, short, shaven-headed, and was wearing a roll down commando cap, a jacket and boots. He was going to tell me his story: as the man who had been approached to be Palme's assassin.

First, we walked around to some of the main Palme murder sites. I filmed footage of him at Palme's grave, a large tumulus stone with his name inscribed on a plaque. Then, I filmed him at the Grand cinema – the distances were all very short. Then, a few hundred metres south at the Sveavägen Tunnelgatan corner. The whole office complex, which included the Dekorima shop property, was being renovated. The Skandia Insurance company, one of Sweden's largest companies, which had been there for decades, had moved out.

We caught a suburban train to Southern Stockholm. On the journey, Birchan made some disobliging comments about Jews. The alleged Jews in question were two seats away. But he also opened doors for a couple of women with a kind of old-fashioned chivalry; the women showed their appreciation, and Birchan flirted back in a most ostentatiously un-Swedish manner. He thought of himself as a ladies' man, I could see that.

He lived in a block of flats in an immigrant suburb. After a quick lunch of meat and potatoes served up by his Polish girlfriend, we conducted the interview in his living room, with carpeted walls and heavy old Russian furniture, under a portrait of Yuri Gagarin and photos of the young Birchan in the African bush, next to a Land Rover. Born in 1952, Ivan Birchan grew up in Yugoslavia, descended from Russians who had fought for the Nazis and so were unable to return to the Soviet Union. His grandfather had been a tsarist general. Birchan very much embraced the mythology of the white Russian, the Russian in exile.

Birchan deserted from Yugoslav military – Yugoslav military intelligence, which was "a joke" - in the early seventies and found himself in Rhodesia, then still under white rule. He trained as a helicopter pilot. The ZANU and ZAPU liberation movements – supported by Palme's Sweden – were the enemies of the Ian Smith regime. Helicopter pilots transported Rhodesian special forces, the Selous Scouts, dropping them into engagement situations out in the bush. They also did some less savoury stuff: killing rebels by pushing them out of the helicopters. "Dropping the baboons from helicopters, teaching them how to fly," Birchan said.

One of his friends at the time was the American mercenary Charles Morgan, another helicopter pilot, who had served in Vietnam.

He and Charles bumped into one another in Libya, where Birchan was working for a while. In the early eighties, Birchan found himself in Stockholm, working as a doorman at the Sheraton hotel. "From the heaven to the Hell." He did well, won the doorman of the year award, even though he felt like a clown. But he soon learned that he was expected to do things by his managers that were not in the official job description: to guide guests to an illegal casino on the seventh floor; another was to procure prostitutes and send them to the rooms. Birchan refused to participate in this, and blew the whistle on the corrupt hotel manager.

Birchan contacted a journalist; He appeared in a couple of stories published by the small left-wing magazine, Gnistan ("The Spark"), whose editor, Karl Gustav Kohler, published a book on the subject. Birchan showed me a copy of the book, a slim paperback, published by a reputable publishing company, which was a journalistic investigation into corruption, crime and Stockholm's big hotels. Birchan was the hero of the book. It caused a scandal, but it was Birchan who was sacked. While he took the case to an Employment Tribunal – in the process of which he was in touch with one of Stockholm City council's deputy mayors – he was jobless.

Every day, he passed the time by reading Swedish and foreign newspapers, and went down to the International Press Bureau newsagents at the central station. One day, in November 1985, he bumped into an old friend: it was his old helicopter pilot colleague from Rhodesia days, Charles Morgan. Morgan had been looking for him at the Sheraton.

THEY HAD breakfast at the Hotel Intercontinental – Morgan was paying. After a while, they got into a kind of vulgar and funny banter, like the old days, when Morgan suddenly got serious and asked what Birchan would do to assassinate someone. Birchan thought for a while and said he would choose a Magnum .357 with a long barrel. He went on to explain some more technical reasons why it would be effective. They separated and promised to stay in touch. In early January 1986, Morgan came to Stockholm again. This time, they met at the pub restaurant Hamlet next to the Sheraton. It hadn't been spelled out at the previous meeting; but the unspoken sense was that Morgan would be offering Birchan a job – a respectable job.

They had three beers each and then Morgan disappeared for some moments.

Morgan came back; he admitted he was on a job for "the company". They had decided Birchan was a very capable candidate and that his method of assassination was a good one. He said they were targeting Olof Palme.

Morgan took out an A4 Manila envelope and spilled out its contents on the table: photographs of Olof Palme, the results of a medical check-up for Palme, a photo of Sten Andersson (the foreign minister), Stig Malm (trade union chief), Kjell Olof Feldt (finance minister), plus short typewritten profiles in English on each of them, and a map of central Stockholm, marking out certain locations. Birchan knew now Morgan was being serious.

Morgan said he would be offered two million dollars for it and would be supplied they weapon. He would be told the time and place for the assassination. Birchan told Morgan that, at the last meeting, he treated the talk about assassinations and so on as a joke, or as if giving advice on a thriller plot. "Agatha Christie or Alfred Hitchcock." And bantered along. But this was going too far. He added that he had "never seen the envelope" and would "never tell anyone." Their meeting ended very shortly after. He hasn't met Morgan since.

It was January 1986, six weeks before the murder. Birchan immediately contacted three people: Alf Karlsson, the head of the anti-terrorist section at SÄPO with responsibility for politicians' security. His journalist friend Karl Gustav Kohler from Gnistan. And Ingrid Båvner, the Social Democrat deputy mayor whom he had been in touch with over the unemployment tribunal issue. His message each time: The CIA are planning to kill Olof Palme.

He called Alf Karlsson cold. Karlsson sounded sceptical. Birchan called three more times to Karlsson. But Alf Karlsson showed no interest. So in the beginning of February he turned to Båvner, who was also the chairwoman of the Police Governing Board of Stockholm City. He talked to Båvner's secretary and said the same thing: that the CIA were planning to kill Olof Palme. After meeting Birchan, I contacted journalist Lars Borgnäs, who did a story about Birchan in 1992. He informed me that the fact that phone call had taken place has been confirmed by Båvner to the Palme investigators.

A week before the assassination, Birchan contacted police inspector KG Olsson at the Stockholm police. KG Olsson confirmed both to Borgnäs and to the Palme police that Birchan had contacted him before the murder. Olsson wrote down the information and passed it on immediately to Alf Karlsson.

Alf Karlsson, however, told the Palme investigators that Birchan had contacted him first after the murder. In an interview with Swedish television, Hans Ölvebro, the head of the Palme investigation, said he believed Alf Karlsson's version. When Borgnäs reported back to Birchan the results of the phone call to Ölvebro, Birchan was enraged: Karlsson could get away with lies because he had a "police ID badge". Karlsson retired from the police a year later and joined a private security company belonging to a former SÄPO chief, PG Vinge, who had to resign as chief of SÄPO In 1970 after calling Palme a "security risk". Right wing sentiments and widespread hostility, even hatred of Olof Palme, were very strong in Sweden's security police/military intelligence establishment.

It seems very probable that Birchan was telling the truth, (and he had been an honest whistleblower in the Sheraton case, at some personal cost) and very likely it was the same team that was casting around for an assassin in London's underworld circles. But where were they from? Were they South Africans who posed as CIA when they came to Sweden? Was Birchan reading a CIA origin into a South African/Swedish plot? Was it a plot under joint ownership?

Was it a third party plot claiming South African alternately CIA origins? Was it the CIA using the South Africans for "plausible deniability?" Did the CIA or MI6 know of a South African/Swedish plot, but did not interfere, wouldn't have been unhappy that he disappeared, in the same way the CIA had encouraged but not actively commissioned military coups in Brazil in 1964 and Chile in 1973?

Of course, planning a plot does not mean they actually carried it out. The CIA planned to kill Castro, Palme's old chum, and that never came off. It could be that they were mulling it – and someone else came first.

Another whistleblower, who appeared on Swedish television in 1994, casts some doubts on that.

CENNETH'S STORY

There was another man approached by the commissioning team behind Palme's murder: a criminal and mercenary called Cenneth Neilberg. He had a long list of crimes behind him. Assault and battery, illegal possession of weapons, accessory to robbery, fencing and illegal coercion. He had also carried out activities he did not want his television interviewer to know about. This was what he told a Swedish current affairs TV programme in 1994. His testimony was that murder was carried out by a mixed international hit team of five people:

"I had an acquaintance in the south of Sweden who was called Mille, and I had known him for years. In the autumn of 1985, he asked me if I was interested in making some money by eliminating a person. Half a million before and half a million after everything was over. At that stage I was not told who was going to be snuffed out. My only worry was to shoot the person. Everything else would be taken care of by others."

"I met Mille about 10 to 15 times, and of course, became very curious. But I did not answer yes or no, but was mostly inquisitive. The more I talked, the more I understood that this was no ordinary Swede. My last contact with Mille was at the turn of the month January/February 1986. Then I said that I wanted some time to consider. I also told him that I thought the risk was too big – it was after all a human being that was to be eliminated. But then, he answered once more that I did not have to worry about a thing. Everything was prepared. People close to the person were involved in the planning."

Neilberg paused then added:

"And then this incident with Palme occurred. Some days later, I met Mille and asked him, 'Was this the job I was to have done?'

'Well, you could say that', he expressed himself in a refined way."

"Then, I became very curious, and again asked about the circle around this, who had fixed it, and all that. And I got the impression – well, he said so straight out – that two Swedish police officers and three men probably from abroad had carried this out. And then I got the impression that 'forget all this', it was nothing I should be messing about with. He himself had got the task from somebody else. And like I said, he had worked many years within SÄPO, and as an agent. So I don't know what conclusion you should draw from this. But I understood that this was serious."

"Afterwards a tragic accident happened to Mille in May 1992. So I took this chance because I didn't dare while he was alive. If there is any sort of game or some connection with this, then... If you can bring it out into the open, I think you should do it."

Hans Ölvebro, the head of the Palme investigation for ten years from 1987, was cool on Neilberg's testimony when confronted by a reporter. An inspector from Sweden's SÄPO security police, which had employed Neilberg as an informer, interviewed Neilberg on tape in early 1993 and sent the interview to the Palme investigators.

ÖLVEBRO THEN told Swedish television Neilberg "wasn't interested in being interrogated" and set a number of difficult conditions which Neilberg's lawyer, asked to respond, said was a lie. "There were no conditions," lawyer Bertil Andersson told Swedish TV.

Ölvebro then said Neilberg lacked credibility since he was a person who had appeared on television. Neilberg repeated that he was happy to talk to the police but thought they wouldn't dare to because what he had to say was too potentially explosive.

Who was Mille? His real name was Milan Heidenreich, an exile Czech who had worked as a police informer. He lived near Gothenburg and had acted as an informer on drug deals and art thefts. Not much else is known about him in the public domain except that he once posed for press photos with Czech president and human rights campaigner Vaclav Havel. This was confirmed in the documentary made about Neilberg in 1994 by the head of the criminal squad Tommy Lindström, who paid Mille hundreds of thousands of kronor over the years. Another policeman familiar with Neilberg confirmed on TV that Neilberg had worked with the Swedish police and had always been a truthful source about the whereabouts of stolen art.

In the early hours of 1 May 1992, it was reported that a driver was killed when his car overturned on the E6 motorway in southern Sweden. When the car turned over the driver was thrown out of the roof hatch and lay dead in the middle of the motorway when the ambulance came. It was Mille.

Ölvebro seemed incredibly obtuse about pursuing some trails. He was nonchalant about South Africa and seems to lie blatantly when explaining away why he and his team had not been interested in Birchan's and Neilberg's stories, which pointed away from Christer Pettersson and towards an international plot. Ölvebro was not hauled over the coals for this, either by Swedish politicians or the media. He avoided difficult questions because perhaps he felt he had a licence from the top of Swedish politics to do so. Especially since one of the stories points to inside the Swedish security police. Experts have said that, even if it was the South Africans or the CIA, they would have needed local expertise to stake out Palme's routines, and for help with bugging his phone. As said, according to Neilberg, the killing team consisted of a mix of foreign and Swedish police/secret operatives.

If they did come from military intelligence or the police, Palme's death represented a kind of century-old culmination of the battle between the forces of Social Democracy and pacifism on the one hand, and rightist business and military forces with an anti-Russian slant, that so defined the Swedish 20th century. History had come full circle.

It was a likely a foreign-Swedish operation, with the foreigners being the CIA/and or the South Africans. A former senior official in the Swedish government to whom I spoke last year in a cafe, a quick, unrecorded interview, where I wanted to know so much more, said the CIA was behind the operation, hired a killer with no connection to the Americans – in the language of the trade, a "cut-out" to create "plausible deniability" – and that the South Africans, who were in Stockholm to monitor the anti-apartheid congress, were on hand to provide a decoy element. But they worked as separate teams.

EPILOGUE: THE NEW SWEDEN

It is 2018, and the murder hunt was, and is, technically still ongoing. Five policemen are still on the case, though you have to wonder what they do on a day to day basis, and whether the belief that the killer was Pettersson and thus been dead and buried since 2004 is still prevalent. A new senior investigator, with a good track record, Dan Andersson, took over a few years ago. He was supposed to lend the hunt a new dynamism. But no indication of where they are going or what they have concluded have emerged from the Police House.

There is supposed to be more material on the Palme murder, filling up a whole floor of the police house, than any other criminal investigation – anywhere. Bigger than Lockerbie, bigger than the JFK material. Senior ANC figures, when interviewed a dozen or so years ago on a visit to Stockholm, are convinced that the South African intelligence services carried out the murder of Olof Palme.

BUT THERE are still those who believe Pettersson did it: on the 29th anniversary of the murder, the Expressen newspaper published a testimony from a journalist friend who said Pettersson had confessed to him at the Zum Franciskaner restaurant in Stockholm's old town months before he died. Was Pettersson telling the truth, or was he just playing along in a role others had created for him, or perhaps he had helped play a part in creating too?

The few officers still at have often been diverted to other issues, like identifying and counting the dead after the Indian Ocean tsunami in 2004, where hundreds of Swedish tourists died. These days, a much more prosperous Sweden regards Palme in a more golden glow and frankly revisionist biographies win literary prizes.

It is hard to find anyone in the Reagan administration prepared, on the record, to say anything good about Palme. "Olof Palme was an uncomfortable person for us," said Edward Luttwak, political adviser to the Reagan administration, to a Swedish interviewer in 1998. "In Europe at the time, the USA was painted as the aggressive party and the Soviet Union as wishing for peace and understanding, and the Soviets depended on people like Palme." He denied the USA had an interest in damaging him politically. Richard Burt, deputy secretary of state for Europe 1983-85, said to the same Swedish interviewer: "Sweden without Palme became a more normal country." He added that Sweden had stopped trying to change the world.

With the Soviets it was different. There was considerable regret at his death. Would Palme's Social Democracy would have been an appealing social model for Soviet moderates Palme's peace commission had good links with the emerging democrats in the Soviet Union associated with Gorbachev. In the event, the Soviet Union ended up with a kind of bandit capitalism. Mikhail Gorbachev, interviewed in 1999, said "Olof Palme was someone who more than anyone else the insecurity the word was in due to rearmament. He was a humanist in that he understood that Sweden's role as a small country was to take initiatives and his important and his initiatives were important and valuable." Gorbachev was convinced the murder was political. "I don't think the murder happened by accident. He was a man who threatened powerful interests, groups not interested in a safer world, who exploit insecurities in the world. Such murders are always hard to solve, because they are planned in secrecy and the truth is deeply hidden."

Gorbachev took a lot of inspiration from Palme. We have seen that, on the first anniversary of the murder, Soviet TV made a documentary about Palme, in which he was praised as a man of peace. The Soviet parliament, the Congress of People's Deputies, had a silent minute for the Sweden after the assassination. In his book, Prophet for Change, published in 2012, Gorbachev said that Palme was one of those "figures from northern Europe" who came up with "major initiatives in the spheres of peace and disarmament". (Another was Brundtland, the Norwegian prime minister). His "vile assassination shocked the Soviet people", he added.

The political climate in Sweden is different now, much more right-wing, both in domestic politics and in international politics. It had an influential right-wing government between 2006 - 2014: unlike the milquetoast non-Socialist governments of the seventies, during Palme's interregnum, it has been both ideologically right wing and stable. Taxes have been cut; the welfare state, in certain areas, is up a third smaller than what it was.

In foreign affairs, Sweden – with Palme's old enemy Carl Bildt at the foreign ministry – it took the lead in anti-Russian agitation over the Ukraine crisis – unthinkable under Palme, who would, in my correctly, taken a much moderate view of supposed Soviet aggression. For all his faults, like his exaggerated idealism about Africa, far reaching social reforms paid for by demotivatingly high taxes and his domineering character, he understood a few things. He did not take the Western powers at their self estimation, and knew, like few politicians seem to do, that you cannot win a nuclear war.

OLOF PALME was recently nominated the most important leader of Sweden's modern history. One man who knew him well, the economist Klas Edlund, reckoned his most important legacy is in the field of social legislation, and for Sweden's self-identity as the world's conscience, Equality with the help of public, subsidised childcare, cheap student loans, these were things Swedes thirty years later take for granted. At the time, they helped women into the workplace and helped children from working-class backgrounds into education. Edlund felt Palme had made Sweden a mighty force in the third world, an agitator against all forms of colonial domination. He made politics real, stimulating and essential. He made the Swedish working class feel important and global.

There are streets and squares named after Olof Palme in Moscow, Buenos Aires, Copenhagen, Berlin, Cologne, Bonn Nuremberg, Madrid, New Delhi, Budapest and Athens. In Britain, there is just one geographical reference named after him: Olof Palme Grove in the small pottery town of Longton, Staffordshire. There are no streets named after Olof Palme in the United States. Palme probably loved some aspects of the United States – at least his idea of it, Kennedy's dream for America- But he had so many powerful enemies.The American Deep State most assuredly did not love Olof Palme. Neither did the Swedish military class and business right. Neither did the apartheid regime in South Africa. Was there a coordination among these forces that led to the prime minister's assassination and one of the most intriguing murder mysteries in history? Now, 30 years on, for sure, with its post Erlander experiment in a moral, independent, progressive foreign policy extinguished with Palme's murder, Sweden is truly lodged in the Atlantic policy fold. Sweden may be prosperous, but in a sense lost its political freedom after 28 February 1986.

London-Skara 2011-2018 Dedicated to CS, AN and RT. For your help and support

35698678R00112

Made in the USA
Lexington, KY
06 April 2019